THE DOLMEN ARCH
A Study Course in the Druid Mysteries

Volume 2
The Greater Mysteries

THE
DOLMEN ARCH
A STUDY COURSE IN THE DRUID MYSTERIES

VOLUME 2
THE GREATER MYSTERIES

COMPILED BY
JOHN MICHAEL GREER

2023

First Paperback Edition
published 2023 Azoth Press
ISBN 978-1-935006-17-6

First Limited Hardcover Edition
published 2020 Azoth Press

Text copyright ©2020 John Michael Greer

This edition, its design and illustrations copyright ©2020 Azoth Press. Full-page duotone illustrations of the *Mabinogion* are by Zach McCain. Other illustrations are by Adam P. Forrest.

All rights reserved. No part of this book may be reproduced or utilized in any form or by any means, electronic or mechanical, including Internet, photocopying, recording, or by any information storage and retrieval system, with the exception of short excerpts used in reviews, without prior permission in writing from the publisher.

Azoth Press
Portland, OR
USA
www.azothpress.com

Printed in the United States of America
on acid-neutral paper.

CONTENTS

VOLUME 2 · THE GREATER MYSTERIES

List of Illustrations   vii

Gradd y Gwyddon y Ffordd   1

- Introduction to the Grade   3
- Healing, Magic, and Initiation   7
- The Tree of Light   13
- Introduction to the Art of Druid Healing   17
- Introduction to the Art of Druid Enchantment   25
- Introduction to the Art of Druid Initiation   33
- The Mabinogion: Lludd and Llefelys   39
- Druid Philosophy: Non-Human Beings   51
- The Magical Memory: The Laws of Memory   71
- Completion Exercises: The Doctrine of One   87

Gradd y Gwyddon y Cylch   93

- Introduction to the Grade   95
- The Cycle of the Cantrefs   99
- The Magic of the Grail   105
- The Art of Druid Healing   109
- Practical Enchantment   115
- The Game of the Cantrefs   123
- The Mabinogion: The Dream of Macsen Wledig   129
- Druid Philosophy: The Seven Cosmic Laws   141
- The Magical Memory: A System of Memory   167
- Completion Exercises: Mastering the Opposites   179

Gradd y Gwyddon Rhydd   185

- Introduction to the Grade   187
- The Cycle of the Cantrefs in History and Initiation   191

᚛᚜	A Guide to Initiation in the Dolmen Arch Tradition	201
᚛᚜	The Secret Work of the Grail	205
᚛᚜	The Initiatory Game of the Cantrefs	211
᚛᚜	The Mabinogion: The Story of Taliesin	217
᚛᚜	Druid Philosophy: The Powers of Mind	231
᚛᚜	Addendum to Druid Philosophy: Practical Mentalism	253
᚛᚜	The Magical Memory: Practical Memory	265
᚛᚜	Completion Exercises: The Way of the Dolmen Arch	277

About the Author   280

About the Publisher   281

LIST OF ILLUSTRATIONS

Volume 2

Fig. 1.	*The Tree of Life*	16
Fig. 2.	*The Mabinogion • The Plague of Dragons*	47
Fig. 3.	*The Cantref Awyr*	100
Fig. 4.	*The Cantref Dŵr*	101
Fig. 5.	*The Cantref Ufel*	101
Fig. 6.	*The Cantref Daear*	101
Fig. 7.	*The Cantref Maen*	102
Fig. 8.	*The Cantref Nef*	102
Fig. 9.	*The Cantref Byw*	103
Fig. 10.	*Standard Dominoes*	124
Fig. 11.	*Two methods of joining dominoes 2/1 and 4/2*	126
Fig. 12.	*The Mabinogion • The Dream of Macsen Wledig*	133
Fig. 13.	*The Cantref Awyr*	192
Fig. 14.	*The Cantref Dŵr*	193
Fig. 15.	*The Cantref Ufel*	193
Fig. 16.	*The Cantref Daear*	193
Fig. 17.	*The Cantref Maen*	194
Fig. 18.	*The Cantref Nef*	194
Fig. 19.	*The Cantref Byw*	195
Fig. 20.	*The Cantref Awyr*	196
Fig. 21.	*The Cantref Dŵr*	196
Fig. 22.	*The Cantref Ufel*	196
Fig. 23.	*The Cantref Daear*	197

Fig. 24. *The Cantref Maen* — 197

Fig. 25. *The Cantref Nef* — 197

Fig. 26. *The Cantref Byw* — 198

Fig. 27. *The Mabinogion* • *Gwion Bach receives the Three Blessed Drops from the Cauldron* — 221

Gradd Y Gwyddon Y Ffordd

The Grade of the Loremaster of the Path

INTRODUCTION TO THE GRADE

MANY CONGRATULATIONS! With this lesson packet, you have completed the work of the Lesser Mysteries and begun the work of the outermost grade of the Greater Mysteries. Over the year or more of your studies so far, you have learned a great many teachings and practical techniques. The task that lies ahead of you now is to synthesize what you have already learned into a working toolkit of approaches you can use readily, and to integrate the more advanced teachings and methods of the three higher grades of the Dolmen Arch course.

What is it that defines the difference between the Lesser and the Greater Mysteries? From one perspective, it is simply the difference made by lengthy study and practice in a single system of mystery school training. In the mysteries, as in anything else, a mastery of the basics makes it possible not only to proceed to more advanced studies, but to begin the process of applying those studies to achieve the goals of the practice. A beginning pianist, to use an example that will be developed at more length later in this lesson packet, occupies herself with scales and etudes. After a certain stage in her education, she works on more complex scales and etudes, but also begins to apply her skills to the playing of actual music, beginning with simple tunes simply accompanied, and proceeding to more demanding and more beautiful works, until at last the melodies of the great composers take shape beneath her fingertips.

In the same way, a student of the mysteries begins with the five-finger exercises of spirituality, the basic studies, meditations, and ritual workings that develop skills essential for the work of a mystery tradition, and then proceeds, not only to more advanced exercises, but to practical work with the skills thus gained. One important difference between the mysteries and music, however, is that few pianists start off their practice with a heap of lumber, ivory, and scrap metal that must first be assembled into a piano, made to work, and brought into tune, all the while learning the rudiments of music theory and essaying five-finger exercises on an instrument not yet built! Yet this is a fair comparison to the work required of a beginning student of the mysteries, for the mind of the novice is not yet a well-tuned instrument, waiting for the touch that will awaken music from it; it resembles much more closely a scrap-heap, accumulated over the course of a lifetime, from which such an instrument must be built.

Your completion of the work of the Lesser Mysteries marks the point at which, to continue the metaphor, you have assembled a workable instrument and may now begin to refine and tune it, while beginning to apply the skills you have learned in five-finger exercises to play simple melodies and chords. In less metaphoric terms, your studies of Druid theory and practice will now begin to bear fruit in the form of the three core applications of this course—healing, enchantment, and initiation, the privileges of the initiated Druid. All three of these studies are introduced in this lesson packet.

As befits training in the Greater Mysteries, the work in this lesson packet will require more time and effort than those in previous grades. You should expect to put at least four months into the studies and practices that follow, and as always in this course, if you need more time to become proficient at the practices or to grasp the concepts thoroughly, you should certainly take it. There is no virtue in hurrying through the course at the expense of depth and comprehension, and much to be gained by taking extra time if you need it.

This lesson packet contains nine instructional papers, instead of the seven in each of the lesson packets of the Lesser Mysteries:

    Healing, Magic, and Initiation .... p. 7
    The Tree of Light .... p. 13
    Introduction to the Art of Druid Healing .... p. 17
    Introduction to the Art of Druid Enchantment .... p. 25
    Introduction to the Art of Druid Initiation .... p. 33
    The Mabinogion: Lludd and Llefelys .... p. 39
    Druid Philosophy: Non-Human Beings .... p. 51
    The Magical Memory: The Laws of Memory .... p. 71
    Completion Exercises: The Doctrine of One .... p. 87

Like the lessons of the preceding grades, these are to be worked through at your own pace, with the Completion Exercises reserved for last. The practical work of this lesson packet builds on that of all the previous grades. Once again, remember that rushing through the exercises benefits no one, least of all yourself. A few extra weeks, or even a few extra months, devoted to mastering some exercise that seems more than usually challenging, will pay substantial dividends further as you move toward the completion of the Path.

Wishing you all the best in your journey on the Path of the Druid Mysteries,

 *John Michael Greer*

HEALING, MAGIC, & INITIATION

THE PRIVILEGES OF THE INITIATED DRUID, as mentioned in the introduction to this lesson packet, are healing, enchantment, and initiation. This triad of disciplines is common to all the mystery schools, whether Eastern, Western, or of any other part of the world, and it is important at this stage in the education of the student that the reasons behind this fact be well understood. There is in fact a common theme uniting these practices: all three permit the expanded awareness of the individuality to be applied to relieve the difficulties attendant on human existence in the world of Abred or material embodiment.

Consider the art of healing in this light. Healing can be carried on in a purely material manner, as with medicines, surgery and the like, but sharp limits exist to what can be accomplished in this way, for many of the roots from which illness springs are not material in nature. It may be said, for example, that a germ entered the body and caused an illness. With the aid of a microscope, however, it may readily be shown that the air we breathe, the water we drink, the food we eat, and all other things with which we come into contact are replete with germs of many different kinds. What is it that causes one of these germs to become the source of illness, while the others remain innocuous for the time being? What is it that causes that germ to make one person ill while others who shared the same home, ate the same meals, and breathed the same air as the person who was taken ill, nevertheless remain unharmed?

The key to this mystery is simply that there is more to illness than the presence or absence of germs, just as there is more to accident than the presence or absence of some hazard. In both cases, the personal element is paramount.

It may be admitted that this is true of catching an illness, but insisted that once an illness has come into being, the material aspect predominates. The best of today's medical practice and the teachings of the ancients unite in opposing this belief. Successful doctors rapidly learn and constantly apply the dictum that a good bedside manner is equal to many a medicine. More surprisingly, it has been found that patients may be cured of many illnesses by the use of some harmless substance given to them under the assurance that it is a powerful medicine.[1] Much the same effect, in all probability, is the source of those sudden cures of illness and debility brought about by religious ceremonies, sacred objects, and the like. The term "faith healing" may be more apposite than many of its modern practitioners suspect, and the words of Jesus—"Thy faith has healed thee"—subject to a more literal meaning than they are often given.

Thus health and illness have a dimension other than the purely material, a dimension that relates the condition of the body to states of mind, to thoughts and emotions—or, in the terms introduced in an earlier lecture in this course, to the astral plane of existence, the aspect or realm of the Cosmos in which what are usually called mental activities take place. As the astral plane of manifestation in the Cosmos as a whole contains the patterns or forms that descend into the material plane to create material phenomena, so the astral aspect of the individual—that is, the personality primarily, and secondarily the body of vitality, the animal form and the magical mirror of the Cosmos, as explained in a previous lesson—contains the patterns or forms that descend into the material plane to create the *corff* or material body. This implies in turn that action on the astral plane, by affecting the astral aspect of the individual, can influence the health of the material body.

Can the same principle be applied to the highest of the three great planes of existence—the spiritual plane? The teachings of the mysteries hold that it can.

Just as the material world comes into being following the forms or patterns that exist in the astral world, the astral world comes into being following the principles that exist in the spiritual world. Just as the material body takes its form and its state of health or illness from the astral body, in turn, the astral body takes its form and functions from the spiritual body. What is this spiritual body? In the unawakened person, it is simply that common spiritual principle from which the astral and physical bodies draw their form; it is shared alike by

---

[1]. The term "placebo" dates from 1920 and was apparently unknown to the authors of this essay, but the placebo effect has been part of medical practice for many centuries.

all human beings, as all animals of a given kind share a common *hunan* or reasonable soul, and all plants of a given kind a common *nwyd* or passionate soul.

In the awakened person, by contrast, the individuality or *elaeth* is the spiritual body. The awakening of the elaeth thus transforms the relationship between the initiate and the very core of his being; no longer merely a part of a spiritual collectivity, he stands apart from the rest of humanity while sharing more fully in the spiritual inheritance of the Cosmos.

The capacity for spiritual healing, in the proper sense of that word, is one outcome of the change from a collective spiritual body to an individuality. Before that change, a student of the mysteries can practice astral healing of various kinds, many of which are commonly misnamed "spiritual." Afterwards, the initiate becomes able to complete the change of causation, drawing on the potent influences of the spiritual plane to bring the astral plane into balance and harmony, and then project that balance and harmony downward into the plane of matter.

Between these two points—in the midst of the awakening of individuality, which commonly unfolds over an extended time—glimpses of the spiritual plane, and rays of influence from the gradually emerging elaeth suddenly appearing and suddenly disappearing—the "trembling of the veil" of the old mystics—show themselves from time to time in the midst of every kind of spiritual practice and in the everyday affairs of life as well. In the work of healing, they are particularly common, and this is among the reasons why healing is especially assigned to the first grade of the Greater Mysteries.

Yet the explanation of healing just given is equally an explanation for the remaining privileges of the initiated Druid, the arts of enchantment and initiation. Enchantment, like healing, commonly begins with the manipulation of material substances. Much that nowadays is called science was counted among the magic of our forefathers, in the days when all forms of high learning were counted among the privileges and practices of initiates; while even today what is called folk magic, the common practice of those peoples not yet deprived of contact with the subtle realms of existence by a too narrow faith or a too materialistic education, is a matter of herbs, stones, charms, amulets, and other material objects and substances.

These things have their place, just as the material side of medicine has its place, but there is also an astral side of enchantment, and much of the training of the apprentice in the magic arts has for its purpose the weaning away of the imagination from material substances, so that the mind of the magician can perceive and influence the powers of the astral plane more directly. The Sphere of Protection ceremony, which you have been studying and performing since the beginning of your work in this course, is one version of a training method used throughout the mystery schools for this purpose: the regular practice of a basic ritual that acts upon the astral plane, so that the developing will can learn to shape, and the developing mind to perceive, the subtle phenomena of that plane. Beyond this, in turn, lies the awakening of individuality and the descent, into forms created by enchantment, of power and insight through the trembling veil of consciousness, but of this more will be said in a later grade.

The third privilege of the initiated Druid, initiation itself, may usefully be contemplated according to the same principles. The fundamental and basic aspect of initiation is material: a ceremony enacted on the material plane which confers on the initiate certain privileges, and places upon him certain responsibilities, both of which bear principally on his actions in the material world. In the case of the Dolmen Arch system, for example, the initiation that concludes these lessons grants the initiate the privilege of teaching that system to others and initiating them in turn, and imposes certain responsibilities relative to the process of instruction and initiation. All this, however, is simply the lowest of the three levels of initiation.

The second or astral level has its effect on the thought, will, and memory of the initiate, who is given certain symbolic keys and instructed in their use. By the regular application of these keys, there is unfolded to the initiate a range of applications of the teachings already given, and certain clues to higher modes of working not covered in this or any other course. Of this very little can be said at this time, for it must be experienced through practice. Finally, the third or spiritual level of initiation consists of means for furthering the awakening of individuality in the initiate, and thus fostering the ability of the initiate not only to receive those powers and insights that descend through the trembling veil, but to ascend to that veil, rend it asunder, and pass within into the light and freedom of Gwynfydd.

What these parallels may suggest, and indeed should suggest, is that healing, enchantment, and initiation are three expressions of one general pattern. In all three of the privileges of the Druid initiate, a mastery of the three great levels of being—material, astral, and spiritual—becomes the basis for constructive change. In most mystery schools, and the system of Druid teaching on which this course is based is among them, a common set of practices are used to facilitate all three of the initiate's privileges, and a common way of thought is used to understand them.

In the lessons you have already received and studied, most of the individual elements of that set of practices have already been introduced; a few more remain to be added, and their assembly into a working system also remains to be done. These two steps will fill the pages of this and the next two lesson packets of the course. As you work with the lessons and practices of this grade, you will doubtless notice suggestive parallels and connections among different parts of the course, both those you have already received and those you have yet to receive. Other connections will remain obscure for the time being. With perseverance and a great deal of steady, patient work, the keys will be revealed.

THE TREE OF LIGHT

HE PRACTICE OF AWAKENING THE ONE LIFE in the psychic centers of the body enters its final stage in this lesson packet. In previous grades, you have learned to concentrate the telluric, solar, and lunar currents in the three cauldrons of the body, and to draw upon the secondary currents of the Red and White Dragons to purify and energize the cauldrons. In this third phase, the centers are linked to the great primary flows of the solar and telluric currents that sustain life on Earth.

The symbolism of this phase of the working follows an ancient pattern. Many of the world's mythologies picture the entire Cosmos as a mighty tree with its roots in the underworld, its branches holding the worlds in place, and its crown reaching up to the highest realms of spirit. This is a powerful image and, like all myths, it can be understood on many different levels. It has obvious relevance to the path of the Druid mysteries, because trees draw their life from above and below at the same time—their roots bring up minerals and water from deep within the earth, while their leaves soak up sunlight and carbon dioxide from the heavens—just as the adept of the Druid path draws power from both the solar and telluric currents.

The image of the cosmic tree likewise touches on some of the greatest secrets of spiritual transformation. Consider the ancient mystery teaching concerning the Norse god Odin, the patron of the Nordic mysteries, who pinned himself with his own spear to the world-tree Yggdrasil for nine days and nights to win the secret of the runes. In the same way, Gautama the Buddha achieved nirvana while seated at the foot of the Bo tree, and the Gnostics taught that the self-surrender of Jesus on the cross was an act of the same kind. It is for this reason that many depictions of the Crucifixion from the Middle Ages portrayed the cross as a living tree.

These myths of revelation at the world tree relate to one of the hidden potentials of the human *enaid* or energy body. Many people nowadays have heard of kundalini yoga, the art of rousing the "serpent power" at the base of the spine and leading it up through the seven chakras of the spine to the crown of the head. This is one expression of a widely known magical technique—the opening of a central channel of *nwyfre* along the midline of the body.

Different magical and mystical systems use this channel in different ways. Some, such as kundalini yoga, draw energy up from below, while others draw it down from above. In the work of the Druid mysteries, as the attentive student may already have guessed, the central channel is opened to a twofold flow of nwyfre from the macrocosm—upwards from the telluric current and downwards from the solar current. This strengthens and balances the generation of the lunar current from the solar and telluric currents within the body, and greatly amplifies the effects of practices already done. It thus brings the work established in the two previous phases of the working to a higher level of intensity; at the same time, it sets in motion a process of transformation that extends beyond the individual self.

According to the teachings of the Druid philosophy, all life on Earth is produced and sustained by the interplay of the solar and telluric currents. The solar current descends, as discussed in a previous lesson, from the Sun and the upper atmosphere into the soil; the telluric current ascends in the same way, rising from the heart of the Earth through stone and soil to penetrate the lower reaches of the atmosphere. In the region where these two currents overlap, life exists as a manifestation of the lunar current, and it thrives as much on the flows of subtle energy brought by the solar and telluric currents as on any more physical nutriment.

The ordinary processes of nature, however, do not always permit the combination of the two currents to proceed as fully as it otherwise might, and the acts of human beings very often interfere in one way or another with the descent of the solar current and the responding ascent of the telluric current. A great variety of magical and spiritual workings have thus existed since ancient times to reestablish and rebalance the connection between Sun and Earth, thereby fostering the fertility of the land and the prosperity of the people. The standing stones and holy trees reverenced by the ancient Druids were important features of this work.

The regular practice of the Tree of Light working, as part of your daily Sphere of Protection practice, also participates in this same process. It is a relatively simple working along these lines, but an efficacious one. In the course of that working, a channel is opened through which the solar and telluric currents may flow freely, and the two currents are set in motion through that channel. Practiced repeatedly in the same location, this working will dispel negative and unbalanced energy patterns and generate increased fertility in the soil and the vegetable life that grows nearby; it will also produce beneficial effects on human beings and other living things in the vicinity of your working.

Thus the work of the Sphere of Protection begins the transition between work on yourself and work on the world around you. In a broader sense, of course, both dimensions of work are present in the ceremony from the beginning, for any transformation of the self sets in motion changes in the environment, and any change enacted in the environment calls up corresponding changes in the self. Still, the focus may rightly vary from one to another stage of training, and as you proceed from the Lesser to the Greater Mysteries, such variations are appropriate.

The Tree of Light

Begin this phase of the work by performing the Sphere of Protection, beginning with the Elemental Cross as usual, and invoke and banish the elements of Air, Fire, Water, and Earth in the standard way. Next, invoke the elements of Spirit Below, Spirit Above, and Spirit Within to fill the three cauldrons. Bring the ray of solar light down from above to the center of the earth, summon the two dragon currents, and bring them up through your body and the three cauldrons.

At this point in the working, imagine a point of light descending from your cauldron of the moon to your solar plexus center, as though you were about to begin the Circulation of Light. Instead of expanding it into a sphere, though, hold it at your solar plexus center for a time, imagining it as a seed. Let the seed of light sprout, sending a slender stem of light upwards and a root of light downwards. Watch it grow into a sapling, and then into a tree, putting out branches and leaves of light above you and roots of light below. Feel sunlight and wind on the leaves, soil, and water around the roots, the firmness of the trunk connecting them. Spend as much time as you need to make the image of the tree as clear and solid as possible.

Next, turn your attention to your breath. As you breathe in, imagine the leaves drawing in air, sunlight, and the nwyfre of the solar current, and sending them down through the trunk all the way to the deepest root. As you breathe out, imagine the roots drawing in water, nutrients from the soil, and the nwyfre

Fig. 1. The Tree of Light

of the telluric current, and sending them through the trunk all the way to the highest leaf. Repeat this process three times in all.

Finally, turn your attention back to your solar plexus, and imagine that the seed of light is still there, in the heart of the Tree of Light. Expand it into a sphere as usual, making the sphere large enough to surround the entire Tree of Light, and then perform the Circulation of Light in the same manner as usual.

Regular practice of this exercise, in conjunction with the other phases of the Sphere of Protection ritual and the other disciplines of the Druid mysteries presented in this course, will open door after door to your magical and spiritual advancement. As your practice ripens, so will your ability to sense and shape nwyfre and work magic in yourself and the world around you. Thus you should perform this working daily as part of your regular practice of the Sphere of Protection, and record your experiences in your practice journal.

INTRODUCTION TO THE ART OF DRUID HEALING

THE EXERCISES FOR AWAKENING THE INNER POWER included in the fourth lesson packet of this course, as explained therein, form the foundation for much of the practical work of the Greater Mysteries. Of those exercises, the practice of awakening and charging the palm centers has a central role. The following instructions explain how to use the energy and energy centers you have awakened for the practice of the art of healing, which corresponds to the Fifth Cantref and therefore has a special applicability to the grade of Loremaster of the Path. During your work on this grade, you will work on learning to heal yourself; extending your healing abilities toward others comes later in the process of training, and will be covered in detail in the lesson packet of the next grade.

Nwyfre and the Palm Centers

The energy centers in each palm are specially adapted to direct the flow of nwyfre. The laying on of hands, which is practiced as a way of healing and an aspect of the practice of initiation in mystery schools around the world, derives its effectiveness from this fact.

Those students who are familiar with the way that the palm centers are used in other traditions of healing and magic may notice a difference between methods of energy work presented elsewhere and those covered in this paper. Very often, other traditions rely either on the solar or the telluric current for the energy used to heal, bless, and empower, and for this reason one or the other of the two hands takes an active role, as a source of energy, while the other hand receives the energy and has a passive function.

Most commonly, the solar current is used, the right hand is usually active, the left hand passive, and the energy that flows into the palm centers is seen as descending, perhaps through the crown of the head, perhaps through some other energy center above the waist. Less common are the healing methods that rely primarily on the telluric current; in these, the left hand tends to be active, the right hand passive, and the energy that flows into the palm centers is seen as ascending, perhaps through the soles of the feet, perhaps through some other energy center below the waist.

Here as elsewhere, the tradition of the Druid mysteries from which this course derives uses both currents together, rather than one alone. In the mode of healing that follows, both palms emit energy and both receive it; the right hand emits a flow of energy derived from the solar current and receives the balancing flow of energy from the telluric current, while the left hand emits energy derived from the telluric current and absorbs the solar flow. In the space between them, as always when the solar and telluric currents come together in balance, the lunar current is born.

In the process of healing, the currents therefore flow through the human body in a double motion, comparable precisely to the double flow practiced in the Tree of Light exercise. The path of this double current through the body follows a slightly more complex path, however.

In the course of healing work, the solar current descends from above through the crown of the head and continues in a straight line to the sun cauldron in the vicinity of the heart, whence it flows to the right shoulder, and then down the right arm to the palm center of the right hand. From there, it flows into the left palm center, up the left arm to the left shoulder, and then angles down through the body to the earth cauldron in the vicinity of the navel. Then, following the currents established in the working of the three cauldrons, it divides into two streams, flows down both legs to the feet, and proceeds out through the soles of the feet and descends into the ground, finally coming to rest at the heart of the Earth.

The telluric current follows the same course in the opposite direction. In healing work, it ascends from the heart of the Earth to the soles of both feet and rises up through the feet and legs to the earth cauldron at the level of the navel, where it unites into a single current. From that point, it flows up at an angle to the left shoulder, and then down the left arm to the palm center of the left hand, where it radiates out. It is then absorbed by the palm center of the right hand, and flows up the right arm to the right shoulder, across to the sun cauldron at the level of the heart, and then up the midline of the body to the crown of the head and beyond, into the sky, where it finally comes to rest at the heart of the Sun.

Most students of the Druid mysteries will find that one of the two currents is easier for them to direct than the other. When you have determined which of the currents you have more trouble directing, make a special effort with it so that both currents flow together in a balanced manner.

Awakening the Palm Centers

During the time you spend on this grade of the Dolmen Arch course, as already mentioned, you will be practicing healing on yourself. You will need to set aside some time for this at least once each week; this may be done just after your meditation, or at a separate time, and will take an extra five to ten minutes. The healing work may be done more frequently than once each week, up to once per day, but less than once per week will not give you enough experience in the healing work to progress to healing others in the next grade.

Your healing practice will begin, then, seated in the ordinary meditation posture. You will want to sit as far forward in your chair as you comfortably can, so that your lower back and the backs of your thighs can be reached easily. If you are practicing healing directly after your meditation, you may proceed at once to the healing work; otherwise, take the few minutes necessary to relax your body, perform the Cleansing Breath, and then do at least a few minutes of color breathing using the color green, which is the color of healing and balance.

When you have finished the meditative preliminaries and are ready to proceed, activate your palm centers in the way you were taught in the lessons of the preceding grade—that is, trace the symbol of water in blue, and the symbol of earth in green, on your left hand, using the index finger of your right; then trace the symbol of fire in red, and the symbol of air in yellow, on your right hand. Notice that the hand corresponding to the solar current awakens the symbols linked to the telluric current, and vice versa; as noted in an earlier lesson packet, an important esoteric teaching is contained in this detail of practice.

When you have traced the symbols, place your hands together in front of your chest as you have been taught, with the bases of your palms joined. The slight hollow at the base of each hand marks the point at which the energy channel that runs up the center of your arm reaches the surface of your hand on the palm side, and spreads out through the palms and fingers; by joining the two hands together as described in the last lesson packet, with the fingers of the left hand pointing forward and those of the right hand pointing up, these two energy gateways are brought into close contact, completing a circuit that can then be used to direct the solar and telluric currents through your body.

This is the next phase of the work. As you did in the Tree of Life exercise, draw in a breath, and with that breath draw down a stream of the solar current from high above you. Visualize it as a stream of warm golden light. Bring it in through the top of your head, and down the midline of your body to the sun cauldron at the level of your heart, and then let it flow along the course already described, out to the right shoulder, through the right arm to the right hand, and through the joined energy gates into your left hand. It then continues around through the left arm and shoulder, angles down to meet the midline of the body again at the earth cauldron, and descends through your legs in two streams to descend deep into the earth.

On the outbreath, visualize the telluric current following the same course in the opposite direction; visualize it as a stream of cool green light, the color of sunlight through leaves. Do this for a total of nine cycles of breath, so that you have brought both currents through your body nine times. This completes the process of awakening the palm centers for healing work; the same process, as you will learn, is also used to activate the palm centers for magic and initiation.

The first few times you work your way through the process of awakening the palm centers, it can be educational to test the energy flow between the palms. To do this, once you have completed the nine breaths, draw your hands slowly apart and turn them so that the fingertips are pointing the same direction. When they are a foot or so apart, pause, and imagine the energy still flowing from one to the other, the solar current from right to left and the telluric current from left to right. After a minute or so, begin moving your palms slightly toward one another and then away again. The total distance each hand moves should be no more than an inch or two. Notice the sensations in your palms. Many students find the results of this practice very unexpected!

When you have finished whatever work you intend to do with the awakened palm centers, a simple closing process should be performed. To do this, bring your hands back together in front of your chest as before, then turn them so that the fingers point the same direction, and clap your hands together once. This brings the energy flow through your hands back to the normal level and prevents you from leaking nwyfre.

The Practice of Self-Healing

Once you have awakened the palm centers, you can use the resulting energy flows to restore balance to your enaid. Since all physical ailments are rooted in large part in imbalances in the body of nwyfre that surrounds and interpenetrates your corff, or body of dense matter, balancing the enaid can be an extremely effective technique for healing on many levels.

It is important to remember, however, that no healing method is suited to all health issues. When the corff itself is significantly damaged, whether by injury, infectious illness, or long-neglected energy imbalances, that damage has to be dealt with directly on the material plane. Energy healing of the sort taught in this and the next lesson packet can be used to assist physical methods of healing, and have great value in this role, but should not be considered a replacement for them. The great strengths of energy healing are, first, in responding to imbalance before it reaches the level of serious illness, and second, in working with chronic conditions of the kind that do not respond well to physical treatment. For these uses, regular treatments of energy healing can be extremely valuable.

The practice of self-healing with nwyfre involves a sequence of passes made by the hands. These have two features not always used in other forms of energy healing. First, the hands remain a short distance away from the physical body; that is, your hands do not touch your body physically during the healing process. Second, each pass is followed by a quick shaking of the hands, as though scattering drops of water from the fingertips. Leaving space between the hands and the body allows you to learn to sense the flow of nwyfre more clearly, while the shaking movement clears away excess nwyfre and readies the hands for the next pass.

The basic sequence of passes for self-healing is done as follows:

First, place the hands side by side above the top of your head, perhaps an inch from your scalp, with the fingers pointing backwards. The hands should be relaxed, not tense. Draw the hands slowly down and forward in front of your face, leaving the hands parallel and side by side, and maintaining roughly the same distance between the palms and your face, and continue down the front of your neck. When they reach the top of your chest, allow them to rotate so that the fingertips point toward each other; in this position, draw them down the front of your body to the level of your hips, and then down the thighs to the knees. Here the fingertips turn down, and you pass the hands down the front of your lower legs, as low as you can comfortably reach. End the first pass by sweeping the hands forward a foot or so, and then giving them a good crisp shake to clear them of excess energy. Repeat this pass a total of three times.

Second, return the hands to the top of the head, with the fingertips close together but the palms angling diagonally outward, toward your temples. Draw them slowly down and forward along the sides of your face, in front of the ears, and then down your neck to the shoulders. At this point they rotate as before, so that the fingertips point to one another, but some inches should lie between them—the exact distance will depend on the breadth of your chest. Pass them down your chest to your hips and then down your thighs, passing over areas just to the sides of the areas you covered in the first pass. By the time you reach your knees, your fingertips will naturally have rotated forward; here you allow them to turn downward and pass down the outside front of each lower leg as far as you can reach. Finish the same way as you did the first pass, and repeat this pass a total of three times.

Third, return your hands to the top of your head, but now the fingertips are pointing toward one another above the crown of your head and your palms are to the side, above your ears. Draw your hands slowly down the sides of your head and neck, then rotate them around the front of your shoulders so that they end up at the sides of your chest, as close to your armpits as the conformation of your arms and body will permit, with the fingers pointing down. Move them down your sides to your hips, down the outside of your thighs, and down the sides of your lower legs as far down as you can reach. Finish the same way as you did the first two passes, and repeat this pass a total of three times.

Fourth, return your hands to the top of your head, and put them in the same position as they were at the start of the third set of passes. This time, though, move the hands slowly backward, down the back of your head and neck, turn them so that the fingers are pointing downward, and sweep them outward along the back of your shoulders, ending with a quick shake. Put them behind your back, palms facing your back and fingertips pointing toward each other, and slide them as far down your back as you can without hitting the seat of your chair; sweep them out along your hips and end the movement again with a quick shake. Finally put them under your thighs, fingertips pointing toward each other, and slide them down the backs of your legs, letting the fingers turn downward naturally as you go; reach down as far as you can, and then end by sweeping the hands outward and shaking them again. Repeat this whole sequence a total of three times.

Fifth, place your left arm comfortably on your left thigh, palm up. Put your right hand above the top of your head, palm down, and then draw it slowly down the left side of the head and neck, over the left shoulder, and down the inside of the left arm, right out past the fingertips. Shake the hand briskly, then repeat the movement a total of three times. Then turn the left arm over, so that your hand rests on your thigh with the palm down, and repeat the same movement with the right hand three times. Then switch hands, doing three passes on the inside of the right arm and three passes on the outside, using the left hand.

Sixth, give your hands a thorough shake, and then place your hands in front of your forehead with the palms facing your forehead and the fingertips pointing toward each other. Let your hands curve a little, so that the fingertips bend inwards toward your forehead without touching the skin. Take three slow breaths, allowing the energy to flow from your fingertips into the moon cauldron at the center of your head. Then move your hands down to heart level, keeping them in the same position, and take three more slow breaths, allowing energy to flow into the sun cauldron at the center of your chest. Then move your hands down to your belly, keeping them in the same position as before, and take three more slow breaths, allowing energy to flow into the earth cauldron just below your navel. When you have finished, draw your hands away and shake them.

Seventh, bring your hands together in front of your belly, with the fingers pointing down and the backs of the hands facing each other. Raise them up the midline of your body as you breathe in, allowing the hands to change position naturally until the fingers are pointing up. Rotate the hands so that your palms are facing outwards, spread your fingers slightly, and sweep them out and down. Let them come to rest at your sides; pause until you feel the energy flowing out of them, and then give them a good shake. Repeat this whole process three times. This concludes the basic sequence of passes for self-healing.

Applying the Healing Forces

The seven passes just described provide a general balancing of nwyfre for your entire body, and will help maintain it in good health. If any part of your body feels unwell, however, more focused work is needed, and this is done between the fifth and sixth passes.

The form of work you will do should depend on the quality of the illness or imbalance you sense in your body. Some conditions are a product of insufficient nwyfre, while others are the result of excessive accumulations of nwyfre. These have different symptoms and are treated differently.

Conditions that involve inadequate nwyfre feel cold and empty, physically and energetically. The cold, hollow feeling many people get in their sinuses or chests immediately prior to coming down with a cold is a good example of this feeling. To treat a condition of this kind, place one or both hands near the part of the body where the cold and empty feeling is apparent, and concentrate on imagining solar and telluric energies flowing into that part of the body, filling it with light and life. Do this for as many breaths as you wish, depending on the apparent severity of the condition, and then continue with the rest of the healing process.

Conditions that involve excessive nwyfre feel hot, congested, and inflamed, physically and energetically. The heat and swelling that take place around an injured joint provide good examples of this. To treat a condition of this kind, use one or both hands to stroke over the part of the body where the hot, inflamed feeling is present. The direction of stroking is important; it should always follow the same natural pattern of flow used in the passes already given, that is, away from the top of the head and toward one of the extremities. For example, a condition on an arm that involves excessive nwyfre should be treated by strokes in the air just above the skin that start just above the ill or injured place and pass over it, moving down toward the hand. Repeat this as many times as you wish, depending on the apparent severity of the condition, and then continue with the rest of the healing process.

As previously mentioned, you should practice the self-healing passes at least once each week during the time you spend on this grade. Pay close attention to what you experience, both while doing the healing work and afterwards; this will be invaluable when you reach the point of performing healing on other people. As with all the practices in this course, keep detailed notes of your practices and their results in your practice journal.

INTRODUCTION TO THE ART OF DRUID ENCHANTMENT

THE PARALLELS DRAWN IN AN EARLIER LECTURE between healing and enchantment extend to practice as well as theory. Just as in the healing work you have learned, the magical work of the present grade takes its starting point from the practices for awakening the inner power introduced in the previous grade of this course. The regular practice of the Grand Psychic Breath and the seven nwyfre exercises, building on the work of earlier grades, have prepared your enaid or body of nwyfre for the magical practices of this grade and the grades to come. It is important to continue the exercises just mentioned, and to supplement them with practices that will be described in this lecture, just as it is important to understand what enchantment is and how it can be invoked.

The Nature of Enchantment

The term enchantment, rather than any of its synonyms, is used in this tradition of the Druid mysteries deliberately, in large part due to the literal meaning of the word: en-chant-ment, putting a chant or rather (since the word came to English from the French language) a song in something. Practitioners of the magic arts in some traditions do this in the most literal sense possible, singing or chanting words of power over some physical object to fill it with magic influences, while others do so in a somewhat more metaphoric manner of working.

In either case, the sense of bringing about a conjunction of meaning and matter, magical life and physical form, is of the essence of enchantment. That which is enchanted is not simply passive and inert; it has an indwelling life and meaning, which flow out from it to affect all that is around it and all that comes into contact with it.

Consider what occurs when you find, lying in some box or drawer, a memento of a time long past that strongly affected you. A moment beforehand, you were in some other state of mind, your thoughts and feelings shaped by other influences. Then you found the memento—your thoughts leapt back to the time that it represented—the memories of that time, filled with old emotions, filled your awareness—the rest of the day, perhaps, was changed for good or ill by the impact of those memories and emotions. If they were good memories and happy emotions, you might put the memento in a place where you will see it more often, to encourage reflection on the memories and reawakening of the emotions; if they were unpleasant memories and troubled emotions, you might go to the extent of casting the memento into the flames of your fireplace to be rid of it, and as it burns, you might well feel a sudden sense of freedom as the memories and emotions lose their anchor in the world of matter.

Many athletes, gamblers, and others make use of the same effect in a more deliberate way. It is far from rare for baseball players, for example, to have some lucky token they insist on having with them when they go to bat, and the closer the score, the greater their reliance on whatever it is that, in their belief, brings them their luck. The omnipresence of luck-charms in the life of the professional gambler is too well known to need comment. Even in less chancy fields of endeavor, the same thing often appears; there are many famous authors, for example, who insist on writing the first draft of a new story with a particular fountain pen, and if questioned, will confess that to do otherwise would be to condemn the story to failure.

Such habits are often dismissed as superstitious folly, but there is a great deal of common sense to them, as indeed there is in most so-called "superstitions." Central to all these things is the phenomenon of enchantment. The memento, like the writer's pen and the gambler's luck-piece, is not simply a material object like any other; it has become charged with a distinct astral pattern and an equally distinct spiritual force. This charge may be perceived even by those who have no knowledge of its presence; it is a matter of common experience, for example, that most people find it acutely uncomfortable to handle a weapon that has been used for murder or suicide, even if they have never been informed of its history.

The violent act in which the weapon had a central role impressed the terrible and passionate emotions of that act into the very substance of the weapon, and left behind a species of bloodstain that no cloth can wipe away. Nor is the repulsion so many people feel for objects and places thus charged an error or a superstition, for the presence of these influences can all too easily bring about a repetition of the unpleasant events that charged the object in the first place. It is fortunate that the same phenomenon works in the opposite direction as well, and a place or an object that has been central to some event that released strong positive emotions very often bears the imprint of those emotions, and can bring about the repetition of a similar event.

What can be done by the accidents of strong emotion, in turn, can also be done by the focused intention of the initiate of the mysteries, and the potential effects of such workings can reach far beyond the psychological realm. The art of enchantment, in the tradition of the Druid mysteries communicated in this course, is the art of doing exactly this, for a purpose the Druid chooses, in a deliberate and intentional manner.

The Ethics of Enchantment

This last sentence, however, points up an important issue that must be addressed before the practicalities of enchantment may be considered. The purposes for which enchantment may be used are many and varied; indeed, as wide as—or perhaps wider than—the human imagination can make them. With every form of human action, there are differences between those goals which are possible and those which are appropriate. It is the task of ethical philosophy to outline the principles upon which such differentiations can be made, and the task of practical ethics to apply them to specific cases. Thus the ethics of enchantment must be considered in this place.

Much confusion over the centuries has surrounded the ethical dimension of occultism. Still, the student who has carefully studied the material previously covered in this course will have little difficulty coming to a clear grasp of the issues involved. To understand the role of fate in shaping the present and future lives by means of character, as explained in the lecture on philosophy in the third lesson packet of this course, is to realize the importance of using the powers of the awakening self in ways that will not hinder the emergence of the individuality. To understand the laws of character, effort, and grace that act on the plane of will, as explained in the lecture on philosophy in the fourth lesson packet of this course, is to realize the importance of moving beyond the automatisms of habit, desire, and fear, and seeking guidance from the promptings of the superior rather than the inferior aspects of the self.

What these realizations make plain, in turn, is that many of the familiar moral rules handed down in the traditions of outward religion have an importance and a value that deserves respect. To use the power of enchantment to steal, to dominate, to harm, or to kill is to set in motion causes that will inevitably rebound upon the one who does such things, weaving a net of fate that cannot be escaped and leading the soul into such sufferings as are necessary to balance and purify his character. Since stealing, dominating, harming, and killing are nearly always done under the influence of desire, fear, and habit, the laws of the unawakened personality, such acts also hinder the awakening of individuality by bringing the one who performs them back under the rulership of the lower aspects of himself.

It is true in turn that acts of the opposite character can also be performed out of desire, fear, and habit, but the patterns of fate such acts weave are of a favorable character, and one expression of a favorable fate is that it brings opportunities for awakening and development to the soul. Thus a man who begins to practice enchantments of healing and blessing, say, from motives belonging entirely to the personality—because he finds it pleasant to be surrounded by happy people, or fears that the unhappiness of other people might inconvenience him, or simply because it becomes his habit to do so—will find over time that the influences of desire, fear, and habit give way imperceptibly to those of character, effort, and grace.

For these reasons among others, the student of these lessons is earnestly cautioned never to use the powers of enchantment to harm or dominate any being, and as earnestly encouraged to use the same powers to benefit others at least as often as he uses them to benefit himself. It is also well to meditate thoroughly on any proposed enchantment, to determine whether the motivation for that enchantment is desire or fear, on the one hand, or will directed by reasoned thought and motivated by character, on the other.

The Practice of Enchantment

The specific method of enchantment that will be taught in the following grades of this study course is only one of several that are part of the broad tradition of Druid mystery school teachings from which this course derives.[2] Most such methods require a mastery of ritual forms, and therefore are difficult to practice outside a suitably consecrated grove. The method taught here differs, in that it works with nwyfre directly, with a minimum of ritualism, using the capacities you have developed in the exercises of the previous grades.

---

2. One of the others has been published in my book *The Druid Magic Handbook*.

The first key to this method is revealed, in a certain sense, in the instructions concerning the Grand Psychic Breath given in the Grade of the Philosophizer. It is this: that the body may absorb and release nwyfre through any part of its surface, and accumulate nwyfre in any part of its structure. The second key to the method is revealed, also in a certain sense, in the Sphere of Protection exercise. It is this: that nwyfre may take on and communicate any quality that is impressed upon it, whether the quality is that of one of the seven Cantrefs or of some other nature. Combine these two keys with the third just discussed—that material objects are capable of taking and holding nwyfre charged with a particular emotional state—and the method will be readily understood.

While the practice of enchantment can be performed anywhere and under any conditions by those who have learned and mastered the art, learning and mastering it is best done in a place and under conditions made suitable for the work by the disciplines you have already learned. Begin, therefore, by placing a chair suitable for meditation on the northern side of a space suited to the practice of the Sphere of Protection. Perform the Sphere of Protection ceremony in its ordinary form, including the Elemental Cross, the Calling of the Cantrefs, and the Sphere of Light, but not including the awakening of the cauldrons, the rousing of the dragons, or the establishment of the Tree of Light. When you have completed the ceremony as just described, take your seat and perform the usual preliminaries for meditation, up to the point at which you would normally begin color breathing.

At this point, as in the practice of color breathing, imagine yourself at the center of an ocean of color, corresponding to one of the seven Cantrefs—it need not be the one that corresponds to the day on which you perform this practice. Proceed to imagine, not merely the color of the Cantref, but all the influences of the Cantref as well. Supposing that you are working with the first Cantref, Awyr, for example, imagine yourself surrounded not only by yellow light but by the light and nimble feeling of air, the qualities of the eastern quarter of the world, daybreak, springtime, and all the other symbols and correspondences of Awyr. Concentrate on this for some minutes, until you feel yourself surrounded by an ocean of the influences of the Cantref.

Then, as in the practice of color breathing, draw the influences of the Cantref in through your solar plexus to fill your body, but with this difference: do not exhale them again at once. Instead, draw them in through your solar plexus seven times with seven slow inhalations, and each time feel the influences accumulating there. The second breath thus adds its force to the first, the third to that already brought in by the first and second, and so on, until you reach the required count of seven. With practice, you will soon feel the accumulation of nwyfre in your body as a pressure almost physical in its nature.

The next step is to exhale the influences of the Cantref you have drawn inside your body. This is done in seven slow exhalations, to balance the seven inhalations. In each exhalation, one part of the influences you have brought into yourself flows back out into the ocean of color and nwyfre around you. At the end of the seventh slow breath, you will have expelled all the influences of the Cantref from your body. At this point, dissolve the ocean of color and influence, concentrating on this until the space around you has returned to balance.

Your first task is to work through all seven of the Cantrefs in order, concentrating and then expelling their influences in your body. Perform this practice no more often than once in any day. When you have completed the sequence of Cantrefs, start from the beginning and go through all seven a second time, again working with only one Cantref on any day.

When you have completed the sequence twice, perform it a third time, with this difference. Before you begin to formulate the ocean of color and influence, trace all four of the elemental symbols on your palms to awaken the palm centers, place your palms together, and draw the solar and telluric currents through your body three times, as though you were about to perform a healing. When you are finished, instead of drawing the influences in and expelling them through your solar plexus, draw them in and expel them through the palms of both hands.

Should you be performing this practice with the first Cantref, Awyr, for example, you would separate your palms and turn them away from your body, keeping them as relaxed as possible. You would then draw in seven slow breaths, and with each breath, you would draw in yellow light and the influences of Awyr through both palms into your whole body, filling your body more completely with the influences of Awyr with each breath. When this is completed, you would then breathe out seven slow breaths, and with each breath, you would expel a part of the light and influences you drew into yourself, until at the end of the seventh breath, your body has returned to its normal state.

Like the previous practices, this one should be done no more than once in any day. It will thus take you twenty-one practice sessions on twenty-one successive days to complete this stage of your preparation for magic. Keep detailed notes on your experiences in your practice journal.

The Material Basis

The final stage of training in enchantment in this grade of the Dolmen Arch course builds on the exercises just described. The ability to concentrate the influences of any one of the seven Cantrefs in your body leads naturally to the ability to concentrate these same influences in objects separate from the body. This is the bridge to the art of enchantment, for it is precisely the ability to place an indwelling life and meaning in an object not normally so charged that is the key to this form of the magician's art.

The choice of a proper material basis for this work is of some importance, and will be covered in more detail in a later lesson. For the time being, a small stone or pebble will be suitable. Find such a stone, wash it thoroughly with cold water, and leave it to dry in a place where sunlight can fall upon it. When it has dried for at least three days, you may begin the final sequence of exercises for this part of the work of this grade.

Prepare for these exercises as you did when learning to concentrate the influences of the Cantrefs in your body, and perform the exercise in exactly the same way, with the following exceptions.

First, as you sit down to begin the gathering of the influences, take the stone and hold it between the palms of your two hands, which face one another.

Second, as you begin to work with nwyfre, draw in each breath laden with the influence of the Cantref through your solar plexus, receiving the influence in your body, and breathe it out through the palms of your hands into the stone. Feel the stone absorbing the charge and becoming energized with the influence of the Cantref you are gathering into it. When you have done this seven times, reverse the process, and breathe the influence of the Cantref out of the stone with seven inbreaths, receiving that influence in your body, and expel it through your solar plexus with seven outbreaths. The stone should feel perfectly inert at the beginning and end of the practice, and filled with life and magical force at the midpoint. Eventually you will charge objects and leave them charged for a period, and then discharge them—but that time is not yet.

Do this practice seven times during the time you spend in this grade, charging the stone with the influence of a different Cantref on each occasion. As before, keep detailed notes on your experiences in your practice journal.

INTRODUCTION TO THE ART OF DRUID INITIATION

THE THIRD OF THE PRIVILEGES of the initiated Druid, as mentioned in the first lecture in this lesson packet, is the art of initiation. Like healing, that art has a twofold dimension; just as the healer begins by healing himself, and then proceeds to apply his gifts to heal others, the initiator must first receive initiation, and become an initiate, before transmitting that gift to others.

There has most likely been more nonsense written about initiation over the centuries than about any other single subject, with the possible exception of the lost continent of Atlantis. The reality is far simpler than most of this outpouring makes it seem, and at the same time far more interesting. The authentic secrets of initiation are the same factors which bring success in any other human activity. Because these factors are too often wrapped in layers of mystification when they are applied to spirituality, it may be helpful to look at them in a different setting.

A more than adequate example may be found in the experience of a person who desires to learn to play the piano. That desire remains ineffectual until it enters into manifestation through action, and even then, action alone is not necessarily enough. Three steps must be taken in order to pass from the desire to its fulfillment. First, the prospective pianist must determine on a particular course of study that will lead toward her goal; she must enroll in a class, make an appointment with a teacher, or acquire a self-teaching course suitable to her background and talents. Second, she must set aside time to practice playing the piano as often and as regularly as possible. Third, she must learn from her practice, and make a habit of comparing each lesson's work and each performance against the yardstick provided by a set of realistic goals as a guide to improvement.

These same three factors—clarity of purpose, persistence of effort, and the ability to learn—are also the keys to initiation. They are ways of working with the three aspects of the hunan or conscious personality, which are will, thought, and memory, and which are also the foundation of the powers awakened by initation in a mystery school. Thus the work of the mysteries is simple, but of course "simple" is not always the same as "easy."

Most of the techniques used in any mystery school, from the simplest to the most complex, are ways of strengthening or supplementing the ordinary faculties of will, thought and memory, so that the initiate can become familiar with the possibilities of these aspects of his own hunan, and can put them to work in the practices of the mysteries, many of which demand more from the human mind than can commonly be applied to the purpose by the ordinary person. This is where the practices enjoined in this study course, such as study, meditation, and ritual work, come into play. Every serious student of the mysteries devotes time to these practices on a daily basis, establishing a routine that soon takes on a life of its own—and this although much of what attracts people to the mystery schools is that the training to be had there seems to offer an escape from the routine, the ordinary and the predictable. Still, human beings are creatures of habit, and the mystery schools learned a very long time ago to put this fact to good use. Productive habits are supports for the will, and difficulties that cannot be overcome by willpower alone can quite often be worn down step by step through the deliberate cultivation of helpful habits.

It is for this reason that most mystery schools teach their students to set aside a short period of time, perhaps half an hour, every single day for their spiritual practices, as indeed you have been advised to do in this course. Establishing a regular routine in this way has valuable benefits, for the student's practice time becomes an ordinary feature of his or her day; as practice time approaches, the mind automatically turns to the work at hand, and skipping a practice produces the same kind of internal upset as does skipping a meal.

Another advantage of this approach to training is that nearly anyone can put half an hour daily into spiritual practices, if only by setting the alarm thirty minutes early so that the work can be done before the rest of the family wakes up. When more free time becomes available, it can be put into the work of the mysteries, but more is not always better; especially in the early stages of the work, the mind and body both need plenty of time to recover from the unfamiliar efforts and transformative effects of spiritual practices. This is another reason why attempting to rush the gates of higher consciousness is not a good idea. Inner development is a natural process that takes its own proper time, and attempting to force it along by exotic means is no more helpful than trying to speed up the growth of flowers by pulling them out of the ground.

In the full sense of the word, then, the entire Dolmen Arch course is an exercise in initiation. The capacity of a student of this course to make use of the teachings and disciplines of the Dolmen Arch system, after completing the course, will be precisely measured by the effort the student puts into learning those teachings and practicing those disciplines before completing the course. There is no other way; just as no one can teach others to play a musical instrument who has not first learned to play the instrument skillfully, no one can teach others to share in a mystery tradition who has not first pursued the appropriate course of training in that tradition, and achieved a certain degree of skill in its practices.

Still, there is a further dimension of initiation that must be received by the aspirant before it can be transmitted to others, and this may be done in one of two ways.

The first way, and the oldest and most common way practiced in the world's mystery schools since earliest times, is the way of formal ceremonial initiation. To enact such an initiation, there must be an initiator who has not only mastered the disciplines of the mystery school conferring the initiation, but has also learned certain specialized skills that enable him to shape energy and consciousness in a ritual setting. The initiator, with or without the help of others, performs a ritual in which the candidate for initiation has an essentially passive role. The initiator invokes and directs currents of nwyfre; the candidate receives them, and as a result certain subtle transformations in the enaid, or body of nwyfre, take place. These transformations further the work of mystery training in a variety of ways. They also lay the foundations for the candidate, if he perseveres in his training, to become an initiator in turn.

It has sometimes been argued that this first form of initiation is the only valid form. Still, such insistences evade a question of great importance: where did the founders of the mystery schools receive their initiation?

The answer is that the repeated performance of certain practices by the aspirant alone will have the same effect as the performance of a single ritual of initiation by an initiator for the candidate's benefit. It was by practicing some such set of practices themselves, over a period of months or years, that the founders of many of the mystery schools gained the capacity to initiate. The practice of formal ceremonial initiation, in fact, had its origins in an effort to spare students the labor of performing the disciplines of solitary initiation for themselves. That decision was understandable, and even today it has much to recommend it, but it has under some circumstances had the unfortunate effect of preventing some of those who might have benefited from initiation from receiving it.

It is for this reason that the initiation of the Dolmen Arch may be transmitted by either or both of these methods. As a student of this course, approaching your own initiation, you have been practicing the preliminary disciplines of self-initiation, and should you persevere to the highest grade of this course, you will complete the process of self-initiation and enter into the possession of the privileges of an initiated Druid. As you do so, in turn, you will be instructed in the way that you may confer this same initiation upon others in a formal ceremonial manner. From that time on, should you choose to teach students of your own, you will be able to choose freely which method you use to confer the privilege of initiation upon those students—either by guiding them through the process of self-initiation, or by performing a formal ritual of initiation for them once they have completed the preliminary training that gives such a ritual its power and effect, or—which is in many ways the best option—by combining the two, and conferring formal initiation at the conclusion of a sequence of self-initiation practices.

Preparation for Self-Initiation

The practices that will be central in your own self-initiation have already been communicated to you, some in previous lessons and others in this one. The complete Sphere of Protection ritual is one of these; the practices of self-healing using the energy centers in the palms comprise another, and the disciplines of Druid enchantment explored in this lesson are the third. In the lesson packets to come, these practices will be combined, expanded, and interwoven in a specific way with certain symbolic patterns, some known to you and others not yet introduced, to perform the work of initiation that will lead to the ripening of your awareness of individuality and the awakening of your capacity to heal, enchant, and initiate.

Three additional preparations, however, may usefully be added at this time. The first of these is an ancient practice of purification that has been part of the mystery teachings since long before the beginning of recorded history. It begins the preparation for initiation on the material plane, but its effects reach well beyond that plane.

This is simply the practice of washing the body each day with cold water, into which a pinch of pure salt has been added. The water should be as cold as you can bear it, or failing that, as cold as you have available. The salt should be sea salt or kosher salt; it should not be ordinary table salt, which has iodine and other adulterants added to it. Simply add a pinch of salt to the water, use a cloth soaked in the water to wash your entire body, and then towel off and dress. This is best done on rising, if your schedule permits it. If you are not able to perform this daily, at least once per week is an acceptable minimum.

The second preparatory practice is to drink water that has been charged with the lunar current, to begin the preparation for initiation on the astral plane. To do this, you will need a glass of clear water, which should be placed within easy reach of a chair where you can perform the preparations for healing work discussed in an earlier paper in this lesson packet. Once you are ready, awaken your palm centers and fill yourself with the solar and telluric currents in the way already described.

Then, instead of performing the sequence of passes, simply draw your hands apart and place them to either side of the glass of water, with the palms facing the glass. Imagine the energies of the solar and telluric current flowing from your palms into the water, the solar current from the right hand, the telluric from the left. Imagine them fusing to create the lunar current in the water, so that the water glows brilliant white, with greater and greater intensity, until it seems too bright to regard directly. When you feel the water has absorbed as much of the lunar current as it can hold, take the glass in both hands and slowly drink the water, feeling the healing force being absorbed by your body and permeating every cell. When you are done drinking, set the glass down and close the practice in the usual way. This should be done at least once each week during the time you spend on this lesson packet; if it is convenient for you to perform it more often, you may certainly do so.

The third preparatory practice is meant to begin the preparation for initiation on the spiritual plane. Since the spiritual plane can only be accessed directly by the fully awakened individuality, it is accessed in this practice through its astral reflection. To do this, each night just before going to sleep, after the review of the day you learned to practice in the memory exercises of the first lesson packet, call up before your mind's eye the image of the sun reflected on the surface of a pool of water. Do not think about the image or meditate on it; simpy imagine it, and if possible, drift off to sleep with the image still in your mind.

This should be done each night during the time you spend in this grade. The importance of the image will be explained at a later time.

THE MABINOGION: LLUDD AND LLEFELYS

The Four Branches of the Mabinogion form a complete sequence of tales keyed to the four material elements, the four seasons of the year, and many other fourfold patterns in Druid lore. This has been noted not only within the Druid community, but outside it as well, and it is not hard to find books and essays discussing the four branches in these terms. Still, the initiatory dimension of the four branches has rarely been grasped. This will now be outlined.

The story of the four branches, as already explained, is the biography of a single figure, who begins his journey as Pryderi the Mabon and completes it as Llew the Og. Understood more deeply, however, the four branches comprise the biography of every person who has ever awakened to the call of the inner life. All the characters of the four stories are parts of the whole self of that person, or aspects of the Cosmos within which he grows toward spiritual maturity. Among these Pryderi/Llew is central, for as Pryderi he is the seed of the individuality, and as Llew he is the individuality itself.

The Meaning of the Four Branches

The process of initiation thus begins when Pwyll, whose name means "intelligence" and who represents the personality, encounters death in the form of Arawn the king of Annwn, and love in the form of Arawn's wife, the queen of Annwn. These encounters are tests, and Pwyll passes them through self-restraint: he strikes Arawn's foe but once, according to the instructions he was given, and refrains from making love to Arawn's wife, according to the rules of hospitality that govern his conduct as a guest. It is because he passes those tests of forbearance that he is guided to the mound of Gorsedd Arberth and to Rhiannon.

Rhiannon represents the mystery teachings as embodied in any one school or tradition; these are portrayed as a beautiful maiden because the mysteries appear to the personality, at first, as the fulfillment of all its desires. In Pwyll's first interactions with Rhiannon, he unwisely allows his nwyd or passionate self, symbolized by Hafgan, to take over the relationship, and must recover himself by disciplining his passions. Once this is accomplished, he enters the mystery school—the sexual pun this phrase suggests would have been appreciated by the Welsh audience of the Mabinogion—and the result is the birth of Pryderi, the first seed of the awakening individuality.

This seed appears at first only as a brief, soon-vanished glimpse, and the personality must contend thereafter with the conflict between the irrational parts of the self, which rage against the mystery teachings and the restrictions and changes they impose, and its own commitment to the work of the mysteries. In time, the spark of individuality becomes stabilized within the self, or in the language of the story, Pryderi is returned to Pwyll and Rhiannon.

With the beginning of the Second Branch, Pryderi is lost sight of for a time in a tremendous clash of forces. Nisien, Efnisien, Bran and Manawyddan define the four great phases of human life and the four basic orientations toward the idea of the good. Nisien represents the child's attitude, which sees the good as a matter of following rules handed down by others; Efnisien represents the youth's attitude, which sees the good as a mater of fulfilling the inclinations of the nwyd or passionate self; Bran represents the adult's attitude, which sees the good as a matter of accomplishing great and good things in the world; and Manawyddan represents the initiate's attitude, which sees the good as a process of awakening the higher potentials of the self.

All human beings pass through the first stage; many pass to the second; some reach the third, and a few complete the process and achieve the fourth. These are also the four material elements and the first four Cantrefs—Nisien is Awyr and air, Efnisien Dŵr and water, Bran Ufel and fire, and Manawyddan Daear and earth—and their contention with the Irish king represents the great cycle of the seasons and the stages of life, in which every initiate is caught up as long as he remains incarnate as a living human being. It is out of these struggles that Pryderi returns from Ireland and his wondrous experiences with the head of Bran—the knowledge gained by his striving with the world—having with him the guidance of Manawyddan to lead him through the outward forms of his initiation.

The Third Branch is the story of that outward initiation. Pryderi—or rather the whole person of which Pryderi is one part, the others involved being Cigfa the material body, Rhiannon the teachings of the mystery tradition, and Manawyddan the aspiration toward the higher—goes to the mound of Gorsedd Arberth, the portal of initiation, and enters into the lonely journey of initiation. Isolated from all others in an inward sense that is symbolized by the vanishing away of the kingdom of Dyfed, laboring and suffering what seem like pointless persecutions, the initiate enters that terrible passage when the individuality can no longer be perceived and the teachings of the mysteries seem like empty dross, and only the lower aspects of the self and the raw will to spiritual attainment remain. Finally, that will achieves its end; the passionate self, which frustrates the work of the mysteries by treating Gwynfydd itself as another object of craving, is brought under discipline at last; and Pryderi approaches his full awakening as Llew.

At this point new names and powers come into play, for the story is being told thereafter from the point of view of the initiator rather than that of the initiate. The events of the Fourth Branch are the same events as those already chronicled in the first three Branches. From that inner perspective, it is not the initiate's personality (Pwyll) or the seed of his individuality (Pryderi) that sets the initiation in motion, but the mysteries themselves that call the initiate, first luring him by means of his desires in the form of the stolen swine, and then sending him through two cycles of death and resurrection separated by a process of education and challenge.

Thus the Fourth Branch reenacts all the events of the first three Branches, but in an order and a significance transformed by its new perspective. The birth, disappearance, and recovery of Pryderi here take the form of the death of Pryderi and the mysterious birth, after an interval, of Llew; the role of Rhiannon in the outer world is taken on by the challenging figure of Arianrhod in the inner, while the role of Manawyddan is taken on by that of Gwydion; challenged by the one and guided by the other, the initiate wins a name, weapons, and a bride; translated out of symbolic terms, these acts represent the individuality gaining mastery over the hunan or personality, which exists in the realm of names and words; the nwyd or passionate self, which exists in the realm of conflicting desires; and the bywyd or animate self, which forms and vivifies the enaid and material body. Thus Bloduewedd, the bride fashioned from the vegetative world, has the same meaning as Cigfa, the "house of flesh" wedded by Pryderi, but her role as seen from the initiator's side is far different from her role as seen from the initiate's.

It is the physical body, in this sense, that leads the initiate to his final encounter. This is the confrontation with death, represented by Gronw, who appears—like Arawn in the First Branch—in the form of a huntsman chasing a stag. Given over to death by the physical body, the initiate receives the guidance of the initiator through the journey between lives; he attains that new life which is Gwynfydd, and conquers death and the limits of material embodiment to complete his journey into the fullness of initiation.

There is much more to be found in the Four Branches than this outline has described, and careful study of the texts, combined with meditation on them, will reveal many secrets of Druid philosophy and magic. Yet it is too rarely remembered that the Mabinogion contains tales other than the Four Branches, and these—or, to be more precise, certain of these—complete the teachings presented here in the form of myth.

Beyond the Four Branches

According to the tradition of the Druid mysteries from which this course is derived, an important but rarely noticed line runs through the Mabinogion and, indeed, the whole body of Celtic legend from Wales, Cornwall, and Brittany. Those stories that traditionally date from long before the age of King Arthur comprise one body of lore; those that traditionally date from the Arthurian age, which extends from the birth of his uncle Ambrosius, King of Britain, through that of his last successor Cadwallader, comprise a separate body of lore. The two embody parallel teachings, but—again, according to the tradition of the Druid mysteries taught here—the older stories represent the original teachings of the ancient Druids, while the Arthurian stories represent a modification of those teachings, adapted to the teachings of Christianity.

A total of twelve stories are commonly included in the Mabinogion,[3] and some of these belong to each of these two categories. The first six—the Four Branches already given in this course, and the stories of "Lludd and Llefelys" and "The Dream of Macsen Wledig"—and the final tale, "Taliesin," are set be-

---

3. This was true when the original course was written, and the Lady Charlotte Guest translation was the standard version accessible to English-speaking readers. Most modern translations omit the story of Taliesin, leaving only eleven stories.

fore the time of Arthur, while the remaining five belong to the Arthurian age. Like other sets of seven in the old lore, the seven ancient tales correspond to the seven Cantrefs of Druid lore, as follows:

- "Pwyll, Prince of Dyfed" to the First Cantref, Awyr;
- "Branwen daughter of Llyr" to the Second Cantref, Dŵr;
- "Manawyddan son of Llyr" to the Third Cantref, Ufel;
- "Math son of Mathonwy" to the Fourth Cantref, Daear;
- "Lludd and Llefelys" to the Fifth Cantref, Maen;
- "Macsen Wledig" to the Sixth Cantref, Nef;
- "Taliesin" to the Seventh Cantref, Byw.

The three latter stories, as representatives of the three forms of Spirit, contain teachings of great importance. The story of Lludd and Llefelys, which corresponds to Spirit Below and thus belongs to this lesson packet, is a relatively brief and cryptic tale full of hints and echoes of ancient mystery teachings. Students familiar with the Arthurian legends will notice certain potent similarities here; for example, the teaching concerning the two dragon currents within the earth, also central to one part of the legends of Merlin and also to certain phases of the work of this course, appears in this tale. In the course of the story, three terrible plagues appear and are overcome by the tale's hero using unexpected means.

In their nature and the means taken to overcome them, some of the secrets of the telluric current are revealed. Notice particularly the role that alcoholic beverages (wine and mead) and water (with or without added insects) play in the banishing of the three plagues.

Most of the characters in the story are not named, and some of those who are named are not who they seem to be; your experience with the Four Branches may be useful in identifying the characters with the principles they represent. The figure of Llefelys in particular has been left deliberately obscure by the author of the tale. The text itself points out that he is not actually a brother of Lludd, but is simply called that "according to the story." His identity, actions, and relationship to Lludd is a useful theme for meditation.

LLUDD AND LLEFELYS

Beli[4] the Great, the son of Manogan, had three sons, Lludd, and Caswallawn, and Nynyaw; and according to the story he had a fourth son called Llefelys.[5] And after the death of Beli, the kingdom of the Island of Britain fell into the hands of Lludd his eldest son; and Lludd ruled prosperously, and rebuilt the walls of London, and encompassed it about with numberless towers. And after that he bade the citizens build houses therein, such as no houses in the kingdoms could equal. And moreover he was a mighty warrior, and generous and liberal in giving meat and drink to all that sought them. And though he had many castles and cities this one he loved more than any. And he dwelt therein most part of the year, and therefore was it called Caer Lludd, and at last Caer London. And after the stranger-race[6] came there, it was called London, or Lwndrys.

Lludd loved Llefelys best of all his brothers, because he was a wise and discreet man. Having heard that the king of France had died, leaving no heir except a daughter, and that he had left all his possessions in her hands, he came to Lludd his brother, to beseech his counsel and aid. And that not so much for his own welfare, as to seek to add to the glory and honour and dignity of his kindred, if he might go to France to woo the maiden for his wife. And forthwith his brother conferred with him, and this counsel was pleasing unto him.

So he prepared ships and filled them with armed knights, and set forth towards France. And as soon as they had landed, they sent messengers to show the nobles of France the cause of the embassy. And by the joint counsel of the nobles of France and of the princes, the maiden was given to Llefelys, and the crown of the kingdom with her. And thenceforth he ruled the land discreetly, and wisely and happily, as long as his life lasted.

After a space of time had passed, three plagues fell on the Island of Britain, such as none in the islands had ever seen the like of. The first was a certain race that came, and was called the Coranians;[7] and so great was their knowledge,

---

4. Beli: "Bright," a title of the Sun and of the ancient Celtic sun god.
5. The names Manogan, Lludd, Caswallawn, Nynyaw, and Llefelys, like that of Beli, are drawn from the traditional history of Britain chronicled by Geoffrey of Monmouth in the twelfth century. Except for Beli and Caswallawn ("Foe-scatterer"), they have no clear or traditional meaning in Welsh, and in fact scholars have not yet agreed on their origins and meanings.
6. The Saxons, the forebears of today's English people.
7. Coranians: a race of magical dwarfs, related by name and nature to the Korrigans of Brittany. According to legend they came from the country of Pwyll, that is, from Annwn.

that there was no discourse upon the face of the Island, however low it might be spoken, but what, if the wind met it, it was known to them. And through this they could not be injured.

The second plague was a shriek which came on every May-eve,[8] over every hearth in the Island of Britain. And this went through people's hearts, and so seared them, that the men lost their hue and their strength, and the women their children, and the young men and the maidens lost their senses, and all the animals and trees and the earth and the waters, were left barren.

The third plague was that however much of provisions and food might be prepared in the king's courts, were there even so much as a year's provision of meat and drink, none of it could ever be found, except what was consumed in the first night. And two of these plagues, no one ever knew their cause, therefore was there better hope of being freed from the first than from the second and third.

And thereupon King Lludd felt great sorrow and care, because that he knew not how he might be freed from these plagues. And he called to him all the nobles of his kingdom, and asked counsel of them what they should do against these afflictions. And by the common counsel of the nobles, Lludd the son of Beli, went to Llefelys his brother, king of France, for he was a man great of counsel and wisdom, to seek his advice.

And they made ready a fleet, and that in secret and in silence, lest that race should know the cause of their errand, or any besides the king and his counsellors. And when they were made ready, they went into their ships, Lludd and those whom he chose with him. And they began to cleave the seas towards France.

And when these tidings came to Llefelys, seeing that he knew not the cause of his brother's ships, he came on the other side to meet him, and with him was a fleet vast of size. And when Lludd saw this, he left all the ships out upon the sea except one only; and in that one he came to meet his brother, and he likewise with a single ship came to meet him. And when they were come together, each put his arms about the other's neck, and they welcomed each other with brotherly love.

After that Lludd had shown his brother the cause of his errand, Llefelys said that he himself knew the cause of the coming to those lands. And they

---

8. Note that this happens on the eve of *Calan Mai*, the same date as the disappearance of the foals in the First Branch, and involves a similar loss of the fruits of fertility.

took counsel together to discourse on the matter otherwise than thus, in order that the wind might not catch their words, nor the Coranians know what they might say. Then Llefelys caused a long horn to be made of brass, and through this horn they discoursed. But whatsoever words they spoke through this horn, one to the other, neither of them could hear any other but harsh and hostile words. And when Llefelys saw this, and that there was a demon thwarting them and disturbing through this horn, he caused wine to be put therein to wash it. And through the virtue of the wine the demon was driven out of the horn.

And when their discourse was unobstructed, Llefelys told his brother that he would give him some insects whereof he should keep some to breed, lest by chance the like affliction might come a second time. And other of these insects he should take and bruise in water. And he assured him that it would have power to destroy the race of the Coranians. That is to say, that when he came home to his kingdom he should call together all the people both of his own race and of the race of the Coranians for a conference, as though with the intent of making peace between them; and that when they were all together, he should take this charmed water, and cast it over all alike. And he assured him that the water would poison the race of the Coranians, but that it would not slay or harm those of his own race.

"And the second plague," said he, "that is in thy dominion, behold it is a dragon. And another dragon of a foreign race is fighting with it, and striving to overcome it. And therefore does your dragon make a fearful outcry. And on this wise mayest thou come to know this. After thou hast returned home, cause the Island to be measured in its length and breadth, and in the place where thou dost find the exact central point, there cause a pit to be dug, and cause a cauldron full of the best mead that can be made to be put in the pit, with a covering of satin over the face of the cauldron. And then, in thine own person do thou remain there watching, and thou wilt see the dragons fighting in the form of terrific animals. And at length they will take the form of dragons in the air. And last of all, after wearying themselves with fierce and furious fighting, they will fall in the form of two pigs upon the covering, and they will sink in, and the covering with them, and they will draw it down to the very bottom of the cauldron. And they will drink up the whole of the mead; and after that they will sleep. Thereupon do thou immediately fold the covering around them, and bury

Fig. 2. The Mabinogion • The Plague of Dragons

them in a cistvaen,[9] in the strongest place thou hast in thy dominions, and hide them in the earth. And as long as they shall bide in that strong place no plague shall come to the Island of Britain from elsewhere."

"The cause of the third plague," said he, "is a mighty man of magic, who takes thy meat and thy drink and thy store. And he through illusions and charms causes every one to sleep. Therefore it is needful for thee in thy own person to watch thy food and thy provisions. And lest he should overcome thee with sleep, be there a cauldron of cold water by thy side, and when thou art oppressed with sleep, plunge into the cauldron."

Then Lludd returned back unto his land. And immediately he summoned to him the whole of his own race and of the Coranians. And as Llefelys had taught him, he bruised the insects in water, the which he cast over them all together, and forthwith it destroyed the whole tribe of the Coranians, without hurt to any of the Britons.

And some time after this, Lludd caused the Island to be measured in its length and in its breadth. And in Oxford he found the central point, and in that place he caused the earth to be dug, and in that pit a cauldron to be set, full of the best mead that could be made, and a covering of satin over the face of it. And he himself watched that night. And while he was there, he beheld the dragons fighting. And when they were weary they fell, and came down upon the top of the satin, and drew it with them to the bottom of the cauldron. And when they had drunk the mead they slept. And in their sleep, Lludd folded the covering around them, and in the securest place he had in Snowdon, he hid them in a cistvaen. Now after that this spot was called Dinas Emreis, but before that, Dinas Ffaraon.[10] And thus the fierce outcry ceased in his dominions.

And when this was ended, King Lludd caused an exceeding great banquet to be prepared. And when it was ready, he placed a vessel of cold water by his side, and he in his own proper person watched it. And as he abode thus clad with arms, about the third watch of the night, lo, he heard many surpassing

---

9. *cistvaen*: a container made of slabs of stone, buried underground, and traditionally used for the ashes of the dead.

10. *Dinas Emreis* means the city of Ambrosius, while *Dinas Ffaraon* means the city of Pharaoh. Students of Arthurian lore may remember that Ambrosius was the personal name of Merlin, or more precisely—since Merlin was a title rather than a name—that Merlin who counseled the kings of Britain, including Arthur, after witnessing the two dragons rise. The reference to Pharaoh, the traditional title of the kings of Egypt, is held to refer to a colony of Egyptian adepts who fled political turmoil in their homeland, settled in north Wales in very ancient times, and added their lore to the Druid tradition.

fascinations and various songs. And drowsiness urged him to sleep. Upon this, lest he should be hindered from his purpose and be overcome by sleep, he went often into the water. And at last, behold, a man of vast size, clad in strong, heavy armour, came in, bearing a hamper. And, as he was wont, he put all the food and provisions of meat and drink into the hamper, and proceeded to go with it forth. And nothing was ever more wonderful to Lludd, than that the hamper should hold so much.

And thereupon King Lludd went after him and spoke unto him thus. "Stop, stop," said he, "though thou hast done many insults and much spoil erewhile, thou shalt not do so any more, unless thy skill in arms and thy prowess be greater than mine."

Then he instantly put down the hamper on the floor, and awaited him. And a fierce encounter was between them, so that the glittering fire flew out from their arms. And at the last Lludd grappled with him, and fate bestowed the victory on Lludd. And he threw the plague to the earth. And after he had overcome him by strength and might, he besought his mercy. "How can I grant thee mercy," said the king, "after all the many injuries and wrongs that thou hast done me?"

"All the losses that ever I have caused thee," said he, "I will make thee atonement for, equal to what I have taken. And I will never do the like from this time forth. But thy faithful vassal will I be." And the king accepted this from him.

And thus Lludd freed the Island of Britain from the three plagues. And from thenceforth until the end of his life, in prosperous peace did Lludd the son of Beli rule the Island of Britain. And this Tale is called the Story of Lludd and Llefelys. And thus it ends.

DRUID PHILOSOPHY: NON-HUMAN BEINGS

THE LECTURES ON DRUID PHILOSOPHY included in earlier lesson packets in this course have summarized, respectively, the teachings of this tradition of Druidry concerning the fundamental principles of the Cosmos; the nature and powers of nwyfre, the One Life pervading all things; the process of evolution by which the One Life enters into manifestation; and the laws governing manifestation on each of the three great planes of the Cosmos. Important as these themes are, they may appear somewhat abstract at first glance. Most students can readily see the value of knowing something about the Cosmos as a whole, but to glimpse the practical applicability of these teachings to the everyday life of the initiate generally takes a great deal of study, meditation, and experience.

As explained in the first lesson packet you received in this course, it was the custom in earlier times to begin the study of any subject from the highest and most apparently abstract point, and to work down from there gradually to the practical application. That rule has been followed in this series of lessons. At this point, as you begin the study of Druid philosophy from the point of view of the Greater Mysteries, the descent from the abstract to the practical takes a further step, and the themes under discussion are those other entities with whom the Druid initiate will at times have to deal, some of them human souls, some of them having other origins and natures.

To speak of human souls, of course, is in one sense a misnomer, because those souls which today are embodied in human form were in long ages past embodied in vegetable and animal forms, and in ages to come—unless they fail utterly, and return to the Cauldron of Annwn to come forth no more—will be embodied in the subtler and mightier forms indwelt by those who dwell in Gwynfydd. Still, there is an important distinction to be made here, because not all souls belong to the class or, better, current of souls whose destiny it is to rise up from Annwn to the heights of Gwynfydd. There is, in fact, another class or current of souls whose nature is distinct and complementary to those of the current to which we belong, and a third class that holds the balance between ours and the complementary current.

The nature and destiny of these alternative currents of evolution is useful for the Druid initiate to understand, and this for two reasons. First, in that the contrast between the different kinds of souls casts no small light on the human soul, for many times it is easiest to understand a thing by seeing it alongside its opposite or complement. Second, in that the work of the Druid at times may bring him into contact with the beings of these other currents of evolution, or the effects of their work in the Cosmos, and a clear understanding of the differences separating the currents confers certain advantages, and a significant degree of protection, in such work.

The following three triads propound the secrets of the other evolutions of the Cosmos.

Triad I.

Three distinct natures of beings having life: the Folk of the Path of Ascent, the Folk of the Path of Descent, and the Folk of the Region of the Summer Stars.

Triad II.

Three stations along the Path of Descent: the Halls of the Elements, the Halls of Nature, and the Halls of Splendor.

Triad III.

Three great families in the Halls of Splendor: the Children of Annwn, the Children of Don, and the Children of Llyr.

Triad I.

Three distinct natures of beings having life: the Folk of the Path of Ascent, the Folk of the Path of Descent, and the Folk of the Region of the Summer Stars.

Druid tradition teaches that this planet, the earth we know, is the field and theatre for three distinct kinds of manifestation—that of the living forms that we know, whether human, animal, and vegetable; and two other realms of a different order, each with its own varying life forms, as different from one another as a human being, a bee, and an oak tree are different from one another.

Those who are familiar with occult literature or the traditions of folklore will be familiar with the nature of the entities of which we speak. One of these two distinct sequences of evolution comprises those entities that occultism commonly terms "elementals" and "elementaries," and folklore from around the world calls by countless names. The other of these sequences comprises those beings to whom occult tradition and popular thought alike give the name of gods and goddesses. In the tradition of Druid spirituality on which this course is based, those beings that belong to the former class are termed the Folk of the Path of Descent, and those beings that belong to the latter are termed the Folk of the Region of the Summer Stars. Those beings that belong to our current of evolution, in turn, are termed the Folk of the Path of Ascent.

Behind these titles lies an important teaching of Druid philosophy hinted at, yet not openly expressed, in the lessons you have already studied. The seventh of the Cosmic Laws or creative principles presented in the previous grade of this course is the Principle of Circularity, which teaches that all phenomena in the Cosmos follow circular paths. The ascent of souls from Annwn through Abred to the heights of Gwynfydd is no exception to this law. Where, then, is the other half of the circle, the descending arc that proceeds from the limits of Ceugant down to Annwn?

This teaching concerning three sequences of evolution answers that question. The descending arc of the circle is the province of a different evolution, comprising those beings called the Folk of the Path of Descent. Their evolution differs from ours; each soul upon the Path of Ascent rises up individually through all the modes and forms of being from the borders of Annwn to the heights of Gwynfydd, but the souls on the Path of Descent do not themselves descend through a similar sequence of levels, for the descending flow of nwyfre has not yet divided into individual beings, as it will when it turns and begins to ascend; rather, it generates individual beings by its flow without dividing in substance.

A metaphor may be useful for understanding this teaching. Imagine a great river rushing toward a waterfall. Once the water leaps over the brink of the falls, it divides into countless droplets that follow their own destiny. Before that point, the water is a unity, but not a featureless one. The shape of the river bed and the continued movement of the water produces visible forms—a surge here, a spray of white foam there—which remain in place even as the water that forms them rushes past. These visible forms are analogous to the Folk of the Path of Descent, who evolve in place, remaining what they are but becoming ever more richly and completely what they are, while the droplets flung into the air by the waterfall are analogous to the Folk of the Path of Ascent, who are divided into separate existence and move through the planes of being as they evolve from form to form and life to life.

Distinct from both these are the Folk of the Region of the Summer Stars, who complete the arc of the circle that passes through Ceugant. The Region of the Summer Stars is an alternate name for Ceugant, for reasons partly poetic and partly rooted in an ancient tradition of starlore; its inhabitants are those timeless and all-experiencing beings whom the lore of countless lands calls gods and goddesses. According to the Druid teaching, there are as many of these beings as there are souls traveling the Path of Ascent or manifested in the Path of Descent; they differ from both in that, being timeless, they do not evolve in any sense we can understand. Existing outside of time, they possess the full potential of themselves eternally, and regard different moments in time as we might regard two locations in space that can be viewed in a single glance.

It must be understood that these other forms of life, separated from us in nature, are not separate from us in space or time. All three forms of life share the same world, and it is purely because the humanity of today has closed its eyes to the existence of the other manifestations of life that we do not experience them, as our ancestors did and our descendants will do, surrounding us at every moment and interacting with our lives in many ways.

Triad II.

Three stations along the Path of Descent: the Halls of the Elements, the Halls of Nature, and the Halls of Splendor.

The Folk of the Path of Descent play an important role in the advanced work of the Druid mage and initiate, and for this reason their nature and characteristics will be discussed more fully in this lecture. These beings may be grouped into any of several schemes of classification, although any ordering of these multifarious beings is unsatisfactory and imperfect at best. One of these classes comprise the entities which many occult writers have called elementals. These entities have been described in occult lore under various names, including earth-spirits, or gnomes; water-spirits, or undines; air-spirits, or sylphs; and fire-spirits, or salamanders. In the lore of Druidry they are described as dwelling in the Halls of the Elements, which are not, however, physical or astral places so much as states or stations of being.

The Halls of the Elements represent that portion of the arc of descending nwyfre immediately prior to its final descent into the forms of physical matter, poetically described as the Cauldron of Annwn. Here the forms of manifestation are those of the four material elements, earth, water, air, and fire, and the beings who exist in that state of existence take their bodies from these forms. These Elemental beings are the lives of so-called inanimate matter, and provide it with form and beauty. When we look on the varied patterns of the rocks, the play of light on water, the billowing shapes of clouds, or the brightness and dancing forms of flame, what we perceive takes its shape and elegance from the activities of these elemental lives.

The Halls of Nature represent that portion of the descending arc above the realm of the elements themselves, and the forms of manifestation on these levels correspond to the forms of living nature, which are compounded of the four material elements. In occult writings, the beings who dwell at this station of existence are often called elementaries. In folklore, they have been given countless names, such as nature spirits, fairies, pixies, elves, brownies, peris, djinns, trolls, fauns, kobolds, imps, goblins, little people, good people, and so forth.

Their forms vary, but they most frequently appear to human beings in human shape, though often diminutive in size. They are able to assume any appearance at will, but they have favorite forms, which they wear when they have no reason to take any other. Under ordinary conditions they are not visible to physical sight, but they have the power of making themselves so when they wish to be seen. There are an immense number of subdivisions or races among them, and members of these subdivisions differ in intelligence and disposition precisely as human beings do.

The great majority of them prefer to avoid humanity altogether, as our habits trouble them, and the currents set up in the nwyfre by our unbalanced thoughts and emotions disturb and annoy them. On the other hand, it sometimes happens that these nature spirits befriend human beings, and offer them such assistance as lay in their power. In most cases when they come in contact with humanity, however, they either display indifference or dislike, or take an impish delight in deceiving us and playing tricks upon us. Many a story that illustrates this characteristic may be found among the village gossip of the people in any rural district; and anyone who has been in the habit of attending seances will recall instances of practical joking of this kind, which indicates the presence of some of these entities.

The third state or station of the Folk of the Path of Descent is that of the Halls of Splendor. The elementals or dwellers in the Halls of the Elements are in most respects less developed and intelligent than man, and parallel the animal creation. The elementaries or dwellers in the Halls of Nature, though they embrace a great range of levels and kinds, are broadly equivalent to human beings in their development and intelligence. The dwellers in the Halls of Splendor, in turn, are of a grade of development and intelligence that surpasses the level of incarnate humanity, and corresponds to that of those members of our current of evolution who have entered into Gwynfydd. Concerning them, the following triad has more to teach.

Triad III.

Three great families in the Halls of Splendor: the Children of Annwn, the Children of Don, and the Children of Llyr.

This triad reveals a dimension of the Four Branches of the Mabinogion that has not been discussed in previous lessons. Some of the characters of the Four Branches are traditionally assigned to three great groupings belonging to the highest grade of the Folk of the Path of Descent. These are the *Plant Annwn* or Children of Annwn, who correspond to Spirit Below; the *Plant Don* or Children of Don, who correspond to Spirit Above; and the *Plant Llyr* or Children of Llyr, who correspond to Spirit Within.

The Children of Annwn play only a minor role in the Four Branches, but have a much greater role in Welsh legend generally. The *Gwragedd Annwn* or "women of Annwn" are magical beings frequently encountered, according to legend, by the shores of lakes, beneath which they have their dwellings; the Lady of the Lake in Arthurian legend is one of them, and Lancelot du Lac was fostered among them and connects to their mysteries. The remaining families are well chronicled in the Four Branches. They are and remain powerful spiritual beings, with whom Druid initiates may at times hold converse and from whom much wisdom comes.

According to the teachings that have come down to us, among the events that are chronicled in the Four Branches are those that accompanied the change from one great age of the world to another, and likewise a change in the rulers of these three great families or classes of spiritual beings. In the previous age of the world, the Plant Annwn was ruled by Arawn; in our age, its rulers are Gwyn ap Nudd and his wife Creiddylad ferch Ludd. In the previous age, the Plant Don was ruled by Math ap Mathonwy; in our age, its rulers are Gwydion ap Don and his sister Arianrhod ferch Don. In the previous age, in turn, the Plant Llyr was ruled by Bran the Blessed; in the present age, it is ruled by Manawyddan ap Llyr and Rhiannon ferch Hefeydd Hen. The change from a single ruler to a pair, male and female, deserves careful meditation.

The following three triads discuss the relations which men may have with beings of the two other kinds just discussed, the Folk of the Path of Descent and the Folk of the Region of the Summer Stars, as well as with those of his own evolutionary current who are not presently embodied in Abred, or who have passed beyond such embodiment.

Triad IV.

Three doors that open upon the worlds of spiritual beings: the door of invocation, the door of evocation, and the door of vision.

Triad V.

Three spirits whom it is well to call upon: a spirit of Ceugant, a spirit of Gwynfydd, or a spirit of the Halls of Splendor.

Triad VI.

Three spirits whom it is ill to call upon: a spirit of Annwn, a spirit of Abred, or a spirit of the Halls of the Hollow Forms.

Triad IV.

Three doors that open upon the worlds of spiritual beings: the door of invocation, the door of evocation, and the door of vision.

The arts of invocation, evocation, and vision belong to that general class of occult phenomena which enable a human being to come into contact with entities other than those presently embodied in material form in Abred. Each of these terms has its own meaning in the tradition of Druid wisdom fundamental to this course, and that meaning differs somewhat from the meanings the same terms are given in more common use, or in other occult writings.

These three words each came to English from the Latin language. The word "invocation" means "calling in," the word "evocation" means "calling forth," and "vision" means "seeing." Certain occult writings use the term "invocation" to refer to "calling in" other beings into the body, as in possession and Spiritualist mediumship, and the term "evocation" to refer to "calling forth" other beings outside the body; however valid these descriptions may be within these other traditions, they are not those used among Druids.

Rather, what is "called in" in the act of invocation is an influence from without the self, which enables the self to perceive entities normally beyond the reach of its perceptions. It has been said, and truly, that we walk unawares amidst angels and archangels, and could be as truly said that we walk unawares amidst devils and arch-devils. In his play *Doctor Faustus*, Marlowe[11] pictures the sorcerer Faustus asking Mephistopheles the devil why he does not remain in his proper place in hell, and has Mephistopheles reply, "Why, this is Hell, nor am I out of it." Faustus by his incantation has invoked into himself the baleful influences of what occult tradition would term a lower plane of existence than his own, termed "hell" by ordinary religion, and thus can see and speak with one of the dwellers of that plane.

The same action performed in an opposite sense happens when a saint, a sage, or an ordinarily devout person prays to the god or goddess of his belief, and is rewarded by a vision of the deity or a sense of the deity's living presence. The god or the goddess was always there; it was the influence invoked by the prayer that enabled the devotee to perceive that fact, to whatever degree the influences of the invocation are capable of providing him.

Evocation is by contrast a calling forth, and what is called forth is a power that exists within the individual soul, or more precisely in the magical mirror of the Cosmos, the third aspect of the astral body discussed in a lecture in the lesson packet of the preceding grade. This magical mirror of the Cosmos contains

---

11. Christopher Marlowe, second only to Shakespeare as a dramatist in the time of Queen Elizabeth.

reflections of everything in the Cosmos, colored to one degree or another by the habitual thoughts and feelings of the individual. What is perceived through the magical mirror of the Cosmos, in an act of evocation, commonly takes the appearance of imagination, and only after appropriate training and much practice can the student learn to keep evoked images and entities distinct from the products of his own imagination, that is, to distinguish between those images projected upon the magical mirror from within and those projected upon it from without.

Vision, finally, is that inborn capacity to perceive and experience other planes that in the lore of the Scottish Highlands is called the "second sight," and has had many names in other places and times. The forms and expressions of vision differ from person to person; for some, it may be set in motion by some charm or formula, while with others it comes and goes of its own accord. There are seers—men possessed of this gift or, more often, women, for it more commonly appears in the female sex—whose visions are limited to glimpses of the next person to die in the parish where they reside, or some similarly restricted class of event, while the visions of others range far and wide. In ancient times, such people in Celtic lands who were possessed of the gift of vision were counted among Druids, and received Druidical instruction; in the world of today, it is only now and then that one gifted with the Second Sight takes up the path of the Druid mysteries, and so instruction relevant to vision is not continued here.

Triad V.

Three spirits whom it is well to call upon: a spirit of Ceugant, a spirit of Gwynfydd, or a spirit of the Halls of Splendor.

The invocation of spiritual beings by means of prayer and ceremonial forms is seemingly as old as humanity. All the ancient peoples invoked greater and lesser deities, as well as many beings who were by no means regarded as divine, and down to the present time we find prayer and other modes of invocation actively employed in all forms of religious worship. Evocation, for its part, has been much practiced down through the centuries, and history displays many instances of invocation of the power of genii and similar beings by means of ceremonial magic and the like. The better class of magical books from earlier times are filled with directions for ceremonial workings of this kind.

The modern mind regards evocation as a product of credulity and ignorance, and this prejudice generally extends to the once respectable religious practice of invoking the power of angels, saints, and other beings that, while not divine, are higher than man. Even so, the most ardent objector to the invocation of these lesser beings, if he remain in the bosom of the churches, is apt to adhere to the old custom of calling upon his own deity for assistance in the affairs of his life, often going so far as to offer his deity ample advice concerning the conduct, operation and management of the Cosmos as a whole, as well as whatever corner of it he happens to inhabit.

Despite the embarrassing nature of these latter excesses, we must not lose sight of the too-often overlooked fact that prayers are indeed answered—that heartfelt prayer very often does seem to bring about favorable results, not alone in those situations in which faith and confidence has a great role to play in bringing success in place of failure, but even when the undoubted influence of some exterior factor has been at work. Furthermore, these "answers to prayer" come to people of all shades of religious belief—to heathens, pagans, and idolaters around the globe, and in all times—as well as to believers in the particular faith which happens to be orthodox in our particular land at this particular time. Thus the unbiased investigator must either accept the polytheistic idea of the existence of many gods of many people, all of whom hear and answer the prayers of their worshippers, or else the alternative idea that all of these various worshippers, while worshipping at their respective shrines and altars, bring themselves in communication with higher spiritual powers, and thus set in operation natural psychic forces which tend to bring to them their desire; or must accept both of these.

The Druid tradition holds that both these ideas are by and large correct. There is, according to the Druid teaching, one source from which the whole of the Cosmos takes its beginning and its order, which is Awen; there is one life which flows through all things, which is nwyfre; but there are many beings who are of a level above that of humanity, who may be contacted by the methods of invocation taught in ordinary religion as well as those communicated in the mystery schools, as well as the methods of evocation properly restricted to the initiates of the mysteries; and that spiritual influences pass through these beings from the One Life, in accordance with Awen, to bring the blessings brought by prayer.

What is essential in this process, whatever the details of the method by which it is performed, is that the being called upon be of a grade higher than that of the one who invokes or evokes. The beings enumerated in the triad are of this nature; the spirits of Ceugant are those previously named the Folk of the Region of the Summer Stars, or the gods and goddesses; the spirits of Gwynfydd are those of our own evolution who have already passed beyond Abred, while the spirits of the Halls of Splendor are those beings of the Path of Descent who are in grade above those of humanity presently embodied in Abred. They are closer to the source of all things than are the embodied humanity of today, and thus may be contacted by means of invocation or evocation with favorable results, provided only that the contact is made with a laudable motive and the man who thus seeks contact with the higher realms of existence has some understanding of the forms and processes involved.

Triad VI.

Three spirits whom it is ill to call upon: a spirit of Annwn, a spirit of Abred, or a spirit of the Halls of the Hollow Forms.

By the same principle, those beings that are of grades lower than ours, further from the source of being, may not be called forth safely or with benefit, and workings that call upon them should be avoided by all students of the mysteries. Three classes of such beings are named in the triad. The first, the spirits of Annwn, are not to be confused with that great family of beings of the Path of Descent that are known as the Family of Annwn; they have their name on account of their rulership over that realm, while the spirits of Annwn here named are those who inhabit that realm and are subject to the rulership of the great ones of the Path of Descent.

The spirits of Annwn properly so called are those potencies who are outside of and beneath the world of life. They have been named "demons" in some traditions, and condemned as powers of evil, but this is a misunderstanding of their nature, for they are not evil in themselves, only in the consequences they bring when brought into contact with the world of humanity. Though men credit them with cunning and malice, the spirits of Annwn have only the most rudimentary consciousness, and simply follow the laws of their being without regard to what their actions may or may not do to other beings. Just as a flame carelessly handled may burn down a house and cause the deaths of the people dwelling there, a demonic spirit deliberately or accidentally brought into contact with the world of men may cause much harm without any deliberate intention to do so on the part of the spirit.

The spirits of Abred referred to in the triad are the spirits of the human dead who have not yet passed beyond material embodiment, but wait between lives for their next incarnation.

The spirits of the Halls of the Hollow Forms, finally, are those beings referred to in an earlier lesson, who have attempted to refuse the cycle of rebirth by building for themselves astral forms in which to dwell on the coming of death.

There are many manuals of corrupt magic that claim to grant their possessors the keys to commanding spirits or demons, and make grandiloquent promises of the benefits to be gained by such activities. It is rare indeed for the workings contained in such books to enable human beings to come into contact with the spirits of Annwn themselves, for these latter are all but mindless and respond only to the laws of their own nature and the direction of those beings superior to them in grade, who have the right and duty of directing their actions. In most cases, what responds to such a summons is a spirit of the Halls of the Hollow Forms, though it sometimes happens that one of the ordinary dead or a lowly elemental spirit may come in answer to the call.

When a spirit of the Halls of the Hollow Forms is contacted, it may be counted upon to say anything the summoner desires to hear, and to make whatever pretense is necessary of great power and knowledge, for the magician who thus summons such a spirit has the one thing the spirit desires, which is access to the currents of nwyfre that flow through the bodies of the living. By vampirizing the living, such spirits prolong their own existence, while the deluded magician feeds the spirit he has summoned with his own life energy, and is commonly subject to failing health as a result. Misled by the flattering words of the spirit, gulled by lavish promises of wealth, power, and the satisfaction of every desire, the fulfillment of which always remains just out of reach, those who fall under the influence of such a spirit waste their lives and substance, and not uncommonly come to an early end.

The triads that follow discuss, in greater detail, certain phenomena of spirits frequently encountered at the present day.

Triad VII.

Three deceptions suffered by those who traffick in spirits: the deceiving form, the deceiving name, the deceiving mind.

Triad VIII.

Three dealings of men with the creatures of the elements: by right, in the schools of the mysteries; by favor, in the course of nature; by violation, in the rites of those who demand through fear what they cannot claim through wisdom or love.

Triad IX.

Three creations of spiritual beings by men: by repeated thought, by strong emotion, and by will deliberately directed.

Triad VII.

Three deceptions suffered by those who traffick in spirits: the deceiving form, the deceiving name, the deceiving mind.[12]

One of the most common forms of evocation at the present time is the calling forth of disembodied human beings by means of a "medium," or person in the flesh, whose vital power is used by the disembodied entity to manifest itself on the material plane. In some of the instances of this form of evocation the disembodied entity is a deliberate actor in the process, while in others the medium is the active party in the transaction, and calls forth the entity from its astral state. Very few indeed of these manifestations are the entities which they purport to represent. The entities involved are little more than impostors from the Astral Plane, who assume the image of friends and relatives of those present, copying the mental image of the departed one which exists in the mind of those present, and which is called forth into memory by the suggestive atmosphere of the seance.

There are also entities of various classes whose existence keeps them close to the material plane and swarm about ceremonies in which spirits are evoked, whether these be the seances of modern Spiritualism or practices of the same kind in other times and places. These entities often act the part of some celebrated character of history, or some friend or relative of those present. It is entities of this kind that make Shakespeare write doggerel, or Napoleon tell someone what to take to get rid of a cold; or Plato promise a maiden that someone "tall, dark, and handsome" waits in her future. These performances have brought Spiritualistic phenomena into disrepute in many quarters where the

---

12. This triad is largely about Spiritualism, a popular movement at the time when the original version of this course was written. I have left the triad and discussion unchanged, because many of the same habits are common in today's popular spirituality under other names.

state of affairs is not known, and caused much pain and heart-burnings among the sincere early followers of Spiritualism who were not acquainted with these psychic facts, but who accepted as "gospel truth" every communication reaching them from the "spirit world."

The average Spiritualist of today is better informed, and is disposed to be quite as particular in forming "spirit" acquaintances and friendships as he is in forming earthly ones. Much of the testimony given at seances by even reputable and truthful entities is, however, more or less incorrect. These entities, as a rule, are familiar only with their own dim memories of the life they have just left, and with such glimpses of the Cosmos as their current conditions have permitted them to grasp. This accounts for the often contradictory statements offered by such entities about any subject upon which they may be consulted. The result of these three factors is an almost complete lack of veracity in the results of Spiritualist communication. It is for this reason among others that the mystery schools caution their students against dabbling in Spiritualism.

Triad VIII.

Three dealings of men with the creatures of the elements: by right, in the schools of the mysteries; by favor, in the course of nature; by violation, in the rites of those who demand through fear what they cannot claim through wisdom or love.

The art of evocation may also under some circumstances be applied to elemental beings, those creatures of the Path of Descent that correspond, in their own evolutionary current, to the animal creation in ours. These beings are semi-intelligent living forces, which under certain conditions may be evoked and guided by the intelligence of human beings. Those who dwell in Gwynfydd have certain privileges in dealing with the elemental creation, and these privileges have been extended to those who follow the way of the mysteries while still in Abred, though that privilege must needs be used with circumspection and forbearance.

The same privilege, on the other side of existence, allows the high entities of the Path of Descent whom we have termed the spirits of the Halls of Splendor to command the animal creation. This privilege likewise descends to those of their evolution who are somewhat lower down the scale; it is for this reason that the folklore of many lands recounts tales of elves and faeries having special powers over animals.

The exercise of this privilege by human beings embodied in Abred is granted from above, not requested from below, and it may be withdrawn at any moment should it be abused. The same is true of the second form of dealing with the elemental creation, which happens when beings of that creation, or of the levels above theirs in the Path of Descent, come into contact with human beings and establish friendly relations. This is much less common at the present time than in the past, when very many people lived close to nature in regions where human industry had made but little change to the natural order. In such conditions, it was not uncommon for the folk of the two Paths, ascending and descending, to have dealings with one another, and while the conditions placed on such dealings were kept by both sides, many benefits followed.

There remains a third form of dealing with the elemental creation, which is that practiced by certain traditions of evil magic that seek to force elemental beings to pander to their desires. This can be done, at least for a time, but it inevitably brings retribution in its wake. The elementals under compulsion may be forced to grant whatever favors are demanded of them, but will take every opportunity to turn the demand against their summoner, while other spirits of the elements, and those spirits of higher grade that govern the elemental creation, cannot but resent such violence being offered to the inhabitants of their kingdom, and will direct the forces of the elements at their command to harm the magician whenever they can.

Triad IX.

Three creations of spiritual beings by men: by repeated thought, by strong emotion, and by will deliberately directed.

Many of the apparent entities encountered by men, whether in the practice of magic or in ordinary life, are created by the human mind itself. They are the result of strong currents of will and desire generated in the minds of men. The discussion of enchantment in an earlier lecture of this grade may be read again at this stage of your studies with advantage, for the charge placed by strong emotion in an object is one form of the phenomenon under discussion here.

The energies of life and meaning released by thought, emotion, or will may or may not find a home within a particular material object. Those that do not find such a home have a different destiny than those that do. The homeless energies tend to coalesce and combine, and gather in the vicinity where similar mental influences are being exerted. To the clairvoyant eye they are like clouds on the horizon, inactive in themselves, but capable of bursting forth in lightning and thunder under the proper conditions. These conditions are often supplied by persons of strong desire or focused will, who vitalize them by the force of their own habitual thinking, strong emotions or deliberate intent.

These "clouds" of thought and energy may either be directed toward the accomplishment of some desired end, if the person who summons them has the strength of will to manage them; otherwise, they may draw him into a psychic whirlwind until he is overwhelmed. The saying that one who "sows the wind, reaps the whirlwind" is quite true in such cases. The person who draws such patterns of energy to himself by unguarded thought or unrestrained passion is not uncommonly swept along with them, and caused great pain and misfortune thereby. The biographies of many prominent people provide ample evidence for this phenomenon, although the public does not understand it.

What we have described as clouds of thought and emotion, if sufficiently reinforced by the repetition of the same thoughts, the intensity of similar passions, or the deliberate action of a strong will, may develop enough stability and internal coherence to function, in some senses, as an independent being. Being entirely the creation of men, they are linked to him by the closest bonds, and their action upon him is direct and incessant. The realm of these "artificial elementals" is an enormous inchoate mass of semi-intelligent entities, differing among themselves as human thoughts differ, and practically impossible to classify according to any meaningful scheme. The one division which can be usefully made is that which distinguishes between artificial elementals made by the majority of mankind unconsciously, and those made by magicians with definite intent.

The astral level of existence, being that level at which the forces we experience as thought and feeling have their natural home, is singularly susceptible to the influence of thought and emotion. A casual wandering thought sets it in motion, forming a cloud of evanescent and ever-changing forms. When the human mind formulates a definite, purposeful thought or wish, however, the effect produced is of a more striking nature. The thought shapes the astral essence into what may best be described as a living being—a being which when thus created is not under the control of its creator, but lives out a life of its own, the length of which is proportionate to the intensity of the thoughts or wish which called it into existence. It lasts in fact just as long as the energy of the thought that created it holds it together.

Most persons' thoughts are so fleeting that the elementals created by them last only a few minutes or a few hours, but a frequently repeated thought or an earnest desire will form an artificial elemental whose existence may extend to many days. Since the ordinary man's thoughts refer very largely to himself, the elementals which they form remain hovering about, and constantly tend to provoke a repetition of the idea which they represent, since such repetitions, instead of forming new elementals, would strengthen the old one, and give it a fresh lease of life. A man, therefore, who frequently dwells upon one wish often forms for himself an astral attendant which, constantly fed by fresh thought, may haunt him for years, ever gaining more and more strength and influence over him; and it will easily be seen that if the desire be an evil one the effect upon his moral nature may be of the most disastrous character.

Still more pregnant for good or evil are a man's thoughts about other people, for in that case they hover not about the thinker, but about the object of the thought. A kindly thought about any person, or an earnest wish for his good, will form and project towards him a friendly artificial elemental. If the wish be a definite one, as, for example, that he may recover from some sickness, then the elemental will be a force ever hovering over him to promote his recovery, or to ward off any influence that might tend to hinder it. In doing this it will display what appears like a very considerable amount of intelligence and adaptability, though really it is simply a force acting along the line of least resistance—pressing steadily in one direction all the time, and taking advantage of any channel that it can find, just as the water in a cistern would in a moment find the one open pipe among a dozen closed ones, and proceed to empty itself through that.

If the wish be merely an indefinite one for his general good, the astral essence will respond exactly to that less distinct idea also, and the creature formed will expend its force in the direction of whatever action for the man's advantage comes most readily to hand. In all cases, the amount of such force which it has to expend, and the length of time that it will live to expend it, depend entirely upon the strength of the original wish or thought which gave it birth; though it must be remembered that it can be, as it were, fed and strengthened, and its life-period protracted by other good wishes or friendly thoughts projected in the same direction. Furthermore, it appears to be actuated, like most other beings, by an instinctive desire to prolong its life, and thus reacts on its creator as a force constantly tending to provoke the renewal of the feelings which called it into existence. It also influences in a similar manner others with whom it comes into contact, though its rapport with them is naturally not so perfect.

All that has been said as to the effect of good wishes and friendly thoughts is also true in the opposite direction of evil wishes and angry thoughts; and considering the amount of envy, hatred, malice and uncharitableness that exists in the world, it will be readily understood that among artificial elementals these more destructive forms are common. A man whose thoughts or desires are spiteful, brutal, sensual, avaricious, moves through the world carrying with him everywhere a cloud of such beings, harming not only himself, but his fellow men, subjecting all who have the misfortune to come in contact with him to the risk of moral contagion from the influence of the astral atmosphere with which he chooses to surround himself. Many a well-meaning man, who is scrupulously careful to do his duty toward his neighbor in word and deed, is apt to consider that his thoughts at least are nobody's business but his own, and so lets them run riot in various directions, utterly unconscious of the swarms of baleful creatures which he is launching upon the world. To such a man an accurate comprehension of the effect of thought and desire in producing artificial elementals would come as a horrifying revelation.

It occasionally happens, however, that an artificial elemental of this description is for various reasons unable to expend its force either upon its object or its creator, and in such cases it becomes a kind of wandering demon, readily attracted by any person who indulges feelings similar to that which gave it birth, and equally prepared either to stimulate such feelings in him for the sake of the strength it may gain from them, or to pour out its store of evil influences upon him through any opening which he may offer it. If it is sufficiently powerful to seize upon some discarded astral body it frequently does so, as the possession of such a temporary home enables it to survive for a longer period. In this form it may manifest through a Spiritualist medium, and by masquerading as some well-known friend may sometimes obtain an influence over people upon whom it would otherwise have little hold.

Since such results as have been described above have been achieved by the thought-force of men who were entirely in the dark as to what they were doing, it will readily be imagined that a magician who understands the subject, and can see exactly what effect he is producing, may wield considerable power along these lines. As a matter of fact, occultists of many schools frequently use artificial elementals in their work, and can accomplish much by means of the powers of such creatures when they are scientifically prepared and directed with knowledge and skill; for one who knows how to do so can maintain a connection with his elemental and guide it, no matter at what distance it may be working, so that it will practically act as though endowed with the full intelligence of its master.

Such creatures occasionally, for various reasons, escape from the control of those who are trying to make use of them, and become wandering and aimless demons, as do some of those mentioned under the previous heading under similar circumstances; but those deliberately created, having much more intelligence and power, and a longer existence, are proportionately more dangerous when the purpose that created them was harmful or selfish in nature. They invariably seek for means of prolonging their life, either by feeding upon the vitality of human beings, or by influencing them to make offerings to them; and they have now and then succeeded in being mistaken for minor gods. By the vitality they draw from their devotees, they may continue to prolong their existence for many years, retaining the strength to perform occasional phenomena of a mild type in order to stimulate the faith of their followers.

The power of even such deliberately created elementals is far from insuperable, for the human will that created them is also sufficient to overcome them, and they cannot come into close contact with any person who does not share the character of their own mental vibrations. Nevertheless, it is worthwhile to be aware of the existence of such entities, and likewise to know of the consequences of misdirected thoughts, emotions, and intentions. The saying that "no man is an island" contains deep truth, for the influences each person sends forth from what he fondly considers the privacy of his own thoughts are pregnant with good or evil consequences, as much for that person as for all with whom he or she may come into contact.

THE MAGICAL MEMORY: THE LAWS OF MEMORY

Association, Resemblance and Contiguity

MANY OF US FANCY that our thoughts, when not impelled in a certain direction by the will, come floating through our minds at random and in obedience to no law. When we see the apparent lack of connection between succeeding trains of thought we may be excused for holding such an opinion. But this idea is far removed from the real state of affairs, for although not clearly apparent, there is always a connecting link between one line of thought and the one succeeding it. What governs the connection between one train of thought and another is the law of association, and it is just as inflexible as is the law of cause and effect in other fields—just as unvarying as is the law of gravitation. The sequence of our thoughts is as much the result of law as is the fall of the apple from the tree—the rise and fall of the tides. Our ideas are always associated in some way, although in many cases we may not be able to clearly trace the connection. Memories come to our awareness in groups, and each group, in turn, is associated with some other group.

In a previous lesson we spoke of the importance of attention in memory training. Next to attention, a clear grasp of the principle of association may be considered the most important step toward a mastery of memory. The recording faculty of the memory depends largely upon the degree of attention bestowed upon the object or subject to be remembered, while the reproducing function depends very materially upon the closeness of the association by which the impression is linked to other impressions which have been previously recorded. Authorities on psychology go so far as to claim that the law of association is to psychology what the law of gravitation is to physics. The habit of making clear and meaningful associations is thus one of the most important requisites in the cultivation of the power of recollection.

In recording or storing away impressions, the best results are obtained when we concentrate our attention upon the thing under consideration. In recollecting these impressions, however, the best results are obtained by being able to associate the desired impression with one or more other impressions, and the greater the number of associated impressions, the greater the ease of recollection. Unless we have obtained a clear impression, the recalled impression will be imperfect, and, unless the impression be associated in some way with other impressions, we may not be able to recall it at all.

The principle of association is based upon that remarkable tendency of an impression to become so connected with one or more other impressions, that the recalling of one impression will bring into the field of consciousness the associated impressions. Association by resemblance depends upon the fact that an impression, either new or recalled, has a tendency to revive a previously recorded impression which resembles it in some particular, and the two thus become associated in the memory. The first impression may not have been previously associated with the second, and the latter may have been recalled only through a long chain of associations, but when the two have once been closely considered together, they are therefore associated closely and one may recall the other without making use of the previously necessary chain of association. The two impressions may originally have been recorded at times far apart from each other, and at different places, but when the resemblance is close, or is afterward made close by attention, they become as closely associated as if they were contiguous in time or place. The trained mind readily sees points of resemblance between apparently widely separated things, and this perceived resemblance records itself in the memory. Such a mind needs but to be given a start and it will bring into the field of consciousness an amazing chain of associated ideas, facts, incidents, illustrations, etc.

On the other hand, the careless mind, having paid no attention to the relation between things, is unable to recall separated impressions by means of this principle of association by resemblance, and is able to recall only those things which are associated by contiguity. Association by contiguity is like counting a string of beads of all kinds, one after the other, in the order in which they were strung, while association by resemblance is like pulling out a drawer in which has been placed everything we know concerning the matter under consideration, and taking from it article after article as each presents itself, choosing and selecting the best for the occasion, irrespective of the time in which they had been filed away. Impressions so associated are readily recalled when an occasion presents itself which calls for the aid of our past experiences and impressions, the occasion being the primary cause of the recall of all the information and accumulated experiences upon the subject that have been impressed upon our memory.

Association by contiguity depends upon the fact that an impression, either new or received, has a tendency to recall other impressions recorded at the same time, or in immediate succession. Impressions that are recorded in close succession have a tendency to so associate themselves and join themselves together, that the recollection of the one will usually recall the others. There is a strong affinity between an impression and the one which immediately precedes or follows it. It may be said that, generally speaking, there is no such thing as an isolated impression. Each impression is practically a continuation of a preceding one, and the beginning of a succeeding one. Thus when we read or hear a sentence, for example at the commencement of the fifth word something of the fourth word still remains in mind. The end of the fourth word impinges on the beginning of the fifth.

In association by contiguity several impressions are recorded directly after the other, and when one is recalled it will bring the other in its train, and so on, from impression to impression. Thus it is easy to repeat a familiar sentence word for word, as they occurred in the text, but we would find it quite difficult to repeat it backwards or to name in a different order the several words composing it. In a poem, the end of each word being associated with the beginning of the succeeding word, we find it easy to repeat them in that order, each word suggesting the next. The child repeats the alphabet from A to Z readily, but ask him to recite them from Z backwards to A and he will be unable to do it, unless he has practiced it in that order. Some persons who have acquired considerable proficiency in feats of memory are able to repeat hundreds of words by the aid of contiguity, but find themselves unable to commence at any particular part of their task if they are compelled to omit the part preceding it. One famous practitioner of the mnemonic arts in the last century could repeat an entire Act of Parliament from beginning to end, without missing a word, but was unable to take up any named portion of it without going over the preceding sections.

Most of the formal systems of mnemonics have been based upon the principle of contiguous association. The oldest and most famous of these is the famous Art of Memory invented in ancient Greek times by Simonides of Ceos.

In this system, each item to be remembered is turned in the imagination into a picture, and the pictures arranged in the imagination in the inside of a familiar place, such as a house. The habit of mentally "walking" through the house, seeing all the pictures that have been arranged in each of the several rooms, wonderfully develops the habit of associating the pictures together by contiguity; and it becomes easy to call each of the pictures and its associated memory to mind instantly by repeating the imagined walk through the room containing the memories needed in any given case. Furthermore, the imagined house allows the rememberer to leave behind the strict sequence of contiguity; had the mnemonist previously mentioned used this method, and assigned each section of an Act of Parliament to some room in an imagined building, recalling its different sections in any order required would have been a simple process indeed.

Whether or not one chooses to follow any such system, however, the student will find it useful to cultivate this faculty of deliberately associating impressions, as it is much easier to recall impressions when they are closely associated with other impressions along the lines of contiguity. This faculty may be developed by exercises designed to concentrate the attention upon an impression and the one immediately succeeding it, or preceding it, so that the two may become practically welded together. Others may then be added until they are connected in such a way that to remember one is to recall all. The closer the contact the easier the recall—the sooner they are connected the more complete the welding. If the two impressions are not quickly and closely connected, there is always the chance that an irrelevant thought may come in between them and interfere with the contiguous association.

An understanding of this great law of association of impressions shows us that when we wish to store away an isolated fact in such a way that we may readily recall it, we must associate it with some other impression already stored away. The more we can associate a fact with other known facts, the more readily will we recall it and the more associations we can give an impression the better it is for the purpose. Things which were not originally contiguously associated, but which were associated by resemblance, may be made contiguously associated by their recall by resemblance several times in the same order, as they thus fall under the law of contiguity as well as the law of resemblance. The greater and more numerous the resemblances, the easier and surer the recall. The apparently wonderful powers of memory of miscellaneous facts possessed by some well-read and close-observing men, is due to the fact that they are able to find points of resemblance between widely separated facts, and are able to run from one set of facts to another in a way impossible to a man who has not cultivated the power of association by resemblance. Such men will, in effect, take hold of a loose end of thought, and then simply unwind the ball.

Remembrance, Recollection, and Recognition

To understand in greater depth the functioning of the law of association, it is valuable to recognize the difference between three functions of the memory: resemblance, recollection, and recognition. While these three words are frequently used as meaning practically the same thing, each has a definite meaning, and refers to a distinct process of the memory.

Remembrance means that process of the memory whereby previously stored impressions come again into the field of consciousness without an effort of the will, as by the normal functioning of the associative function. Recollection is the word used to describe that process of the memory whereby a man recalls, by an effort of the will, some impression previously stored away. Remembrance is apparently automatic in its action, while recollection is a deliberate act, and is often accompanied with much effort. Recognition is the word applied to that process of the memory whereby, when we see or hear a thing, we know that we have seen or heard it before. It is a conscious association of the present impression with one had before. It is a re-cognizing—literally, a re-knowing. If we see a thing on two different occasions, and do not "know" it when seen the second time, we do not recognize it, and the memory stores away two different impressions of the thing. If afterwards, we become aware of the identity of the two impressions, they become fused into one impression. Authorities in the field of psychology have proposed three laws of remembrance, as follows:

1. All impressions have a tendency to revive previous impressions of a similar character; but a previously received impression will not thus be brought again into the field of consciousness, unless it be sufficiently distinct, unless the originally faint impression has been recalled to the consciousness by recollection and strengthened by repeated revivals.
2. An impression received similar to one previously received, if not recognized as being similar, will be stored away as a separate impression. But if the previous impression be recalled at the same time, and recognized as similar, the two impressions will be associated in the memory, and stored away together.

3. When one part of an associated series of impressions is revived, the other parts may be revived if desired with a minimum of effort; and the revival of an impression renders easier the revival of any impression received about the same time, without reference to resemblance.

In considering the first law of remembrance, we must not forget that one may see a resemblance between things which, to another person, appear to have no connection or resemblance. This difference, of course, is carried out in the application of this law. If the resemblance is not seen or recognized, there is no association in the process of remembering.

The act of remembering is almost altogether a subconscious one and we are not consciously aware of its workings. We may be lost in thought and one subject after another passes before the consciousness, and we do not perceive the connection or association at the time. We can often, however, retrace the steps taken and can see the slight thread of connection between the different subjects of our thought. It was with this retracing in mind that a lecture in the second or Theoretical grade of this study course taught you to trace out the Seven Ways of Thought; you may find it useful to review that lecture and apply its teachings to the memory work of the present grade.

When we remember a thing it is generally because the association is natural to the remembering mind, following chains of associations that have been laid down by repeated remembrance. When we seek to recollect a thing, by contrast, we must use the will to find connections and associations between a number of things before the missing impression is found. There is scarcely any conscious mentation required in the case of remembrance as compared with the process of recollection. The one is automatic, the other deliberate and potentially forced.

We have spoken of the fact that it is difficult to bring into the field of consciousness an impression that has been but faintly recorded, while it is comparatively easy to so bring forth one that has been clearly and distinctly recorded by means of the attention. But a poor impression may be strengthened by a frequent revival, until it will become nearly or quite as distinct, and as easy to recall, as one of original clear recording. Impressions received under circumstances of great importance are apt to be clearly recollected and consequently easily recalled.

We desire to call your attention to an important fact concerning the revival of impressions, and the consequent strengthening of the original impressions by the revival. It is the fact that the gist of the whole strengthening process lies in the conscious revival of the original impression, the holding of it before the field of consciousness by the attention, and the sending it back to the storehouse strengthened by the new amount of attention bestowed upon it. The conscious revival of a previous impression, and the new attention given it, is worth much more to the strength of the memory than the repeated viewing of the object originally causing the impression, at least so far as that particular impression is concerned. Of course a repeated view of the object will probably bring to light details which were not included in the first impression. We have spoken of this in previous lessons.

In the same way, if, when you see a thing, a past impression is recalled and is thus associated, the old impression becomes a part of the new, and thereafter it is hard to separate them. We have much unavailable unused material in our memories, which might be of the greatest use to us if we had occasion to associate it with some other memory. Sometimes we take up a new subject of thought, and form a connection and association between scores of disconnected facts which had been lying around loose in our mental storehouse.

Recollection is always accompanied with an effort of the will to *find* some chain of association which we desire to recall. This process may take but a fraction of a second, as the mind works very rapidly and the chain of association is soon formed. But often it takes some time before we are able to recall the desired thing, and many times we have to acknowledge our inability to bring forth the missing impression, but the orders given will often be taken up by the subconscious mentality and the impression will come into consciousness at some later time, often when we have ceased to think of the desire.

In recalling an impression one has often to recall the circumstances and place of the recording of the desired impression, or what took place just before or just after the fact he desires to recall. The mind instinctively calls upon the strongest faculty to supply the cue to the whole series of impressions.

In considering the matter of recognition, in turn we see that there is a distinction between what may be called *full recognition*, and what may be termed *partial recognition*. When we meet a man whom we have previously met, and recognize his appearance, and remember his name, who he is, what he does, etc., we fully recognize him. But when we meet a man whose face we recognize but whose name we fail to remember, or when we recognize his face, or even recognize his face and remember his name but fail to remember who he is and the circumstances of our former meeting, we have only *partially* recognized him.

There is a common joke about a man who once met a lady whose face he recognized but whose name he could not remember. Falling back on the old expedient he said, "Madam, I have forgotten the spelling of your name. Will you kindly tell me just how you spell it?"

"Certainly," said the lady, "I spell it J-o-n-e-s."

When we meet with a person who accosts us by name, and whose face we dimly recognize, but whom we 'cannot place,' we may remain in his company for a time, and then suddenly some allusion will give us the missing association and we remember clearly all that we have ever known about the individual.

There is a difference between remembering a thing and recognizing it. How many times have we sought for a thing which we distinctly remembered but which we were unable to find! Shortly thereafter, we found the thing in a place that we have looked over several times, and it seems impossible that we did not see it. The trouble is that our faculty of recognition was not functioning properly, and although we saw the object we failed to recognize it. This trouble may be largely overcome by first forming a distinct mental image of the thing sought for, in which case we will recognize the object as soon as seen. This will apply to any object no matter how familiar we may be with it, as unless the mental image is sufficiently clear we will not recognize it even though we see it, our memory of it for the moment being merely a memory of name and not of appearance. A man may hunt for his wife in a crowd, and will not find her, although he may be looking her right in the face. His anxiety has driven away the mental image.

General Principles for Using the Memory

The following principles will give a general idea of the laws governing the receiving, recording and revival of impressions received by the memory. The student will most likely find them interesting, and they may aid in fastening in his mind the laws governing the mental operations known to us as memory. Some of what is said below has already been stated in other words in previous lessons, but we have thought it advisable to bring these things together in one chapter, that the student might more readily associate one principle with another akin to it.

PRINCIPLE 1.

Employ concentration so as to receive an impression sufficiently intense as to render easy a subsequent revival of the impression.

As we have explained before, it is necessary for the mind to be strongly directed toward the object or subject the impression of which we are desirous of recording in the mind in such a way as to be able to recall it with the least amount of exertion. Speaking generally, it may be said that the strength of the impression is in exact proportion to the amount of interest and attention bestowed upon the object or subject. Consequently it is of the utmost importance that we cultivate attention and interest, by practice, so as to be able to register a distinct impression. By doing this we have taken many steps toward the acquiring of a strong memory.

PRINCIPLE 2.

Record definitely and decidedly the primary impression.

Very much depends upon the sharpness of the primary impression. The primary impression is the foundation upon which subsequent impressions must be built, and if it be not distinct, it is very difficult to remedy the carelessness afterward, as in that case there has to be a tearing away of the primary impression, and a substitution of a new primary record, as otherwise there will be a confusion of memory. Therefore, in obtaining the first impression of an object or subject, direct upon it as much attention and interest as possible, and formulate the impression clearly in the mind so that it may be more easily recollected.

PRINCIPLE 3.

At the beginning, avoid including too many details in the impression.

This principle, if applied, will save the student much unnecessary work and waste of energy. The best plan is to master the main points of a subject at the beginning, then gradually add other important points to these. Then on to the less important, finishing up with the comparatively unimportant details. By forming a general idea of the subject to be studied, certain features will stand out more prominently. Study these first, getting a clear impression by omitting the lesser details, then stop and look over the subject again. You will then see other points standing out clearly. Take these up, and so on, until the subject is mastered. In this way you will be able to store away a complete record of the subject "from the ground up," and you will find it easy to recall to mind any part of it and at the same time be aware of the relation of that part to any other part.

This is the most rational plan of study. It will help you in following this method, to think of the subject to be mastered as being a tree. Commence at the ground and thoroughly understand the trunk, then take up the larger limbs, then the branches, then the twigs. In commencing the study of a new subject, accordingly, it is better to read first the most elementary work on the subject to be found, and after mastering this take up a work rather more advanced, and so on. Many make the mistake of reading at first the most complete work on the subject to be had, and the consequence usually is that they master no point completely, and have merely a vague idea of the entire subject. Some teachers advise the careful study of the subject as stated in some standard encyclopedia before even taking up the elementary text book. The rule of Nature is that we shall crawl before we walk, and study and memorizing is no exception to the rule.

PRINCIPLE 4.

By reviving an impression frequently, you increase its intensity.

The whole subject of memory training depends so much upon this one principle, that if we were compelled to take away this principle the whole structure would fall. Remember now, we are speaking of the conscious recollection of the original impression, and not of the receiving of a subsequent impression. By this method, not only is the impression intensified, but the will is trained to assist, and in a short time the recalling of the impression becomes almost automatic. By constant review, a subject becomes almost indelibly impressed upon the mind, and is recalled with the least possible effort. If you have observed the first three rules, you will have received impressions with a considerable degree of clearness, and by regular practice and reviewing you will be able to obtain a wonderfully deep and permanent impression of the subject under consideration. It sometimes happens that a man meeting a stranger and spending a whole evening in his company is yet unable to recognize him when he sees him a few days later. The writer points out that if the stranger had been seen for only five minutes a day for a fortnight, he would have been easily recognized, the constant repetition of the impression recording it strongly in his mind.

PRINCIPLE 5.

When reviving an impression, do it so far as possible without referring to the object itself, thus obtaining the greatest permanent intensity.

We have touched upon this principle in a previous lesson. The idea is that the impression should be revived mentally so far as is possible. Of course, it will be found that details have not been noticed, and it will be necessary to go back to the object to supply the things omitted, but first endeavor to recall plainly that which has been noticed, and thus intensify the impression. The details subsequently acquired are to be treated in the same way, each revival of impression including more details and being more complete. If you were to simply go and look at an object in a general way every day for a month you would not know half as much about it as would be the case if you had studied it carefully the first time, and then tried to mentally reproduce it either in the imagination or on paper with the aid of a pencil, and then repeated the process every day for a week, acquiring fresh details each day. In the latter case the second day's inspection would only include the points that had not been intensely impressed by the first day's view, and the new points closely observed would be added to the first day's impressions when both were reviewed or revived. "An unheard lesson is soon forgotten."

PRINCIPLE 6.

When practicing, first revive the previous impression of the subject or object, rather than attempting to receive a new impression.

This principle closely resembles the preceding one, and teaches that we should rely upon our memory as much as possible, instead of flying back to the subject or object as a whole, as soon as we find that we cannot easily recall any detail. Use the memory and thus strengthen it, instead of using it only when made necessary by the absence of the object itself. To do otherwise would be like keeping a copy of the multiplication tables handy to refer to whenever we had to multiply two figures, because that would be easier than taking the trouble to exercise our memory. If we depend upon receiving a new impression instead of reviving the old one, we will never really learn anything, and will be constantly compelled to go back to learn our lesson over again.

PRINCIPLE 7.

When a subject or an object is being studied for the first time, and therefore no previous impression has been recorded, it is well to think of a similar impression so as to establish a mental association.

This principle renders somewhat easier the receiving of impressions of a new object, as by connecting the new thing with something already learned, you gain the advantage of the association and the benefit of attaching the new impression to one that is already well fixed in the mind. It is akin to the observing of a new detail of an object and the including of that new detail in the next review, thus gaining the advantage of the previous strong impression and having a peg upon which to hang the new impression. If you meet a man named Thompson, and find it hard to recall the name, you will find it a material help to think of that man as having the same name as another friend of yours whose name is also Thompson, and whose name you never forget. The two men and their names are thus linked together in your memory, and you will find it very easy to remember the new acquaintance's name after forming the association. In the study of a new subject, always endeavor to connect it with the subject nearest associated to it, which you already know. If you can connect a thing with something similar to it, the mind will make the new thing a part of the old, and will not treat it as a newcomer. The mind seems to be somewhat conservative, and will get along better with a new acquaintance if it thinks it is related to an old friend.

PRINCIPLE 8.

It is well to establish a series of mental associations, so that one impression may revive the next of the series and so on.

When one part of a thing is remembered, the mind very readily recalls other parts of the same thing, and so when we join a number of things together, thus forming a chain, each link being a part of the whole, we will find it comparatively easy to start at any link and run backward or forward over the entire length of the chain. It is well to form the different parts of a subject into a series, arranging the parts in logical order so far as is possible. A new part may afterwards be inserted in its proper place, and recalled just as well as the old portions. The effect of association in recalling objects or subjects is wonderful. It is very much easier for a child to remember the letter H because he knows G, and associates H with it. We will find that our memory of many subjects is strikingly like that of the child's memory of the alphabet or multiplication table, so far as association is concerned. If you cannot remember a thing just when you desire to do so, the next best thing is to have a loose end which you can unwind until you get the desired thing. It would bother the average man to call off at random the names of the cross streets in the center of his city, but if he will start at the first one he will be able to run them off in proper order without much trouble. In the same way it is easy for the school-boy to name the Presidents of the United States, or the Kings of England, commencing with Washington or William the Conqueror, as the case may be.[13] But ask him to "mix them up" and give you the entire list and he will find it a very difficult task. We will find that the things we remember best are connected in our mind with something that came before or just after, or which in some other way bear some orderly relation to the remembered thing. In forming the mental series, follow the rule of the alphabet, or list of Presidents, and fasten the first one in your mind firmly, then add on the next, etc.

PRINCIPLE 9.

In the study or investigation of a subject or an object, use as many faculties as possible.

---

13. This used to be a standard requirement in elementary school education, which all but the least gifted students accomplished in a short time. Can you recall either sequence?

The value of this principle is perceived when we remember that each faculty registers upon the mind a separate impression, and when we use more than one faculty in the study of a thing, we receive as many sets of impressions as we have used faculties. If we are trying to commit a name or a date to memory, it will aid us materially if, in addition to repeating the name or date, we will write it down and study it with the eye, thus receiving the abstract impression of the thing, its sound, and the visual impression. In recalling it we may be helped either by the general remembrance of it, by its sound, or by our recollection of how it looked when written on paper.

Many persons giving public recitations say that the position of certain words and paragraphs appear before their mind's eye, just as they were on the page of the book from which the lines were read. Preachers who prepare their sermons in manuscript and study them over at home, going to the pulpit with only general notes or with no notes at all, tell us that they will see the position of each paragraph, and the first word of same, just before they reach it, looking just as it did in their manuscript. Public speakers experience the same thing. Many persons find themselves unable to remember a name unless they repeat it aloud once or twice. Many instances of the application of this principle will occur to you as you progress in your work of training the memory.

PRINCIPLE 10.

You may greatly improve weak faculties by exercises adapted to each.

When you find it difficult to recall impressions previously received from any particular faculty, it is well to begin training and developing that faculty to the end that it may register sharper impressions. Other chapters of this book will suggest many methods and ways of doing this. By developing a number of faculties, you will receive a greater number of intense impressions, and will, consequently, find it much easier to recall the thing wanted, as a greater number of impressions have been made sharply, and can be more easily found when wanted.

PRINCIPLE 11.

Difficulty in recalling an impression may be overcome by endeavoring to revive an impression received at the same time, or by trying to recall some associated component.

An instance of the application of this principle is had in the case of one who fails to recall a name. Try as he will, the name will not come into the field of consciousness. He then begins to run over the alphabet, slowly, pausing at each letter and considering it before passing on. Very often the thought of the first letter of the name will bring back the impression of the name itself. The initial letter of a name is often remembered more clearly than the balance of the name, and the latter is brought by association when the mind recalls the first letter. If this method fails, try the plan of trying to remember the person himself, how he looked and talked, when and where you first heard his name, etc., or if it be the name of a thing, apply the same rule, and try to recall the circumstances surrounding it, the qualities connected with the thing bearing the name, etc.

PRINCIPLE 12.

In endeavoring to recall an impression, think of some definite thing connected with it and revive others received about the same time. This is better than trying to recall it in an indiscriminate way.

When you are unable to succeed by the application of Principle 11, and can recall no impression received at the same time or component part, endeavor to recall the impression of something connected with the thing, in some way, getting as close to the object or subject as possible, and, if possible, the circumstances connected with the obtaining of the impression. Imagine yourself back in the position and under the circumstances that existed when the impression was received, and often you will start into operation a train of thought which will bring the desired thing into the field of consciousness.

PRINCIPLE 13.

When a previous impression is recalled, involuntarily, by the mind, after a previous unsuccessful attempt to recall it voluntarily, it is well to note the associated reviving impression, for future use and experiment.

This involuntary recollection of a thing which the mind has previously refused to recall is, of course, an effort of the subconscious function of the mind. But a little careful investigation will show that it came into the field of consciousness following closely another thought, although the connection between the two may not be apparent at first sight. By remembering the reviving impression, that is the impression which came into the field of consciousness just before the elusive impression, you may bring back the troublesome thing at will, no matter how long afterward the time may be when the word is again forgotten. The noting of the dim connection will often open up quite a field for thought and give the key to a further knowledge of the great subject of memory.

Exercise

The exercise for this lesson in memory work is less specific than those in previous lessons. Taking the thirteen principles just outlined for your guide, choose a subject about which you know nothing but would like to learn, study it, and commit what you learn to memory, so that by the time you finish the work of this grade, you can readily bring to mind both the general outline of the subject and such subsidiary details as you have chosen to recall. Test yourself at monthly intervals by writing out an account of some part of the subject you have chosen to remember, using no references other than those provided by your memory.

COMPLETION PRACTICE: THE DOCTRINE OF ONE

THESE EXERCISES, like the completion exercises of the preceding grades, are intended to be performed during the transition period between this grade and the next. You should begin them when you have finished the other work of this grade.

The previous completion practices, in conjunction with the other disciplines and studies of the Druid mysteries, have brought you to the point at which several higher formulae of the esoteric teachings may be applied. The secret of the Doctrine of One is among these core formulas, and is applied in one way or another by most of the occult fraternities. It has been called the keystone of the Mystic Arch. The following aphorism handed down by tradition, and repeated in a previous lesson, is relevant in this context:

> When a person approaches the awakening of individuality he enters into the realm of will, and rises above the realm of desire. Desire and will are the opposite poles of the same principle—the center of balance being reason. On the plane of will, though one remains under Awen, yet he may learn to respond actively to it instead of remaining passive to it. He may learn to balance the manifestations of Awen against one another. Furthermore, and this is the greatest of all, he may learn to will to will, to complete the circle of will. He may learn the secret of the Doctrine of One. When this last secret is learned, man is well on the road to mastery.

You have learned that from the One Life, which is the principle of all lives, the Cosmos has been evolved. The evolution of the Cosmos and everything in it has proceded under the direction of the One Life. In the life of the individual, the active manifestation of the One Life is a continuum of which the negative pole is desire and the positive pole is will. There is thus an unbroken chain of cause and effect extending from the One Life to the individual life, which is but a focused center in the life that is common to all.

At the personal or individual end of this unbroken chain, we find the individual will. But we find that this individual will is conditioned, restricted, bound and hampered by the accumulated burden of fate—that is, the consequences of its own previous actions, which have formulated a personality as a sheath within which the individuality evolves. The idea of separateness is the principle of personality, and the budding individuality fails to recognize that it is identical in nature and substance with the One Life, in which it is a center or focal point. So entangled is it in the bonds of personality, so deluded by the illusions of the "John Smith" nature and characteristics, that it imagines itself to be a thing apart. It feels the personal conscious on all sides, and actually imagines that it, the "I," is really this bundle of mental states, impressions and ideas that belong to "John Smith." It has exchanged its cosmic birthright for the humble mess of pottage of personality.

There is an ancient tale of one of the kings of Britain, Blaedud, who while still a young prince became afflicted with leprosy and fled from his father's court. He found employment as a swineherd, and spent his days driving his charges from their pens to the forests where they fed on acorns and beech mast. As time passed, his childhood at the royal court faded from his memory, and all that he could recall was his life as a swineherd. After some years in which he remained in this state, disfigured by leprosy and living a life scarce different from the pigs he tended, he noticed that some of his swine disappeared from the woods each day, returning an hour or so later coated with mud and seemingly greatly refreshed.

He followed them, and discovered, deep within the forest, a hot spring where healing mineral waters bubbled up through the earth. He took to leading his herd there each day and bathing himself in the waters, and found that the healing virtue of the spring cured his leprosy. As his flesh returned to its natural and wholesome state, his memory also returned to him, and when he was completely cured, he relinquished his swine to his former employer and returned to the royal court, where he was welcomed once again as a prince of the realm. The spring he had discovered is still in use at the town of Bath, in the west of Britain.

This was among the parables that the Druids of old used to teach their students about the difference between the personality and the individuality, and thus between the illusion of a separate personal existence that each of us has, and the reality of One Life of which each of us is a manifestation and an expression. Each of us is a prince or a princess laboring as a swineherd, waiting for the discovery of the cleansing and healing spring that will restore us to our true nature and place in the Cosmos.

In every school of the mysteries, and in the awakening of the individuality of every soul, there sooner or later comes the recognition that the personality is merely a form temporarily taken by the One Life. That recognition can be cultivated and encouraged by meditation, but it cannot be brought to full awareness except by a process of gradual ripening of awareness. At first there come glimpses of the unity of the little life with the One Life, which may be lost sight of for an extended period; then the glimpses lengthen and deepen until finally the awareness of the One Life becomes the consistent background of all life's doings, and the personality is recognized as a vessel or vehicle within which a greater reality moves, for a time, for purposes of its own.

Each person is thus his own jailer and his own liberator, the source of his own suffering and the source of his own redemption. So long as the personality dominates, the imbalances and distortions of the personality inevitably rebound on the whole self in the form of sufferings of many and various kinds. It is when the individual recognizes his own identity with the One Life, not merely as an abstract concept, but as a lived reality; when he takes firm hold of his personality, recognizing that it is not himself, but a vehicle he has gradually and with much pain created on the long journey up through the Circles of Abred, that he passes beyond the limits of the personality and begins to reach to that life beyond personality. You may seek that awakening by turning the attention to the dim light of individuality that always shines within. Regard it steadily, and judge all outward things by its light and that light will grow stronger. Then you may know that your feet are truly set on the path of initiation, and the light will shine brighter and brighter until all else is filled with its radiance.

The Doctrine of One is the key to the turning of attention. Put baldly, in fewest words, it is simply the teaching that "all things are One." Most students of esoteric traditions have encountered this teaching many times, perhaps nodding in assent, perhaps dismissing it as a platitude empty of force or deep meaning. It is only after a certain degree of advancement on the path of the mysteries has been accomplished that a sense of the extraordinary power hidden in this teaching begins to come to the attention of the student.

That power is released by combining the study of this teaching with the exercise of will and attention. The personality defines itself as separate from the Cosmos, and it therefore experiences everything it perceives as being equally separate from the Cosmos and from itself. When the mind, through will and attention, replaces this habitual thought with the opposite realization of the oneness of all things, then the soul, while remaining an individual, yet realizes its real nature and identity with the One Life, and is able to act according to the degree and strength of the recognition. This process of exclusion is slow and gradual—it begins with an intellectual conception of the truth of the Doctrine of One, which then gradually evolves into a greater and broader experience and realization as the student progresses along the path of the mysteries.

By realizing its oneness with all things, the individuality does not cease using the personality as an instrument of expression and life. On the contrary, it is only then that the awakening soul begins to use them. For, previous to this realization, the things of personality have used him, instead of he using them. All things are good for the individual to use, but none of them are good enough to use the individual. The student of the mysteries first learns to set aside the things of personality—learns, when necessary, to do without them—so as to realize that he does not need them to remain himself. Then, having freed himself from them with a mental effort, he returns and uses them, intelligently and properly, and positively. Thus liberation from the personality does not mean abandonment of the personality—it means, rather, the establishment of the correct relationship between the individuality and the personality, the "I" and the "me."

It will be useful at this point for the student to survey the Completion Exercises already given in this source, and to revisit any of them, the point and value of which have not yet become clear or have faded in impact with the passing of time. These exercises and the formulas they teach, in connection with the intellectual perception of the Doctrine of One, as well as the exercises to follow, will bring about a gradual unfoldment of the realization of oneness with the One Life, and further the awakening of the individuality. The following exercise, and others akin to it in the grades that follow, will aid the student in unfolding into this consciousness.

Completion Exercise 1

Let the student place himself in the ordinary position of meditation and pass through the usual preliminaries. Let him then meditate upon the One Life, the Essence or Spirit of the Cosmos. He should picture it as a great ocean of life, upon which and in which he rests as a minute focal point or center of manifestation. He should picture the resistless force and power of this great ocean of nwyfre, and feel its waves and movements. He should endeavor to realize that its tides and rhythms are perceptible in his inner being, and that in every way he is of it, and in it.

As you pursue this exercise, direct your meditation toward the realization that you are part of the One Life, and nothing other than the One Life. Realize that there is no real separation between you and the great ocean of life, and that there can be no such separation. In your meditation, mentally perceive your corff, your enaid, and the threefold structure of the personality—bywyd, nwyd, and hunan—not as yourself but as the veils that clothe and surround yourself, and that yourself—your true self—is the One Life. Realize that you are a center of force in the great ocean of life—a channel for the expression of as much of the One Life as your capacity of the moment will allow. Realize that as you grow and unfold, you will become a greater and still greater and grander channel for the inflow and outpouring of the One Life.

Perform this meditation at least seven times, and as many more times as you find useful.

Completion Exercise 2

As you go about your daily affairs, whenever you encounter something that angers, distresses, or troubles you, pause either at the time or as soon thereafter as circumstances permit, and think to yourself, "This, too, is part of the One Life." Strive to make this more than a mere repetition of words; make the effort to understand that every phenomenon you encounter, whether or not that phenomenon pleases you, is as much subject to the Doctrine of One as you are yourself.

Perform this practice for at least seven days, and as many more days as you find useful.

Gradd
y Gwyddon
y Cylch

The Grade of the
Loremaster of the Circle

INTRODUCTION TO THE GRADE

CONGRATULATIONS AND WELCOME to the second of the Inner Mystery grades of this course, the *Gradd y Gwyddon y Cylch!* In the names of this and the previous grade, the Gradd y Gwyddon y Ffordd, is contained an important teaching concerning the mysteries in general, and the tradition presented in this course in particular. The Path that gives its name to the first of these grades, the Loremaster of the Path, represents the work that is to be done by each initiate of the mysteries to awaken the individuality and enter into that richer and more complete mode of being that the teachings of the Druid tradition call Gwynfydd, the Luminous Life. The Circle that gives its name to the grade upon which you are now embarking, the Grade of the Loremaster of the Circle, is in one sense composed of all those who have followed and are following that Path—your teachers, your peers, and your students.

During the time you spend on this study course, from the first instructional paper to the last, your focus is inevitably on the Path. You have had work to do—a great deal of it—to gain a solid grasp of the philosophy and practice of the Druid mysteries, and to set in motion the process of awakening in yourself the subtle life and consciousness of the individuality. During this time, it may be that you may have had no contact with the corresponding realm of the Circle, or it may be that you have had the company of other students in this work. Even so, this has been a small part of the journey, and had you discovered these lessons in the form of yellowing pages left behind by some long-departed Druid, and pursued the studies and practices of the Dolmen Arch system in perfect solitude, without contacting, or knowing of the existence of, any other Druid in the world, you could still have proceeded step by step, grade by grade, through the work of the Path.

As you approach the end of this study course, you also approach a transformation in the work, in which the Circle will become equal in importance with the Path. The former should never supersede the latter; what you will be able to bring to the Circle depends always on the work you have done, are doing, and will continue to do on the Path. Nor will you reach the end of the Path in this life or any other, for the possibilities open to every human soul, or more properly put, every soul belonging to the Path of Ascent, reach beyond the capacities of our imagination and extend upwards to the very borders of Ceugant.

Still, it is with the conclusion of these formal studies that your relation to the Circle takes on a new importance. As a full initiate of these mysteries, you will have the privilege of applying the teachings and practices you have received to the world around you, through the arts of initiation, enchantment and healing, through the skills of will, thought, and memory you have learned, and more broadly through your thoughts, words, and actions in the course of every day of your life.

It is yours to choose whether you will become a teacher and initiator of the mysteries, and pass them on to students of your own. It is yours to choose whether you will become an enchanter, and direct the flows of nwyfre in the Cosmos to reshape the world that you and others experience. It is yours to choose whether you will become a healer, and wield the solar and telluric currents through the energy centers of your body to restore health and well being to yourself and those who seek your help.

It is *not* yours to choose, however, whether what you have learned and mastered will shape the world around you, the lives of the people with whom you come into contact, and your own life. The work you have done will express itself in your life, whether you will it or otherwise. As you learn the methods by which a Druid initiate exercises the privileges of healing, enchantment, and initiation, therefore, it is well to reflect on how you might best apply what you have learned, remembering that with power always comes responsibility.

This lesson packet, like the one that precedes it, contains nine instructional papers:

> The Cycle of the Cantrefs.. p. 99
> The Magic of the Grail..p. 105
> The Art of Druid Healing.. p. 109
> Practical Enchantment...p. 115

The Game of the Cantrefs .... p. 123
The Mabinogion: The Dream of Macsen Wledig .... p. 129
Druid Philosophy: The Seven Cosmic Laws .... p. 141
The Magical Memory: A System of Memory .... p. 167
Completion Exercises: Mastering the Opposites .... p. 179

Like the lessons of the preceding grades, these are to be worked through at your own pace, with the Completion Exercises reserved for last. The practical work given in this lesson, like that of the Loremaster of the Path Grade, is more advanced than the work of the Lesser Mysteries and will therefore require more time; a minimum of four months should be spent on this work, and as much more as you feel is appropriate. Nothing will be gained, and much may be lost, by rushing through these lessons at a pace faster than your mind can absorb the concepts taught, and your whole self absorb the effects of the practices.

Wishing you all the best in your journey on the Path of the Druid Mysteries,

 *John Michael Greer*

THE CYCLE OF THE CANTREFS

THE TITLE ASSIGNED TO THIS GRADE, Loremaster of the Circle, as you have already learned, is in part a reference to the circle of your fellow students and fellow teachers in the Dolmen Arch mystery school, past, present and to come. This is an important meaning and deserves careful thought and meditation on your part. Still, there is another and, in some ways, a deeper meaning to the title, and it relates to an aspect of the seven Cantrefs that has not yet been revealed to you.

The Cantrefs were originally presented to you in terms of their relationship with the directions of space, and the time-symbolism given in that original presentation derived from this symbolism of space: thus Awyr, for example, was primarily the East, and its assignment to dawn and spring drew from that directional symbolism following an ancient correspondence. This is a common element of training in any system of the Lesser Mysteries: the student must first be taught to orient himself relative to the symbolic Cosmos used in that mystery school, and the orientation is according to the familiar patterns of orientation in space.

Beyond the spatial orientation of any such set of correspondences, however, lies an inner dimension of the symbolism, which is an orientation to time, not bound to the patterns of space but unfolding in its own right. Thus the alchemists of old studied the lore of the four elements, first as static substances, but then as stages in a cycle of change. The mystics of old China similarly contemplated the eight trigrams of the I Ching[1] first as emblematic realities assigned to the directions, and then as a sequence of change giving rise to the sixty-four hexagrams in which all transformations are simultaneously concealed and revealed.

In the same sense, the seven Cantrefs form an order in time as well as a pattern in space, and this order in time or sequence of symbolic changes will become central to much of the remaining work before you in this study course. It has particular relevance to the work of practical enchantment and the art of initiation, and—in a sense that will be made clear to you in the grade to come—it defines a crucial reality that shapes the lives of every initiate of the mysteries, a reality that expresses itself through the phenomenon human beings call "history."

The pattern in time you are about to learn is called the Cycle of the Cantrefs. It follows the ordinary order of the Cantrefs as you have already learned them; and it may best be understood by passing through the Cantrefs in order, and relating their sequence to the patterns of change that may be observed in all things throughout the Cosmos. For the sake of example, we will use the writing of a lesson such as this one to illustrate the Cycle.

The First Cantref: Awyr

This, the first stage in the cycle, stands for the process by which things begin to come to be, the initial ray of dawn sunlight and the first breath of the morning wind that calls the rest of the process into being. It represents the first stirrings of the creative act that brings any new thing into being, and therefore follows the First Cantref's symbolism of mind and consciousness,

Fig. 3. The Cantref Awyr

for every new thing has its first origin on the spiritual plane of the Cosmos, our first faint perceptions of which are the phenomena of the mind and the experience of consciousness. In the example of the lesson, Awyr represents the initial, formless, and purely abstract decision or inspiration that sets the writing process under way.

---

1. This is not merely a system of divination, as it has too often been regarded in the West, but the core document of Chinese mystical philosophy, and a primary text used in the mystery school of China.

The Second Cantref: Dŵr

This second stage in the cycle is the phase of growth, learning, and enlargement, the flowing water of the pool of wisdom and the verdant growth of the hazels that grow around it. It represents the unfolding and development of the first stirrings set in motion in Awyr. Its emblem indicates the descent of cre-

Fig. 4. The Cantref Dŵr

ative energy from the spiritual plane toward the plane of matter, the process by which all creation takes place in the Cosmos. In the example of the lesson, Dŵr represents the process by which the author enlarges the initial abstract inspiration or decision into the concrete and clearly felt sense of what is to be done.

The Third Cantref: Ufel

This third stage in the cycle represents the emergence of choice and conflict, the encounter with alternatives and obstacles that is a part of every process of creation. This is by no means a negative or destructive phase in the Cycle of the Cantrefs, for it is in the course of confrontation with obstacles, challenges, and choices that each created thing takes on its form, potential-

Fig. 5. The Cantref Ufel

ity and power. The emblem of this stage indicates the resistance of the planes below rising up to meet the descending influence from the spiritual plane. In the example of the lesson, Ufel represents the challenge of deciding what will be included in the lesson, and constructing an outline by which the material to be included will be ordered.

The Fourth Cantref: Daear

This fourth stage in the cycle represents the descent into manifestation, in the course of which, through labor and patience, the creative act earths out and embodies itself in whatever its form of manifestation will be. Here the new creation has taken its most complete form. Complexity and elaboration are therefore the keynotes of this stage, as the inspiration of Awyr, the

Fig. 6. The Cantref Daear

growth into form of Dŵr, and the choices and conflicts of Ufel all must find their expression among the intricate articulations of the manifest Cosmos. In the example of the lesson, Daear represents the actual writing process, the work of assembling letters and words in the mind and putting them down on paper to create the lesson as a manifest reality.

The Fifth Cantref: Maen

This fifth stage in the cycle represents the effects and consequences of the descent into manifestation, the results that follow from the first four steps and, especially, the fourth and central stage of the creative process. No act of creation takes place in a vacuum; there is always a context or, to use a modern term, an environment that is affected by the creative act, and

Fig. 7. The Cantref Maen

the effects thus set in motion spread outward to the uttermost edges of the Cosmos like the ripples set in motion by a stone tossed into a pool. Here also belong the encounters of the newly created reality with the limits in space, time, energy, and matter that will determine its ultimate extent and its eventual fate. In the example of the lesson, Maen represents the process of sending the lesson to students, the impact the lesson has on their thoughts and actions, and the further effects set in motion by the changes thus caused.

The Sixth Cantref: Nef

This sixth stage in the cycle represents the response of the Cosmos to the effects and consequences set in motion in the previous stage. Just as every creative act takes place in an environment that is affected and changed by that act, the resulting effects and changes call forth responses from those things affected by them, and these inevitably return to affect creation,

Fig. 8. The Cantref Nef

creator, and creative process alike, perhaps to support, perhaps to transform, and perhaps to destroy. In one, very simple sense, this is the commonly known law that every action calls forth a reaction, but it is more accurate to say that every action either initiates or takes part in a conversation in which every other part of the Cosmos is a participant. In the example of the lesson, Nef represents the responses of the students to the lesson, which affect the writer of the lesson and influence the process by which further lessons come into being.

The Seventh Cantref: Byw

This seventh and last stage in the cycle represents the summing-up and balancing out of the entire previous process. As each individual creative act becomes a past event rather than a present reality, and the consequences and responses set in motion by the descent from abstract impulse to manifestation settle into a stable form, the entire cycle can be experienced and assessed as a whole, and its value, meaning, and implications understood. In the process, the creative act and all its consequences become part of the broader environment in which new impulses and manifestations will emerge in turn; in one sense, therefore, this stage is the final legacy of the creative process, what is left when all is said and done. In the example of the lesson, Byw represents the lesson as part of the existing body of course work in a study program such as this, which the author must take into account when writing the next lesson.

Fig. 9. The Cantref Byw

It will be noticed that the seven stages of the Cycle of the Cantrefs divide neatly into three parts. The first—the triad of creation—corresponds to the first three material elements, Air, Water, and Fire; the second—the point of manifestation—corresponds to the element of Earth; and the third—the triad of completion—corresponds to the three forms of Spirit, Spirit Below, Spirit Above, and Spirit Within.

The Cycle can have different expressions, depending on the nature of the process being considered. In some cases, the first triad is the stage of growth, the central point is that of maturity, and the last triad is that of dissolution. That is, the first triad brings a new creation down the planes from spirit to matter, the point of manifestation sees that process completed, and the last triad brings the now aged creation back up the planes from matter to spirit, passing from manifestation into the unmanifest.

In other cases, the first triad is the stage of differentiation, the central point is that of isolation, and the last triad is of reintegration. That is, the first triad gradually draws a new creation out of the undifferentiated background of which it is composed, the point of manifestation sees that process completed, and the last triad takes the now fully individualized creation back into relationship with the rest of the Cosmos.

The lesson packet of the grade to come will explore the Cycle of the Cantrefs in several different contexts. To prepare yourself for that study, it is important that you take the time to meditate on the Cycle, and to consider the ways in which it applies to the Cosmos around you. In particular, the two expressions just described should be carefully considered, and their application to different kinds of human experience explored, both in and out of meditation.

THE MAGIC OF THE GRAIL

HE WORK YOU HAVE DONE with the expanded Sphere of Protection ritual, including the awakening of the Cauldrons, the rousing of the Dragons, and the establishment of the Tree of Light, is in certain ways the most important part of the training you have received in this course. Every exercise has its value, and all flow together into the greater process of the awakening of the individuality—the heart of this, as of every other mystery teaching—which will continue long after your studies with this course are over. Still, the Sphere of Protection with its additions forms the heart of the process of initiation in this tradition of the Druid mysteries.

It is important to understand why this is, not only so that you may apply its lessons more directly to your own initiatory process hereafter, but so that you may know how to instruct others in the process of initiating themselves. The awakening of the individuality depends on many things, but all of them depend ultimately on nwyfre, the One Life in which you as well as all other beings in the Cosmos share. Nwyfre follows the patterns laid down by Awen, and the most important of these for our purposes is the pattern of unfoldment that leads all dwellers on the Path of Ascent from their origin in Annwn through Abred to the heights of Gwynfydd.

From Annwn upwards through Abred until the upper reaches of human existence are attained, that path is not traversed by any power or gift internal to the one who traverses it. It is nwyfre acting through each soul which leads that soul step by step to the heights. Only when the human level itself is reached does the slowly awakening soul begin to partake in a role in its own unfoldment, and even so that role is very limited at first. Many lives must pass and much progress be made before the soul gains any significant degree of influence over its own course.

Still, the One Life does not stop working for the spiritual development of the individual at any point. The central challenge of each life, and indeed each moment, is to sense the direction in which nwyfre seeks to move the soul, and to choose to move with it, in the direction it wishes to move, rather than across it or against it. Yet there is another factor, for the strength or intensity with which nwyfre manifests in a particular life, or a particular moment, is subject to variation. We are capable of opening ourselves up more fully to the flow of the One Life, and equally capable of closing ourselves off from a portion of that flow. Ultimately, this latter choice is the route that leads to the refusal of the One Life and to annihilation, just as the former choice, the decision to open oneself to the flow of nwyfre, is ultimately the choice that leads to Gwynfydd.

Many of the practices you have learned have the specific purpose of helping you to open yourself to, or to use a more traditional turn of phrase, to participate in the flow of nwyfre more completely on a variety of planes. The Sphere of Protection and its various expansions are the most important of these practices, for they direct the will and imagination to the task of fully participating in the patterns of the One Life and dispelling obstacles and hindrances to those patterns and the flows that move through them.

All this may be found symbolized in a set of ancient legends that have come down to us in partial and heavily rewritten form as the legends of the Holy Grail. The Grail was traditionally the cup with which Christ celebrated the Last Supper; the legend had it that it was brought to Britain by Joseph of Arimathea; that it became a source of blessing, wisdom, and life to the land and all who dwelt therein; that it disappeared on account of a destructive act of violence directed against its keeper, plunging the land into barrenness; and that it could only be recovered if a knight found the Grail castle and, once there, asked the right question; once this occurred, the land was healed and the blessings of the Grail flowed again.

As with all the legends of King Arthur, this represents a Christianized version of a much more ancient teaching story communicating the secrets of Druidry. The original story has not come down to us in its entirety, but references in the poems of a few of the old Welsh bards enable it to be reconstructed in part. In this oldest form of the story, the Grail was a cauldron of healing and fertility, symbolized by mead, which was hidden away in an otherworldly realm each winter and had to be brought back to the world each spring. There are many dimensions to that tale, of which the seasonal is the most visible; on a subtler level, the mead in the sacred cauldron is the One Life, and the hero who restores it to the world is the initiate who opens the hidden cauldrons of his being to the flow of nwyfre, and thus gains not only blessings for himself but the capacity to heal and bless all around him.

The working that follows is a crucial step in learning to turn the flow of nwyfre within yourself into a vehicle for healing and blessing. You are to practice it, during the time you spend in this grade, for a single purpose; the method of applying it to other purposes will be taught in the final lesson packet of this course.

The Grail Working

Begin by performing the full Sphere of Protection ceremony as you have learned and practiced it; proceed to awaken the three Cauldrons, rouse the Red and White Dragons, establish the Tree of Light, and draw the solar and telluric currents through it, using the methods you have been taught in previous lesson packets. Once all this has been done, proceed as follows.

Say the following words, silently or aloud: "From above to below, from below to above, the two currents are awakened. In their presence and power, I formulate my intention. It is (state your intention here)." Pause for a time, focusing your intention on what it is you will to accomplish. Do not "think about" it; instead, hold it in your mind, keeping your thoughts still and your concentration on the intention as you have stated it. Take your time with this phase of the work.

When you are ready to go on, say: "I invoke Spirit Below. Let the telluric current ascend and fill my intention with its power." Visualize a current of light the color of springtime leaves rise up from the center of the earth to your solar plexus, where it forms a sphere of green light. With your imagination, place your intention into that sphere, as though placing a seed in the soil. Again, take your time with this phase of the work.

When you are ready to go on, say: "I invoke Spirit Above. Let the solar current descend and fill my intention with its power." Visualize a second current of light the color of sunshine descend from infinite space above you to your solar plexus, where it flows into the same sphere of light, turning it green-gold. Imagine the solar energy infusing the intention and bringing it life and power. Again, take your time with this phase of the work.

When you are ready to go on, say: "I invoke Spirit Within. Let the lunar current be born within my intention and fill it with the power of Awen. Let my intention become Reality." Imagine the green-gold light suddenly fusing into brilliant white, the color of lightning, and the light expanding outward, slowly at first and then with steadily increasing speed, until finally it rushes outward in all directions to fill the entire universe. Be aware of your intention expanding with it. Then release the imagery completely, and proceed with the Circulation of Light in the same manner as usual.

This working may be used for any purpose or intention, within the limits that are appropriate to enchantment. For the time you spend working through this lesson packet, however, you are requested to use one and the same intention each time, and that is to awaken your individuality. These exact words should be used: "It is to awaken my individuality."

From the regular practice of this exercise, along with the other disciplines of the Druid mysteries presented in this course, the process of your own initiation will unfold at its proper pace. Your ability to make use of the full range of practical methods to be communicated to you, and to confer initiation on others, depends on that unfolding. Thus you should perform this working daily as part of your regular practice of the Sphere of Protection, and record your experiences in your practice journal.

THE ART OF
DRUID HEALING

AT THIS POINT you have had several months to practice the method of self-healing given in the previous grade. This has had two results, which are equally important to your progress. First, you have begun to learn through experience what the healing process is like, how it works, and what subtle variations increase or decrease your own ability to direct energy through your hands. Even if you have not noticed this consciously, be well aware that your nwyd and bywyd have done so, and are subtly adjusting your performance of the healing work to increase the benefit they receive from it.

The second result, in turn, is that blockages and imbalances within yourself that tend to interfere with your capacity to heal have been cleared away or, at the least, ameliorated so that they will hinder your work less seriously. The old saying "Physician, heal thyself" contains much merit; it is a common habit, and a bad one, for those who need healing themselves—especially on the mental and emotional planes—to concern themselves too greatly with healing others, before they have brought themselves back into balance. This leaves them vulnerable to further illness, and it also has the unwelcome effect of tending to communicate their own existing illnesses and imbalances to others.

It is thus of great importance that you continue the regular practice for self-healing that you learned in the previous grade. You should be sure, in fact, to perform that practice more often than you do the practice for spiritual energy work with others given in this grade. This rule may sound unduly restrictive, or even selfish, but it is based on long and proven experience. When you exert your powers to help another person, it is your responsibility to see that your energies, which will be in contact with theirs, are as clean and balanced as possible; it is also important that any imbalances you absorb from those that you treat be cleared away, so that they cause no harm to others that you may happen to treat, or to you.

Ethical and Legal Issues

This brings us to the ethical issues that surround using the methods you have learned for the benefit of anyone besides yourself. Those issues are challenging, and they are made even more challenging by laws in most jurisdictions that are deliberately designed to keep anyone but licensed professionals trained in the officially approved medicine of our day from helping other people in any way related to health. In the United States today, even if no money changes hands, you quite literally cannot describe what you are doing as "healing," "treating," or "curing," or refer to someone you are helping as a "patient," without risking legal charges and the possibility of going to prison. Unreasonable as this is, it is the current reality, and you will need to live with it until such time as the legal and social environment changes. Whenever you practice this work with other people, therefore, you should refer to it as "spiritual energy work," and under no circumstances should you claim to be able to heal, treat, or cure any physical ailment or injury, or even suggest that you will try to do so.

Absurd as these restrictions may seem, there is a valid ethical dimension to them at this point in your studies. As a novice practitioner of Druid spiritual energy work, you have only a very little experience with a subtle and profound art, and your ability to help others will be sharply limited at first, by your lack of experience with the techniques themselves as well as by the slow inner ripening of their inner dimensions of nwyfre, will and imagination. It would thus be unethical for you, during the course of your self-education in this work, to claim to be able to heal, treat, or cure illnesses or injuries.

For the same paired reasons of ethics and legality, you should never accept money or any other exchange of value for performing this work. While you are still a student of the art taught in these lessons, the benefit you get in exchange for your efforts is experience, practice, and self-training in the healing process, which is more than enough recompense. Even after you have reached a high level of skill, you should know that the laws against accepting money for unapproved methods of healing are very stringent, and can land you in a great deal of legal trouble. It is far less problematic to treat the abilities that you will develop as a gift that is to be shared freely with others, for their benefit and the world's.

It is important never to do a working of this kind for someone who does not wish it to be done. In most cases this will not be an issue, since you will normally only do this work for those who have agreed to take part in it. In the case of a child, an unconscious person, or anyone else not able to give legally valid consent, it is crucial for legal as well as ethical reasons to have the consent of the person's legal guardian before proceeding.

Finally, you should never physically touch a person you are helping during a session. In today's society, touching another person carries with it a great many tangled personal, ethical, and legal issues that are best left alone. For similar reasons, a man who performs this work for a woman who is not a relative by birth or marriage, or any person performing this work on a child other than his own, should have another person present at all times during the session.[2]

The Method of Working

When you are ready to perform a session for another person, the first requirement is to explain to the person you are helping what you will be doing, and what he can expect to experience. Explain to him that you will not be touching him physically at any point, but that you will instead be directing energy from the Cosmos into his body to balance and harmonize the body of subtle energy that surrounds and enlivens his physical body. Let him know that he may perceive tingling, a sense of warmth, or other mild sensations, and encourage him to let you know if anything becomes uncomfortable in any way during the session. Should you be asked to perform a session for a person who is unconscious or for a young child, or for anyone else who cannot give consent, explain these things to the person who has arranged for you to do the work.

If at all possible, he should sit on a plain armless chair, such as a dining room chair or a folding chair, with his feet flat on the ground and his hands resting on his thighs. The chair should be placed in such a position that you are able to stand in front of it, behind it, and to the right side. Encourage the other person to sit a little forward, so that his lower back does not touch the back of the chair, and ask him to close his eyes, breathe normally, and relax. If he is not able to sit in a chair for whatever reason, adjust the following procedures accordingly.

Once he is ready, tell him that you will need a minute or so to prepare yourself, and that you will tell him when you begin the session. Sit in another chair

---

2. These suggestions may seem old-fashioned to modern ears, but given the current state of gender relations, they are still wise to follow.

facing him and awaken your palm centers in the way you have already learned. When you are ready, let him know that you are about to begin.

At this point, place your hands comfortably in front of you, palms facing the other person, and allow the solar and telluric currents to flow from your palm centers toward him. You will feel the energies meeting resistance at first, as though you were pushing against something heavy and unyielding. Continue to draw telluric energy up from below you and solar energy down from above you, and let them flow out through your hands. After a few seconds, you will feel the energy begin to flow as you make contact with the other person's enaid, or body of nwyfre. Maintain the flow for a time, until you feel no more resistance.

Next, rise from your chair and approach the other person. Tell him that you are about to make passes with your hands over his body, and remind him that you will not touch him physically. Standing before him, make passes with both hands down the front of the body from head to waist level, keeping your hands six to twelve inches away from his body. Do this three times with the hands side by side in front of the body, then move your hands out to the sides and make three more passes; continue moving your hands apart and performing three passes until the whole front and sides of his body, from head to waist, have been covered by your passes. As before, give the hands a quick shake after every pass.

Now kneel down and do the same thing from the waist to the feet, starting with the hands side by side in front of the other person and making three passes, then proceed outward from there until his hips, legs and feet have been covered by your passes. Continue to shake the hands to clear them of nwyfre after every pass.

Stand up again. Explain that you will be standing behind him; go around behind his chair, and do another series of passes. This time, however, start with passes down the sides of the head, shoulders and arms, down to hip level. Do this three times, then move your hands a little around toward the other person's back and repeat with another three passes. Do this until you perform three passes with your hands side by side on either side of the other person's spinal cord. Again, shake the hands after each pass.

Now move to the other person's right side, and explain that you are about to charge the energy centers of his subtle body. Start by placing your right hand in front of his forehead and your left hand behind the back of his head, again leaving six to twelve inches between your hands and his body. Holding your hands steady, concentrate again on the flow of the solar and telluric currents through your body and hands, and allow the energies to flow into and through the uppermost of his three cauldrons until there is no sense of blockage or imbalance. Move your hands down to the level of his heart, your right hand in front of his chest and your left behind his middle back, and repeat the process with the middle cauldron. Then kneel and lower your hands to the level of his abdomen, so that your right hand is in front of his navel and your left behind the small of his back, and repeat the process with the lower cauldron. Remember to shake your hands after charging each of the cauldrons.

Stand up again and explain that the working is almost over, and you simply need to clear away excess energy from his energy body. This is done with a series of broad sweeping motions down from above the head, well away from the body, with a crisp shake of the hands after each motion. When you are finished, let the other person know, and explain that you need to close off the energy flows in yourself to conclude the working. Encourage him to relax as you do so. Sit in your chair, and close in the way you have already learned.

Distance Work

This same process may be done for someone who is not in your presence, and may be performed in one of two ways, depending on your level of skill. The simplest version of the spiritual energy working for another person at a distance is done by activating the palm centers while facing toward the other person, no matter how far away the distance between you. Once the palm centers are activated, just as in the first part of the ordinary method, place your hands comfortably in front of you, palms facing the other person, and allow the solar and telluric currents to flow from your palm centers toward the other person. Concentrate on the idea that the energies of the solar and telluric current are flowing across the distance to come into contact with the other person's enaid, charge it with energy, and restore it to balance and wholeness. Maintain the energy flow for as long as you desire, or sense to be necessary.

The more complex form of the spiritual energy working for another person at a distance is done by placing a chair as though the other person were with you, visualizing the other person sitting in the chair, and maintaining that visualization as strongly and clearly as possible while performing the full working just as though the other person were present. Since nwyfre is present everywhere and in all things, no barrier separates you from anyone else in the world, and the work you do with nwyfre will have a definite effect even across vast distances. This is among the reasons why it is essential to attend to the ethical dimension of this work, and to perform it only when the recipient of the work has given his permission. The same logic governs all the practical work of the mysteries, and goes far to explain why the teachers of the traditional mystery schools tend to reserve practices that can affect other people, especially at a distance, to those who have advanced sufficiently far to use it with some degree of wisdom.

A Note on Practice

You may or may not have the opportunity to put the instructions just given to practical use during the months you spend in the Grade of Loremaster of the Circle. It is essential, as already explained, that you continue to perform the self-healing exercise given in the previous grade, and so you should continue to do so at least once each week; if you have the opportunity to practice spiritual energy work for other people during the time you spend in this grade, make use of it, and pay attention to the differences that are made by having another person's energy involved in the work. As with all your practices, finally, be sure to write up the details in your practice journal.

PRACTICAL ENCHANTMENT

The preliminary disciplines of enchantment you performed in the previous grade have provided you with nearly everything you will need in order to practice enchantment with good effect. More broadly, the studies and practices you have received all through your work with this course of Druid mystery training has prepared you for success in the art of enchantment, though this is only one of several applications of the skills you have developed and the qualities of character you have attained. To draw on a metaphor much used among teachers of the mysteries, you have been given the workman's tools that you need for the work that is before you. What remains is simply the task of learning how to use them.

This is, however, a more complex matter than it seems at first, because the process that we have termed enchantment deals with some of the most subtle and, outside of the mystery schools, poorly understood aspects of human consciousness. The material you have received so far in these lesson packets has avoided dealing with these subtleties, but the work of the Greater Mysteries depends in the most profound sense on their full and proper understanding. They deal with that dimension of human life and that aspect of the hunan that we have called bryd, the will.

The Nature of Will

> And the will therein lieth, which dieth not. Who knoweth the mysteries of the will with its vigor? For God is but a great Will pervading all things by reason of its intentness. Man doth not yield himself to the angels nor to death utterly, save only through the weakness of his feeble will.

This passage, which appears in a story of Edgar Allan Poe and by him was attributed to the writings of Glanville the Cambridge Platonist,[3] admirably expresses the understanding of the will that has been most common among practicing occultists in the western world for the last century and a half.

There is a real and a valuable truth in that understanding. Much of what keeps the ordinary person mired in unsatisfactory conditions and self-defeating habits is simply a lack of will or, more precisely, an inability to direct the power of the bryd, which is innate in all of us, to productive purposes. A certain degree of training in the conscious use of will is thus inevitably part of any system of training in the mysteries, as it is of any worthwhile education whatsoever.

In the present course, the regular exercises you have been asked to perform fill that role, alongside their more obvious functions. To perform the meditations, rituals, and other practices of this study course, it is necessary to use willpower to set aside the many distractions that would otherwise interfere with the work, and the strength of will thus developed will inevitably have its effects in the rest of life. You may already have noticed that certain difficulties you once had, which were caused by what is commonly called a lack of willpower, have lessened over the time you have spent in your studies of the Druid mysteries. This is a common consequence of training of the sort that you have pursued.

There is also a very real extent to which spiritual training of any kind not only develops but demands a strong will, capable of mounting up above the planes upon which habit, desire and fear dominate the personality. The lecture on philosophy in the fourth lesson packet of this course discusses the will in those terms, as the power by which the transition is made from the plane of personality to that of individuality. This is a basic reality in the work of the mysteries, which is truly work, in the full sense of that word; many of the attainments on the path of the mysteries must be won by the sweat of the initiate's brow.

Yet it is altogether too common for people who have been exposed to the concept of training of the will to treat this insight as fundamental, and to miss the deeper teaching that lies behind it. This same misunderstanding may shape your thoughts as well. Imagine a person exerting willpower, and what comes to mind? A man with clenched jaw, narrowed eyes, and knotted muscles, as though straining to lift a weight in a physical culture competition? All these are signs of conflict; they betray the weakness of the will, not its strength.

---

3. Joseph Glanville was one of a circle of Platonist philosophers at Cambridge University in Britain during the seventeenth century, who opposed the popular materialism of the time and argued for the existence of the spiritual world.

The struggle of the will to rise above the plane of personality, to learn to will to will, is similarly a function of weakness, for the will in such a case is not yet wholly turned toward its goal; it is divided, and this division gives rise to inner conflict and weakness. All weakness of the will is a function of internal conflict, of a will that seeks two or more incompatible things at the same time. When it confronts no opposition and suffers from no conflict, will is effortless. It corresponds, not to struggle and strain, but to what philosophers have called "intentionality," the orientation of the mind that locates meaning in objects of experience.

The Power of Intentionality

An old Hindu teaching story may be of help in understanding this concept of intentionality. Let us suppose that you were walking in the forest and see what looks like a poisonous snake coiled up beside the trail. Your heart pounding, your muscles ready to leap out of range of the snake's fangs, you make a wide circle around it, and only when you have completed the detour do you see that the "snake" is in fact a coil of rope. The perceptions that reached your eyes were the same all along, but your mind gave that perception two radically different intentionalities. When the intentionality changed, everything about your experience changed except the thing you were experiencing.

You may not be able to choose whether the coiled thing beside the trail is a snake or a rope. If you face a window and look toward it, however, you can either look *through* the window at the scenery outside, or you can look *at* the window and examine the glass, frame, and so on. If you look at the scenery it can be very difficult to notice the window glass, and if you look at the glass it can be just as difficult to notice the scenery. Is the glass a way of seeing the world outside, or something to look at in its own right? It can be either one, and the difference is intentionality.

Many things in life can be shaped even more powerfully by your choice of intentionality. If you face a challenge with confidence, for example, your chances of success are much better than if you face the same challenge with a mind full of doubts and worries. Intentionality explains the difference. What the confident person sees as potential opportunities, the worried person sees as potential obstacles, and both are right, because whether something is an opportunity or an obstacle usually depends on how you choose to approach it.

The teaching of the mysteries goes beyond this, for the initiates of all ages have always recognized that where intentionality is directed, nwyfre follows.

Whatever meaning the mind identifies in any object of your experience is taken up and amplified by the flow of nwyfre. The more significant the meaning that is there experienced, the stronger the flow of nwyfre it sets in motion will be, and the greater the power it has to influence the experience of others as well as yourself. This is among the most important keys to practical enchantment, but it also explains many of the failures that trouble newcomers to enchantment, as well as those who attempt to practice enchantment outside the mystery schools.

Very often, motivated by a misunderstanding of the nature of will, the beginner imagines himself browbeating the universe into obedience to his will. This establishes an intentionality of conflict between the would-be enchanter and everything else in the world. Nwyfre, as is its nature, flows along the lines laid down by that intentionality, and he finds himself embroiled in conflict with everything he experiences. The harder he tries to make the world obey his will, the more fiercely and uncompromisingly it resists, because every effort made with the intention of bullying it into submission reinforces the intentionality and heightens the conflict. An intentionality of harmony with the universe avoids these difficulties, but this does not come easily to many beginners at the art of enchantment. Sometimes it takes many repeated experiences of failure before the necessary lesson finally sinks in!

This same effect has a notable influence on the application of enchantment for practical ends. It is inevitable, for example, in a society obsessed by material wealth, that many people try to use enchantments of various kinds to achieve financial prosperity. Far more often than not, their efforts backfire and leave them poorer than they started. Why? In many cases, they focus throughout the working on wanting what they do not have. This establishes an intentionality of wanting and not having, and so they find themselves repeatedly wanting money and not having it. Enchantment can be used to become prosperous, but the intentionality must be one of being prosperous, not on wanting to be prosperous. This may be done, for example, by directing the will and imagination to the task of seeing opportunities for abundance around you. This redefines your surroundings as a source of opportunity, and as nwyfre follows intentionality and shapes experience, opportunities appear.

Working an enchantment for love is another common notion of beginners, and is surrounded by pitfalls at least as significant as those that surround enchantments for prosperity. One of the most common of these unfolds from the principle already explained—that an intentionality of wanting love and not having it will tend to reproduce the experience of wanting love and not having it. There is also very often an intentionality of wanting love and not feeling worthy of it, which has equally unwelcome results. There is, as it happens, one and only one universally effective form of love enchantment, which consists of work on the self to become more lovable. Very few beginners in the art of enchantment, however, are willing to confront the unlovable elements of their own personalities, and so the temptation to pursue the same goal by some other means is common.

The Method of Enchantment

Such workings, however, should not be among your first ventures into practical enchantment, nor should you attempt anything else that ties into strong emotions or desires. These should be left for later, if they are done at all. For reasons discussed in the previous grade's paper on enchantment, it is best to begin with simple workings for the purpose of blessing and healing, and to proceed from there as you gain experience and familiarity with the method.

That method has already been communicated to you in three parts, divided and put in three distinct places. The practices you were taught in the paper on enchantment in the previous grade—the collection of nwyfre charged with the energies of one of the Cantrefs into your body from the Cosmos, and its direction and concentration into a material basis—provide one part of the method. The second is the practice of awakening the palm centers, which was given to you in the Philosophizer Grade and developed further since that time. The third is to be found in the paper on the Grail Working in this lesson packet, where the art of placing an intention in nwyfre is discussed. Combine these and you have a simple, powerful, effective method of enchantment that can be practiced without complex ritual or cumbersome gear. To put it into practice, you will need only two things other than those you bring with you always in the various levels of yourself.

One is an intention you have considered carefully, paying close attention to the intentionality it embodies. If you wish to bless a place, for example, it is important to formulate the intention so that it involves an intentionality of recognizing and entering into fuller and deeper relation with those beneficent powers that are always present in the Cosmos, rather than one of struggling against evil influences. It is also necessary, while considering the intention, to decide which of the seven Cantrefs most closely corresponds to your intention. For an enchantment of blessing, the traditional Cantref to use is Awyr, the First

Cantref, due to its symbolism of light, springtime and morning, but other enchantments will have their own correspondences.

The other thing you will need is a small stone or pebble of the sort you used for the exercises in enchantment in the previous grade. It should be prepared in exactly the same way, by being washed with cold water and left to dry in sunlight for at least three days before using.

When you are ready to cast your enchantment, perform the basic Sphere of Protection ritual—the Elemental Cross, Calling of the Cantrefs, and Circulation of Light—to clear the space, and then begin as you would begin a meditation, by entering into your meditation posture, releasing excess tension, and then practicing color breathing; the color you use should be that of the Cantref that corresponds to the intention of your enchantment. The stone may be placed somewhere within easy reach of your meditation seat, or set on your lap, depending on circumstances.

Once you are ready, awaken your palm centers in the usual way, and then pick up the stone. Place it between the two palms, and press the hands together in the conventional gesture of prayer. Then repeat your intention, silently or aloud, and hold it in your mind for a few minutes, imagining it flowing into the stone.

Now comes the crucial part of the practice. As you breathe in, imagine the colored light and all the influences of the Cantref you have chosen flowing in through every part of your body except the inside surfaces of your two hands, which are pressed together around the stone. As you breathe out, the colored light and influences flow through your palm centers into the stone, concentrating there, and leaving your body completely emptied of the light and the influences. All the while, continue to hold your intention in your mind, imagining it being present in the stone. Repeat the breathing process until you have done it a total of seven times. By this point you should feel the presence of the Cantref in the stone with great intensity.

At this point, open your hands and set the stone aside. Do not discharge the nwyfre you have placed in the stone; leave it there to do its work. Breathe normally for a few cycles, allowing any energies that might have gathered in your body to disperse. Once your body has returned to its normal state, close in the usual way, clapping the hands to seal the energy centers, and proceed with your ordinary activities.

The stone is now fully charged with the enchantment, and will radiate its force into the area around it. You should plan on doing this working at least once during the time you spend on the lessons of this grade, and no more than three times, choosing a different intention for each working.

The process of enchantment establishes a link between the stone and the Cantref, and nwyfre charged with the influences of that Cantref will continue to flow into the stone, replenishing its energy, for some time; depending on the intensity of your concentration and the degree of relationship you have developed with the energies of the Cantrefs over the course of your studies, it may remain active for weeks, months, years, or indefinitely. It is unnecessary and indeed unwise to enchant more than one stone in this way for a single purpose, as that risks imbalance and an excess of one Cantref's energy; if you feel that the stone you have enchanted no longer has the power it should, simply take the stone and charge it again.

Should it ever become necessary to remove the enchantment from a stone, the process just described is done in reverse. Start with the same meditative preparations, without performing the Sphere of Protection first; use the same color breathing, but instead of formulating the intention with which the stone was enchanted, formulate the intention that the enchantment should be dissolved. After you awaken the palm centers and place the stone between them, with each inbreath, draw the color and influence of the Cantref from within the stone into your body, and with each outbreath release it into the Cosmos through your entire body; all the while, the idea that the enchantment is being removed should be held in your mind. Seven breaths done in this way will remove the enchantment. When you are finished, close as usual, and then perform the basic Sphere of Protection ritual to clear away any lingering influences.

THE GAME OF THE CANTREFS

IT IS NOT OFTEN REMEMBERED outside the mystery schools that what are now games of chance and skill, played for enjoyment or even relegated to the nursery for the amusement of children, are in many cases descended from divinatory oracles or methods of mystery school training. Those who have studied the card oracle known as Tarot know that the enigmatic imagery of the Tarot deck originated from the symbolism of a mystery school, perhaps in ancient Egypt, perhaps elsewhere, which was conveyed to the future in the form of a game.[4] The game of Snakes and Ladders played by children in the western world, in the same way, can be traced to an oracle still used by Tantric adepts in India and Tibet, who use it to forecast their future incarnations.

The system of Druid mystery teaching upon which this course is based had, in earlier times, a simple gamelike method for practicing certain mental exercises related to the Sevenfold Wheel of Thought, which was introduced in the Grade of the Practitioner. At some point, perhaps in the nineteenth century, a student of these mysteries discovered that the same practice could be used more effectively with the aid of common dominoes, and the Game of the Cantrefs was born. It is a valuable method both for training the mind and for guiding meditation upon the Druid wisdom, and should be learned and practiced at this stage in your studies.

---

4. This speculation has turned out to be quite correct, although the mystery tradition in question was in Renaissance Italy rather than ancient Egypt. It is now known that the earliest form of Tarot was invented around 1415 by Marziano da Tortona, the secretary to the Duke of Milan, as an instructional game using emblems drawn from the rich occult symbolism of the Renaissance.

To play the Game of the Cantrefs, you will need to acquire an ordinary set of dominoes, which contains 28 pieces. Each of them, as you will find, is divided in half by a line, and on each side of the line is a number of dots between 0 and 6. See Figure 8, for example.

Fig. 10. **Standard Dominoes**

For the purposes of the Game, each number of dots is assigned to a Cantref, with 0 dots serving as a substitute for seven. Thus one dot corresponds to Awyr, two to Dŵr, three to Ufel, four to Daear, five to Maen, six to Nef, and none to Byw. Since the 28 pieces in a domino set include every possible combination of zero through six points, every possible relationship between the Cantrefs—including the relationship of each Cantref with itself—is indicated by one and only one piece.

For the sake of convenience, each domino piece may be indicated by a pair of numbers divided by a diagonal line, such as 3/1, 2/4, or 0/6. In each case the first number is the number of dots on the upper half of the piece, and the second number that on the lower half; the three pieces just denoted will thus be found to be identical to the three pictured in Figure 8.

The Cantrefs, as you learned earlier, correspond in the Sevenfold Wheel of Thought to seven conceptions and seven questions. The conceptions are Being, Becoming, Source, Substance, Power, Purpose, and Value, and the questions are Whether? What? How? Who? Where? When? and Why? Each domino piece can therefore be seen as the application of one question to one conception. This is the key to the basic form of the Game, which may be played in two ways, as indicated below.

In following the examples about to be presented, you will find it useful to have a set of dominoes present, and lay out the pieces indicated in the examples. This will make the examples much less confusing, and aid understanding.

The Game of the Cantrefs: Basic Form

Choose a theme of any kind that is suitable for meditation, either a part of the Druid teaching or an issue that confronts you in your daily life. Consider it in general terms for a short time, and as you do so, take out your set of dominoes and lay out all 28 tiles face down on a table or other surface before you. Without looking at the faces of the dominoes, choose three and put the others aside. Then, one at a time, turn the dominoes you have chosen face up, and read them in terms of the questions and conceptions of the Sevenfold Wheel of Thought;

the upper half of each piece represents the question, while the lower half represents the conception.

We will assume for the sake of the example that the three pieces already mentioned—3/1, 2/4, and 0/6—are the ones you have chosen. As you turn up the first of these, you see that the question is "How?" and the conception is "Being." The first question you ask about the theme, then, is "How does it exist?" "How" in this setting may be taken to mean "In what manner?" or "By what means?" or both. Once you phrase the question, answer it as best you can before proceeding to turn up the next domino piece.

For the second piece, the question is "What?" and the conception is "Substance." The second question you ask about the theme is therefore "What is its substance?" or perhaps "Of what substance is it?" It is entirely allowable to vary the phrasing as needed to fit it to the theme, so long as the question and the conception indicated by the domino piece are included in the final question you ask. Answer the question to the best of your ability before going on.

For the third piece, the question is "Why?" and the conception is "Purpose." The third question you ask about the theme may be "Why is this its purpose?" or "Why does it have the purpose that it does?" or some similar phrasing. Once again, answer the question to the best of your ability.

You will find that when you apply this basic form of the Game of the Cantrefs to a theme drawn from your daily life, the questions that emerge from it are the ones you most need to ask and answer in order to understand that detail of your life. When you apply it to your Druid studies, the questions you ask and answer will guide you most effectively to a deeper understanding of the lore of the Druid mysteries.

The Game of the Cantrefs: Intermediate Form

When you have familiarized yourself in detail with the basic form of the Game of the Cantrefs, and have practiced it enough to have some facility with the process, you may proceed to the more challenging intermediate form of the Game. Here the dominoes are combined in a manner not unlike the one used in playing domino games, that is, joined so that the two ends in contact have the same number of points upon them. (For example, if you have dominoes marked 2/1 and 4/2, you can only join them by putting the ends with two points together—either end to end, or with one end against the side of the other end, as shown in Figure 9.

To play the intermediate form of the Game, begin by choosing a theme and turning all the dominoes face down, as in the basic form. Choose one, and turn it face up; this gives you the first conception and question to consider concerning the theme. Now choose six more, and turn them all face up. These are the options you have available to play the Game, and you must figure out how to combine them with the first piece you chose, so that as many as possible can be played.

For example, imagine that you have drawn 1/2 as your first piece in an intermediate Game, so the first thing you ask about the theme is "Whether it becomes?" The remaining pieces you draw are 4/2, 6/6, 2/6, 1/5, 5/6, and 5/5. Each of these remaining pieces may be played with either end up, so that for example, 4/2 may also be played as 2/4, and 1/5 as 5/1.

You place 1/2 on the table before you, call to mind your theme, and consider "Whether it becomes?" When you have finished this contemplation, you may take any of the other pieces and add it to 1/2, so long as the piece you play has either a 1 or a 2 (that is, a single dot, or a double dot) upon it. To play the piece, you place it in contact with 1/2. We will suppose that you play 4/2, and place the end with two dots against the side of the 2 end of 1/2, as in the second picture above. (You place it on the side because you have another piece with a 2 on it; you may also place it on the end, and put the other piece against the side.)

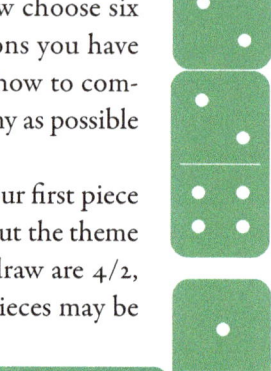

Fig. 11. Two methods of joining dominoes 2/1 and 4/2

The next phase, the interpretation of the move, must be understood with due care. Whenever you join a piece to another piece in the intermediate game, the question or conception that corresponds to the end the two pieces have in common remains in play; the question or conception the two pieces do not have in common changes. In the example just given, the conception, Becoming, remains the same, since the two dots that the two dominoes have in common represent Becoming in the piece already played. The question changes, since the single dot representing Whether? in the piece already played is not to be seen on the piece that is newly joined to it; instead, the question Who? takes its place. This gives the second combination to be contemplated, which is "Who" (or "Whose," depending on the original theme) "does it become?"

Once this has been considered appropriately, the player chooses another piece and adds it. There is a certain amount of flexibility in which pieces to play in what order, though of course the requirement that only equal numbers may be joined restricts this flexibility. Our player, let us say, next chooses the piece 2/6, and places it against the side of the original piece 1/2, in a position mirroring that of 2/4. The original combination "Whether it becomes?" changes again, and the new combination to be contemplated is "When does it become?" The conception Becoming, here again, comes from the 2 that the newly played piece shares with the original piece 1/2, while the question "When?" corresponds to the 6 of the new piece.

Once this has been considered at appropriate length, a new piece is chosen and played. Let us assume that it is 1/5, and is played on the 1 end of the original piece 1/2. In this move, the question remains unchanged while the conception changes, and the new combination is "Whether it has power?" Power, of course, is the conception corresponding to 5.

At this point the player faces a choice which will have a significant influence over the further play of the game. Up to now, each piece played could only have been placed in one location, but the possibilities are far wider from this point on, and each choice means that certain combinations will be considered and others will not be. The piece 5/6, for example, could be placed on the 6 end of 2/6 or the 5 end of 1/5, and in either case it would represent "When does it have power?" If 6/6 is placed on the 6 end of 2/6 and 5/5 on the 5 end of 1/5, though, and 5/6 is played next to one of these, 5/6 will instead represent "Where is its purpose?" (Once again, all this will be much easier to understand if the student actually lays out the game as it is being described here.)

Whichever of these choices is made, the game continues until all the pieces that can be played have been played. It will sometimes happen that one or more of the pieces cannot be played with the others that have been drawn—for example, if one of the pieces drawn for the game just played had been 3/3, 3/0, or 0/0, it could not have been played with any other piece—it is left aside and not included in that game.

As with the basic form of the game, you will find that the process of playing the Game of the Cantrefs in its intermediate form will help you deepen your understanding of any aspect of the Druid wisdom you take as a theme, and the combinations of question and conception that come up in a game will be found more significant in regard to that theme, at least for the person who plays it, than any others. As you proceed through the Gradd y Gwyddon y Cylch, play the Game regularly and use it to explore the teachings of this lesson packet; along with its other advantages, it will give you the background needed to play the still more challenging advanced version of the Game, which will be covered in the final lesson packet of this course.

THE MABINOGION: THE DREAM OF MACSEN WLEDIG

HE SECOND OF THE THREE TALES of the Mabinogion corresponding to the threefold element of Spirit, the Dream of Macsen Wledig is another relatively brief and cryptic tale. Unlike any other of the seven tales used to communicate the secrets of the Cantrefs, this tale begins and ends outside the British Isles; much of the action takes place in the city of Rome and the lands around it, while the brief and gruesome conclusion takes place in Brittany.

There are multiple layers to the story. One of these layers comes from history, albeit history refracted through the prism of folk memory. In the year 368, a Roman officer named Maximus came to what was then the province of Britannia and rose through the ranks to become commander of the Roman legions there. In 383, during a period of troubles in the western Empire, the legions in Britannia proclaimed Maximus emperor. He crossed the English Channel, taking most of the British garrison with him, and brought Gaul under his control. When he crossed the Alps and took Rome, however, the powerful ruler of the eastern Empire moved against him, and Maximus was defeated, captured, and put to death.

A second layer breaks away from history and enters the realm of mythology. Beli son of Manogan, whom the tale names as king of Britain, was also named as the father of Lludd and Llefelys; he is the great solar god of the ancient Druids under one of his names. In traditional Welsh lore, though he does not appear in the Fourth Branch of the Mabinogion, he is said to be the brother-in-law of

Math ap Mathonwy and the father of Gwydion, Arianrhod, and Gilfaethwy, and thus intimately connected to the story of that Branch.

Elen, another important character in the story, is also a divinity, the old goddess of dawn and dusk, and the patron goddess of the ancient roads of Britain—a correspondence referred to in the story. Though she has no genealogical connection to Beli or his relatives, her symbolism also includes a reference to the Fourth Branch, for the part of Wales where she appears in the story is in Arfon in the far north, the same area where the Fourth Branch takes place. The city of Caer Sain at the mouth of the Arfon river, now Caernarfon, was sacred to her in ancient times.

As a teaching story of the Druid mysteries, however, the historical and mythological dimensions are subordinate to a symbolism discussed at length elsewhere in this course, for the subject of the Dream of Macsen Wledig is the awakening of the individuality and its relationship to the personality. There are four stages to the process outlined here. The first is the personality's first visionary glimpse of the realities that are higher than it; the second, the quest to learn about those realities, drawing on the teachings and accounts of others; the third, the journey of initiation that brings personality and individuality into contact with each other; fourth, the descent of the power and influence of the individuality into the realm of the personality to put it in order. This process may well be familiar to you, as you have been engaged in it now for many months.

The Dream of Macsen Wledig

Macsen Wledig was emperor of Rome, and he was a comelier man, and a better and a wiser than any emperor that had been before him. And one day he held a council of kings, and he said to his friends, "I desire to go tomorrow to hunt."[5] And the next day in the morning he set forth with his retinue, and came to the valley of the river that flowed towards Rome. And he hunted through the valley until mid-day. And with him also were two-and-thirty crowned kings, that were his vassals; not for the delight of hunting went the emperor with them, but to put himself on equal terms with those kings.

---

5. Notice the implied reference here to the opening of the First Branch of the Mabinogion.

And the sun was high in the sky over their heads, and the heat was great. And sleep came upon Macsen Wledig. And his attendants stood and set up their shields around him upon the shafts of their spears to protect him from the sun, and they placed a gold enameled shield under his head; and so Macsen slept.

And he saw a dream. And this is the dream that he saw. He was journeying along the valley of the river towards its source; and he came to the highest mountain in the world.[6] And he thought that the mountain was as high as the sky; and when he came over the mountain, it seemed to him that he went through the fairest and most level regions that man ever yet beheld, on the other side of the mountain. And he saw large and mighty rivers descending from the mountain to the sea, and towards the mouths of the rivers he proceeded.

And as he journeyed thus, he came to the mouth of the largest river ever seen.[7] And he beheld a great city at the entrance of the river, and a vast castle in the city, and he saw many high towers of various colours in the castle. And he saw a fleet at the mouth of the river, the largest ever seen. And he saw one ship among the fleet; larger was it by far, and fairer than all the others. Of such part of the ship as he could see above the water, one plank was gilded and the other silvered over. He saw a bridge of whalebone from the ship to the land, and he thought that he went along the bridge, and came into the ship. And a sail was hoisted on the ship, and along the sea and the ocean was it borne.

Then it seemed that he came to the fairest island in the whole world, and he traversed the island from sea to sea, even to the furthest shore of the island. Valleys he saw, and steeps and rocks of wondrous height, and rugged precipices. Never yet saw he the like. And thence he beheld an island in the sea, facing this rugged land.[8] And between him and this island was a country of which the plain was as large as the sea, the mountain as vast as the wood. And from the mountain he saw a river that flowed through the land and fell into the sea. And at the mouth of the river he beheld a castle, the fairest that man ever saw, and the gate of the castle was open, and he went into the castle.

And in the castle he saw a fair hall, of which the roof seemed to be all gold, the walls of the hall seemed to be entirely of glittering precious gems, the doors all seemed to be of gold. Golden seats he saw in the hall, and silver tables. And

---

6. Traditionally, one of the Alps.
7. Traditionally, the Rhine.
8. Ynys Mon, the island of Anglesey, across the Straits of Menai from the province of Arfon in northern Wales.

on a seat opposite to him, he beheld two auburn-haired youths playing at chess. He saw a silver board for the chess, and golden pieces thereon. The garments of the youths were of jet black satin, and chaplets of ruddy gold bound their hair, whereon were sparkling jewels of great price, rubies, and gems, alternately with imperial stones. Buskins of new cordovan leather on their feet, fastened by slides of red gold.

And beside a pillar in the hall, he saw a hoary-headed man, in a chair of ivory, with the figures of two eagles of ruddy gold thereon. Bracelets of gold were upon his arms, and many rings were on his hands, and a golden torque about his neck; and his hair was bound with a golden diadem. He was of powerful aspect. A chess-board of gold was before him, and a rod of gold, and a steel file in his hand. And he was carving out chess-men.

And he saw a maiden sitting before him in a chair of ruddy gold. Not more easy than to gaze upon the sun when brightest, was it to look upon her by reason of her beauty. A vest of white silk was upon the maiden, with clasps of red gold at the breast; and a surcoat of gold tissue upon her, and a frontlet of red gold upon her head, and rubies and gems were in the frontlet, alternating with pearls and imperial stones. And a girdle of ruddy gold was around her. She was the fairest sight that man ever beheld.

The maiden arose from her chair before him, and he threw his arms about the neck of the maiden, and they two sat down together in the chair of gold: and the chair was not less roomy for them both than for the maiden alone.[9] And as he had his arms about the maiden's neck, and his cheek by her cheek, behold, through the chafing of the dogs at their leashing, and the clashing of the shields as they struck against each other, and the beating together of the shafts of the spears, and the neighing of the horses and their prancing, the emperor awoke.

And when he awoke, nor spirit nor existence was left him, because of the maiden whom he had seen in his sleep, for the love of the maiden pervaded his whole frame. Then his household spake unto him.

"Lord," said they, "is it not past the time for thee to take thy food?" Thereupon the emperor mounted his palfrey, the saddest man that mortal ever saw, and went forth towards Rome.

And thus he was during the space of a week. When they of the household went to drink wine and mead out of golden vessels, he went not with any of them. When they went to listen to songs and tales, he went not with them

---

9. Notice the hint here that Macsen and the maiden are one person rather than two.

Fig. 12. The Mabinogion • *The Dream of Macsen Wledig*

there; neither could he be persuaded to do any thing but sleep. And as often as he slept, he beheld in his dreams the maiden he loved best; but except when he slept he saw nothing of her, for he knew not where in the world she was.

One day the page of the chamber spake unto him; now, although he was page of the chamber, he was king of the Romans. "Lord," said he, "all the people revile thee."

"Wherefore do they revile me?" asked the emperor.

"Because they can get neither message nor answer from thee as men should have from their lord. This is the cause why thou art spoken evil of."

"Youth," said the emperor, "do thou bring unto me the wise men of Rome, and I will tell them wherefore I am sorrowful."

Then the wise men of Rome were brought to the emperor, and he spake to them. "Sages of Rome," said he, "I have seen a dream. And in the dream I beheld a maiden, and because of the maiden is there neither life, nor spirit, nor existence within me."

"Lord," they answered, "since thou judgest us worthy to counsel thee, we will give thee counsel. And this is our counsel; that thou send messengers for three years to the three parts of the world, to seek for thy dream. And as thou knowest not what day or what night good news may come to thee, the hope thereof will support thee."

So the messengers journeyed for the space of a year, wandering about the world, and seeking tidings concerning his dream. But when they came back at the end of the year, they knew not one word more than they did the day they set forth. And then was the emperor exceeding sorrowful, for he thought that he should never have tidings of her whom best he loved.

Then spoke the king of the Romans unto the emperor. "Lord," said he, "go forth to hunt by the way thou didst seem to go, whether it were to the east, or to the west." So the emperor went forth to the hunt, and he came to the bank of the river.

"Behold," said he, "this is where I was when I saw the dream, and I went towards the source of the river westward."[10]

And thereupon thirteen messengers of the emperor's set forth, and before them they saw a high mountain, which seemed to them to touch the sky. Now this was the guise in which the messengers journeyed; one sleeve was on the cap of each of them in front, as a sign that they were messengers, in order that

---

10. The journey must be made by means of the Second Cantref rather than the first.

through what hostile land soever they might pass no harm might be done them. And when they were come over this mountain, they beheld vast plains, and large rivers flowing there through.

"Behold," said they, "the land which our master saw."

And they went along the mouths of the rivers, until they came to the mighty river which they saw flowing to the sea, and the vast city, and the many-coloured high towers in the castle. They saw the largest fleet in the world, in the harbour of the river, and one ship that was larger than any of the others. "Behold again," said they, "the dream that our master saw." And in the great ship they crossed the sea, and came to the Island of Britain. And they traversed the island until they came to Snowdon. "Behold," said they, "the rugged land that our master saw."

And they went forward until they saw Anglesey before them, and until they saw Arfon likewise. "Behold," said they, "the land our master saw in his sleep." And they saw Aber Sain, and a castle at the mouth of the river.[11] The portal of the castle saw they open, and into the castle they went, and they saw a hall in the castle. Then said they, "Behold, the hall which he saw in his sleep." They went into the hall, and they beheld two youths playing at chess on the golden bench. And they beheld the hoary-headed man beside the pillar, in the ivory chair, carving chessmen. And they beheld the maiden sitting on a chair of ruddy gold.

The messengers bent down upon their knees. "Empress of Rome, all hail!"

"Ha, gentles," said the maiden, "ye bear the seeming of honourable men, and the badge of envoys, what mockery is this ye do to me?"

"We mock thee not, lady; but the Emperor of Rome hath seen thee in his sleep, and he has neither life nor spirit left because of thee. Thou shalt have of us therefore the choice, lady, whether thou wilt go with us and be made empress of Rome, or that the emperor come hither and take thee for his wife."

"Ha, lords," said the maiden, "I will not deny what ye say, neither will I believe it too well. If the emperor love me, let him come here to seek me."[12]

And by day and night the messengers hied them back. And when their horses failed, they bought other fresh ones. And when they came to Rome, they

---

11. The present castle of Caernarfon dates from the thirteenth century, but there has been a fortification close by since the time of the old Celtic hill forts.
12. The individuality does not descend to the personality; the personality must rise to the plane of the individuality.

saluted the emperor, and asked their boon, which was given to them according as they named it.

"We will be thy guides, Lord," said they, "over sea and over land, to the place where is the woman whom best thou lovest, for we know her name, and her kindred, and her race."

And immediately the emperor set forth with his army. And these men were his guides. Towards the Island of Britain they went over the sea and the deep. And he conquered the Island from Beli the son of Manogan, and his sons, and drove them to the sea,[13] and went forward even unto Arfon. And the emperor knew the land when he saw it.

And when he beheld the castle of Aber Sain, "Look yonder," said he, "there is the castle wherein I saw the damsel whom I best love." And he went forward into the castle and into the hall, and there he saw Cynan the son of Eudaf, and Adeon the son of Eudaf,[14] playing at chess. And he saw Eudaf the son of Caradawc, sitting on a chair of ivory carving chessmen. And the maiden whom he had beheld in his sleep, he saw sitting on a chair of gold.

"Empress of Rome," said he, "all hail!" And the emperor threw his arms about her neck; and that night she became his bride.

And the next day in the morning, the damsel asked her maiden portion. And he told her to name what she would. And she asked to have the Island of Britain for her father, from the Channel to the Irish Sea, together with the three adjacent islands, to hold under the Empress of Rome; and to have three chief castles made for her, in whatever places she might choose in the Island of Britain. And she chose to have the highest castle made at Arfon. And they brought thither earth from Rome that it might be more healthful for the emperor to sleep, and sit, and walk upon. After that the two other castles were made for her, which were Caerleon and Caermarthen.

And one day the emperor went to hunt at Caermarthen, and he came so far as the top of Brefi Fawr, and there the emperor pitched his tent. And that encamping place is called Cadeir Macsen[15] even to this day. And because that

---

13. Notice that this contradicts the story of Lludd and Llefelys, according to which Beli was still king of Britain when he died, and his son Lludd succeeded him.

14. Cynan is "Chieftain" and Adeon is meant to suggest *adeiniog*, "winged." Eudaf is a pun on *eu taith*, "their journey," referring to the later part of the story.

15. *Cadeir Macsen*: "the Seat of Macsen."

he built the castle with a myriad of men, he called it Caerfyrddin.[16] Then Elen bethought her to make high roads from one castle to another throughout the Island of Britain. And the roads were made. And for this cause are they called the roads of Elen Luyddawc, that she was sprung from a native of this island, and the men of the Island of Britain would not have made these great roads for any save for her.

Seven years did the emperor tarry in this Island. Now, at that time, the men of Rome had a custom, that whatsoever emperor should remain in other lands more than seven years, should remain to his own overthrow, and should never return to Rome again.

So they made a new emperor. And this one wrote a letter of threat to Macsen. There was nought in the letter but only this. "If you come, and if you ever come to Rome."

And even unto Caerleon came this letter to Macsen, and these tidings.

Then sent he a letter to the man who styled himself emperor in Rome. There was nought in that letter also but only this. "When I come to Rome, and when I come."

And thereupon Macsen set forth towards Rome with his army, and vanquished France and Burgundy, and every land on the way, and sat down before the city of Rome.

A year was the emperor before the city, and he was no nearer taking it than the first day. And after him there came the brothers of Elen Luyddawc from the Island of Britain, and a small host with them, and better warriors were in that small host than twice as many Romans. And the emperor was told that a host was seen, halting close to his army and encamping, and no man ever saw a fairer or better appointed host for its size, nor more handsome standards.

And Elen went to see the hosts, and she knew the standards of her brothers. Then came Cynan the son of Eudaf and Adeon the son of Eudaf to meet the emperor. And the emperor was glad because of them, and embraced them.

Then they looked at the Romans as they attacked the city.

Said Cynan to his brother, "We will try to attack the city more expertly than this." So they measured by night the height of the wall, and they sent their carpenters to the wood, and a ladder was made for every four men of their number.

---

16. The story amusingly derives Caerfyrddin, the Welsh spelling of Carmarthen, from *caer*, "castle"; *myrdd*, "myriad"; and *dyn*, "man." Its more traditional derivation is from *caer*, "castle," and *Myrddin*, the Welsh spelling of the name of Merlin. (The change from M to F in the name is standard Welsh grammar.)

Now when these were ready, every day at mid-day the emperors went to meat, and they ceased to fight on both sides till all had finished eating. And in the morning the men of Britain took their food, and they drank until they were invigorated. And while the two emperors were at meat, the Britons came to the city, and placed their ladders against it, and forthwith they came in through the city.

The new emperor had no time to arm himself when they fell upon him, and slew him, and many others with him. And three nights and three days were they subduing the men that were in the city and taking the castle. And others of them kept the city, lest any of the host of Macsen should come therein, until they had subjected all to their will.

Then spake Macsen to Elen Luyddawc. "I marvel, lady," said he, "that thy brothers have not conquered this city for me."

"Lord, emperor," she answered, "the wisest youths in the world are my brothers. Go thou thither and ask the city of them, and if it be in their possession thou shalt have it gladly."

So the emperor and Elen went and demanded the city. And they told the emperor that none had taken the city, and that none could give it him, but the men of the Island of Britain. Then the gates of the city of Rome were opened, and the emperor sat on the throne, and all the men of Rome submitted themselves unto him.

The emperor then said unto Cynan and Adeon, "Lords," said he, "I have now had possession of the whole of my empire. This host give I unto you to vanquish whatever region ye may desire in the world."

So they set forth and conquered lands, and castles, and cities. And they slew all the men, but the women they kept alive. And thus they continued until the young men that had come with them were grown grey-beaded, from the length of time they were upon this conquest.

Then spoke Cynan unto Adeon his brother, "Whether wilt thou rather," said he, "tarry in this land, or go back into the land whence thou didst come forth?" Now he chose to go back to his own land, and many with him. But Cynan tarried there with the other part and dwelt there.

And they took counsel and cut out the tongues of the women, lest they should corrupt their speech.[17] And because of the silence of the women from

---

17. This detail is deliberately horrifying. Treat it as a symbol; what meaning lies behind the ghastly image?

their own speech, the men of Armorica are called Britons. From that time there came frequently, and still comes, that language from the Island of Britain. And this dream is called the Dream of Macsen Wledig, emperor of Rome. And here it ends.

DRUID PHILOSOPHY: THE SEVEN COSMIC LAWS

HE SEVEN COSMIC LAWS or Creative Principles were introduced in the Gradd yr Athroniwr with little commentary, other than a suggestion that they be used as themes for meditation, and it was left to the intuition of the student to follow up on the possibilities they present. They could with equal appropriateness have been presented in the first lesson packet of this course, and indeed versions of the same seven laws or principles have been published in books intended for the general public. It may come as some surprise to students of the Greater Mysteries, therefore, to learn that these seven laws or principles are counted among the great practical secrets of the mystery teachings.

It is a common saying in all the mystery schools that the greatest secrets of the mysteries could be shouted from the rooftops without the least risk of communicating them to those who do not know them already. The Seven Cosmic Laws well exemplify that statement. Approached as abstractions, taken on faith, and repeated by rote, they reveal nothing to the uninitiated. It is when they are treated as operative statements to be applied to the everyday realities of life that they reveal their remarkable powers, and treating them so, as realities rather than abstract notions, runs athwart nearly every one of the unexamined assumptions that make up what the world at large is pleased to call common sense.

As a student of the Greater Mysteries, you have already learned how little reliance may be placed on the habitual thinking of everyday society. You have learned that even in the parts of yourself you know best—the hunan or personality, with its three aspects of thought, will, and memory—are found capacities of which most people never dream; you have learned that the less often recognized parts of yourself have additional capacities, waiting to be awakened; and above all else, you have learned of the immense potentiality that lies before you in the awakening of the individuality, and you may well have begun to glimpse a little of the promise of that awakening in the "tremblings of the veil" that occur in the lives of many students of the mysteries, and admit into the dimly lit realm of ordinary life a brief flash of transforming radiance.

It is in the context of the training that you have already received that the Seven Cosmic Laws may be usefully revisited. The following reflections are meant to help start you along the path that will lead to a mastery of one practical application of the Laws, a practical application that has been summed up in the single phrase "Mental Alchemy." The comparison implied in the phrase is precise. Where the physical alchemist transmutes lead into gold using the subtle properties of matter, the mental alchemist transmutes common, leaden, valueless states of mind into the pure gold of the awakened consciousness, using the subtle properties of mind.

As with previous lectures on Druid philosophy, this one makes use of nine triads drawn from the storehouse of the Druid wisdom. The first seven of these triads deal, in reverse order, with the Seven Cosmic Laws. It is to them that we now turn.

Triad I.

Three aspects of the Law of Circularity: the reconciliation of forces, the recurrence of manifestation, and the transmutation into the Creative Spiral.

Triad II.

Three aspects of the Law of Correspondence: the correspondence of the lesser with the greater; the correspondence of the lower with the higher; the correspondence of the part with the whole.

Triad III.

Three aspects of the Law of Vibration: the genesis of motion, the alternation between extremes, and the poise of power.

Triad IV.

Three aspects of the Law of Causation: the reality of compensation, the relativity of happiness and sorrow, and the secret of cosmic justice.

Triad V.

Three aspects of the Law of Polarity: the interrelation of opposites, the mutual defining of opposites, and the transmutation of opposites.

Triad VI.

Three aspects of the Law of Balance: regularity, harmony, and limitation.

Triad VII.

Three aspects of the Law of Unity: the unity of the Seven Cosmic Laws, the unity of the circle and the circumference, and the unity of the self and the Cosmos.

Triad I.

Three aspects of the Law of Circularity: the reconciliation of forces, the recurrence of manifestation, and the transmutation into the Creative Spiral.

The Law of Circularity manifests in the universal tendency of things to move in arcs rather than straight lines, and unless stopped by some other force or barrier, to return to their starting place. In an important sense, circularity is an outgrowth of vibration, a more basic cosmic principle. The primary expression of vibration is action to and fro in a straight line or path, a movement backward and forward between the limits of the poles of manifestation. This would be the invariable movement if the particular force manifested were the only manifestation of force or energy in that particular field of the Cosmos. But when a swinging pendulum, free to move in any direction, is subjected to the conflicting attractions and repulsions of other manifestations of force and energy, then is manifested the universal tendency toward the circular trend—the tendency to convert the straight path of the swing into a circular path or cycle.

The action and reaction, attraction and repulsion, arising from the interplay between the force of polarity working in a straight line on the one hand, and the attractive and repulsive forces from without on the other hand, tend to swing the moving thing in a curved path around a central point, the point of balance of all the forces. Since this process of reconciliation of forces is in operation through the Cosmos, the manifestation of circularity may be noticed on all planes. There is ever a cyclic trend of things and events, following the tendency to move in circles. The electrons in the atoms move in circles, just as do planets around the sun; and just as does the sun move around some other center in space.[18] The highest occult teachings, as well as the highest speculations of science, inform us that there is always a movement in circles around some given point; and the movement of *this* center of motion around some other center; and so on to infinity.

All events tend to move in constant circular movements of continuous recurrence. The experience of man, aided by the reports of history, bears out this statement. The student of human history is struck by the recurrence of forms manifested throughout the ages of history. The student of philosophy is attracted by the same evidence in his own field. And so it is with every field of human thought—the repetition of forms is noticeable everywhere. Peoples and nations rise, flourish, decline and fall, only to be succeeded by others traveling over the same lines. The civilizations of Atlantis, Egypt, Chaldea, Rome, and Greece arose and passed away. Our civilization is traveling over the same general lines. All forms of political government, monarchic, autocratic, democratic, in all their variations, were known in the past as in the present. The same law is observable in the history of philosophical thought. Theories popular in Greece over two thousand years ago that afterward fell into disrepute, are now again forcing their way to the front. The scientific principles of causation, continuity, determinism, and evolution were popular at a particular phase of the classical world; and they were likewise popular in ancient Egypt and in India centuries before that time. Fashions in literature, dress, and manner constantly recur—traveling round and round their little circles. Laugh as we may at the absurdity of fashion in dress, nevertheless it proceeds according to the Law of Circularity. Religious ideas are as old as the world—pantheism, polytheism, monotheism, and atheism, all have played their parts of fashion in religious thought, over and over again—and will play them again. The present-day revival in interest in occult thought arises from the same law.

The life of individuals manifests the same trend and tendency. A little thought will convince you that the majority of people travel in circles in life. The same old thing over and over again, recurs at intervals of greater or lesser duration, according to the nature of the person. The majority of persons are like

---

18. At the time this was written, the existence of other galaxies was an unproven hypothesis, and our Sun's movement around the galactic center had not yet been detected. It is interesting to note how often the advance of science confirms the teachings of the mysteries.

the squirrel in the cage who travels all day on his whirling wheel, but ends where he began.

"But," you may say, "if the Cosmos travels around in a continuous circle it would never progress or advance into increased consciousness." Very true! And if the individual continued in the "constant circular movement of continuous recurrence" he would never advance on the Path of the Mysteries. The triad gives us the secret when it names the third aspect of the Law of Circularity as the transmutation into the Creative Spiral. The only escape from the closed circle is found by transmuting it into a spiral. This is accomplished by advancing the central point. If the central point of a circle is moved forward, then the circle is converted into a spiral. The central point is advanced in the Cosmos by the Cosmic Will urging forward the entire cosmic process, and thus converting the circular process into a spiral trend.

By a similar process, the individual may convert the circle of his life into a rising spiral, which while carrying him around the cycles of life will at the same time take him a stage further at each turn. While apparently traveling around a circle, like the average person, he will be proceeding in the direction of his dreams with each turn. The Mountain of Attainment, around which winds the Spiral Path, is traveled only in this way. Round and round the pilgrims travel, seemingly retracing the same steps—but in reality reaching a stage higher each circle they make.[19] They often complain (until they learn better) saying, "I have gone round and round, and still reach nowhere." But when they compare their present stage with that of a year ago, they see that they have made progress. Is this not the case with you?

By advancing the central point, by the will, the wise convert circles into spirals, and thus attain and advance.

Triad II.

Three aspects of the Law of Correspondence: the correspondence of the lesser with the greater; the correspondence of the lower with the higher; the correspondence of the part with the whole.

---

19. This may be a reference to Glastonbury in Britain, a great center of initiation in Druidic times, which had a spiral path—its traces still visible today—leading from Chalice Well to the summit of Glastonbury Tor.

The Law of Correspondence manifests itself as the universal tendency of things to repeat the same patterns and relationships on different planes of existence. Because the Cosmos is a unity, a unity governed by Awen and guided and shaped by nwyfre, common laws functioning on every plane will have corresponding effects; the law that governs the amoeba also governs man, though man through his complexity has the power to make use of the law's possibilities in ways the amoeba cannot. The same law in turn governs beings as far beyond man as he is beyond the amoeba, and whose capacity to make use of the common law exceeds ours by the same degree. Just as the Law of Circularity depends on the more basic Law of Vibration, the Law of Correspondence depends on the Law of Unity, the first and most fundamental of all the Seven Cosmic Laws.

The simplest form of correspondence for the untrained mind to grasp is the correspondence that exists between smaller and greater realities—a correspondence that extends in both directions. The same laws govern the whirling of great planetary spheres through space, the fall of a drop of rain to the ground, and the inexpressibly minute play of forces in the atom. It is by recognizing this, and applying the laws that shape the world we can see and touch to other aspects of the Cosmos too great or small for our direct perception, that scientists have come to understand many of the laws governing the material world.

This same principle may be traced in everyday life—in fact, you have traced it already, in your study of memory. You have seen how a single object, however small, that serves as a memento of some other time is able to summon up at once the emotions, the memories, the experiences of that past time. Thus the Law of Correspondence functions; a small physical part of that experience enables the whole to be recalled to mind.

Beyond the reach of science as it is presently constituted, however, are those realms of the Cosmos that transcend the material. It is a common habit of thought among the uninitiated to picture the spiritual side of the Cosmos as everything the material world is not. Like so many of the misunderstandings of popular thought, this is a partial truth rather than wholly an error; it is true that many of the properties of the material world are not found in the spiritual worlds; but equivalent properties are found throughout, correspondences that link the material and the spiritual. It is in this way that the human mind even in its earliest days could begin to reason about the higher aspects of existence, reasoning from the lower to the higher by way of analogy, which is one manifestation of correspondence. Simple and even childish as some of those early reasonings often seem to modern eyes, they are pregnant with spiritual truth and deserve the most careful contemplation, for the minds of the most ancient peoples were unclouded by specious reasonings and powerfully grasped the Law of Correspondence by intuition.

On still another plane, the mind applying itself to the phenomena of existence and the principles of the mystery teachings begins to grasp the correspondence that exists between the part and the whole. The modern student has gained an inestimable advantage in this regard from the progress of science, which has revealed examples of this form of correspondence unknown in the days before the microscope and other tools of research. It is a dull mind indeed that can be unmoved, for example, when contemplating the cells that make up his body, by the reflection that each of these cells is a little life of its own, with its own birth, growth, maturity, labor, aging, and death. Does this not inspire you to wonder whether you yourself are but a cell in some greater living thing, filling your own place in its greater life as the cells in your body fill their places in yours?

In the Cosmos, all things are at once parts belonging to wholes, and wholes composed of parts. Study the part and by analogy you understand something of the whole; study the whole and by the same means you understand something of the part. It is with this in mind that the initiate recognizes that his labors toward the awakening of individuality are not done for himself alone, but play a part in the greater life of humanity, which ripens age after age toward the fulfillment of its own role in the Cosmos of which it is one small part.

Triad III.

Three aspects of the Law of Vibration: the genesis of motion, the alternation between extremes, and the poise of power.

The Law of Vibration manifests itself as the universal tendency of things to move and change, and in moving and changing, to alternate between one side of a polarity and another. In the Cosmos everything is in constant motion and undergoes constant change. Everything "beats time." Vibration is universal, and, manifesting according to the Law of Vibration, constitutes the difference of degree existing between things on all planes. Everything moves to and fro between its two poles. Everything rises and falls within the limits of its nature. Everything advances and retreats within the limits of its power.

One lesson that must be learned from this law is that in the Cosmos everything is in constant motion and undergoes constant change. This is one of the fundamental principles of all the mystery teachings, which has been upheld through the centuries, until now the most advanced modern science has adopted the same position.[20] Heraclitus, the famous Greek philosopher, who lived nearly twenty-five hundred years ago, made this principle the basis of his philosophy. Clodd, the English scientific writer, says: "Nothing escapes the law of change. The shrewd speculations of Heraclitus the Ionian, who lived two thousand five hundred years ago, that everything is in a state of flux, and, therefore, that the universe is always 'becoming,' have added confirmation in every discovery of modern physics."

Buddha said: "Everything changes but Change."

Huxley[21] said: "The more we learn of the nature of things, the more evident is it that what we call rest is only unperceived activity; that seeming peace is silent but strenuous battle. In every part, at every moment, the state of the Cosmos is the expression of a transitory adjustment of contending forces; a scene of strife in which all the combatants fall in turn. What is true of each part is true of the whole. Natural knowledge tends more and more to the conclusion that 'all the choir of heaven and furniture of the earth' are transitory forms or parcels of cosmic substances wending along the road of evolution, from nebulous potentiality, through endless growths of sun and planet and satellite; through all varieties of matter; through infinite diversities of life and thought; possibly, through modes of being of which we have neither a conception, nor are competent to form any, back to the indefinable latency from which they arose. Thus the most obvious attribute of the Cosmos is its impermanence."

The ceaseless motion of all things is caused, of course, by the operation of the Principle of Motion—one of the three Cosmic Principles, which acts upon Substance and Consciousness in the many manifestations arising principally from the action and reaction of the dual principles of, or rather the opposite poles of, Attraction–Repulsion. Its forms and varieties are as manifold as are those of Substance, or Consciousness—that is to say, they are practically infinite. The basic activity of motion, however, is that which we call vibration. Vibration is universal, and constitutes the difference of degrees between things on all planes. Everything from the tiny corpuscle or electron, of which the atoms

---

20. A statement as true now as it was when this course was written.
21. Thomas Henry Huxley, the great English biologist and ally of Darwin.

are composed, to the greatest masses of matter known to us, manifest the Law of Vibration.

In previous lessons you have learned that the Cosmos, when resolved into Annwn, is practically motionless—the principle of motion is in its nearest possible approach to a condition of absolute rest. Yet that absolute rest is analogous to motion of such a high degree of vibration as to be practically motionless and at rest. In this condition, or state, the two poles of motion have been resolved into one—the extremes have merged—absolute motion and absolute rest are seen to be identical. From the first dawn of the new cosmic day, however, there is manifested vibration on a constantly descending scale, until the lowest point is reached—then the upward trend begins. In these varying degrees of vibration is manifested every thing that is in the Cosmos, not only the physical things, but also the mental states. Every mental state, of any and all kinds, has its own degree of vibration, which makes it what it is, and constitutes its difference from other mental states. These mental vibrations may be transmitted from one brain to another, in the phenomena of Mentalism.

It should not be necessary here to inform the student that that which we call sound, light, heat, magnetism, electricity, X-rays, and other forms of energy, are but varying forms of vibration. And that even the most solid piece of material substance—a diamond or piece of steel, for instance, is composed of a countless number of tiny atoms, which in turn are composed of minute electrons or particles—all in constant vibratory motion, manifesting intense energy, dashing about and circling around each other, bounding and rebounding from each other, each atom resembling a solar system with its circling planets in constant motion. The elementary text-books on physical science inform their readers that every thing, and all things, of which we have any knowledge through our senses, are but appearances arising from differing rates of vibration. And that, moreover, our only consciousness of them is the result of vibration.

But, what of the second aspect of the Law of Vibration, which causes everything to "beat time," so to speak? This has a very important bearing upon mental states and phenomena. Rhythm, according to the accepted usage, is "movement in measured time," the most familiar instance of which is the time kept in music, which is measured by the beats of the metronome or the baton. Scientific investigation, as well as the ancient mystery teachings, show us that everything in the Cosmos "beats time," and moves in accordance with rhythm. We see this in the swing of the planets; the beating of the human heart; the in-breathing and out-breathing of the lungs; the rise and fall of the tides; and in the operation of vibration on every plane, in every thing.

A moment's thought will show you that all the phenomena in Nature manifest this law of vibratory movement between two extremes. There is always the ebb and flow of things, the rhythmic swing of the pendulum between the two extremes of any existence. Day is succeeded by night; summer by winter; action by reaction; work by rest; activity by inactivity; intermittent symptoms in diseases; "good times" by "bad times" in business; exaltation by depression. On every plane may be observed instances of this universal "pendulum swing" of Rhythm, which carries the thing back and forth between its two polar extremes. Modern science holds that the Evolution of worlds must have had its precedent Involution, and the Evolution must be followed by Devolution—and so on, to Infinity. It holds that just as the suns and planets were evolved by stages from the nebulae, so must they return to the nebulae in time; again to begin a new series of evolutionary world-building. Herbert Spencer makes this law of Rhythm one of the principles of his philosophy.[22]

The Druid Teaching also shows the Law of Vibration to be operative in the form of the Days and Nights of the Cosmos—the swing of rhythm between the Manifest Cosmos and the Unmanifest Cosmos. The Law of Polarity and the Law of Vibration are twin laws—they are bound to each other for eternity. You will notice the resulting effect, that the rise and fall, or rhythmic pendulum swing, is determined, governed and restrained by the length of the scale of polarity. Nothing can swing beyond the limits of its poles—nothing can exceed the limits of its nature or power. Consequently, if a thing swings far in one direction, it swings back equally far in the other. If its swing is great, its extremes are widely apart—if the swing is small, then the extremes are close together. The pendulum illustration may be applied to the phenomena on all planes. A short beat of the metronome allows the rod to move only a short distance each way—the long beat admits of a wide swing. Those who enjoy keenly also suffer keenly; while those whose natures allow of but limited suffering, are also capable of only a limited degree of capacity for enjoyment. The pendulum swings as far in one direction as in the other. Only by a mastery of mental rhythm can man hope to escape the pain that his high development would otherwise bring him.

---

22. Spencer was a leading English philosopher of the late nineteenth and early twentieth century, who made evolution central to his system of thought.

The Druid mysteries therefore instruct their initiates in the Art of Mental Alchemy, by an understanding of which they may apply the energy and power of mental vibrations intelligently and under the control of the Reason and the Will. When it is understood that the difference between mental states is like the difference between states of physical energy—merely a rate of vibration—then Mental Alchemy becomes as real as the physical alchemy of the ancients, which science is now on the eve of rediscovering. An understanding of this gives one the mastery of self, and also the secret of mentalism. Moreover, an understanding of the Law of Vibration enables one to take advantage of the flood-tide of mental rhythm, and a neutralizing or rising above the ebb-tide. With an understanding of the Law of Balance, one may so balance and counterbalance himself that he is not disturbed by the backward swing of the pendulum of Rhythm, but instead may take advantage of its energy and transmute it into desirable things. In this understanding comes the Poise of Power.

Triad IV.

Three aspects of the Law of Causation: the reality of compensation, the relativity of happiness and sorrow, and the secret of cosmic justice.

The role of cause and effect in human life is recognized by all the world's greatest thinkers, although the average person endeavors to deny it, and refuses to look the facts in the face. That wonderful essay upon "Compensation," by Emerson,[23] carries the truth to every open mind. All true philosophers have recognized the force of this principle. Any one may see the fact, if he will stand apart and view the world-picture in the proper perspective. The idea of compensation is simply that of cause and effect treated as a reality of everyday existence, leading to the recognition that nothing comes from nothing, and every action brings its inevitable reaction. In short, life is always a matter of "paying the price." We cannot buy a piece of candy and keep our penny at the same time. We must always give up one thing to obtain another—we must always relinquish to attain—we must always die to live. For every advantage gained, another must be surrendered. This is the Law of the Cosmos, as all wise men know it. It does one no good to deny or ignore it—it is the nature of things: fixed, constant, immutable.

---

23. Ralph Waldo Emerson, the first significant American philosopher, and a leading light of the Transcendentalist movement of the early nineteenth century.

Emerson, in his essay on "Compensation," says:

> The theory of the mechanic forces is another example. What we gain in power is lost in time, and the converse. The periodic or compensating errors of the planets is another instance. The influences of climate and soil in political history are another. The cold climate invigorates. The barren soil does not breed fevers, crocodiles, tigers, or scorpions. The same dualism underlies the nature and condition of man. Every excess causes a defect; every defect an excess. Every sweet has its sour; every evil its good. Every faculty which is a receiver of pleasure has an equal penalty put on its abuse. It is to answer for its moderation with its life. For every grain of wit, there is a grain of folly. For everything you have missed, you have gained something else; and for everything you gain, you lose something. If riches are increased, they are increased that use them. If the gatherer gathers too much, nature takes out of the man what she puts into his chest; swells the estate, but kills the owner. Nature hates monopolies and exceptions. The waves of the sea do not more speedily seek a lever from their loftiest tossing than the varieties of condition tend to equalize themselves.
>
> There is some leveling circumstance that puts down the overbearing, the strong, the rich, the fortunate, substantially on the same ground with all others. Is a man too strong and fierce for society, and by temper and position a bad citizen—a morose ruffian, with a dash of the pirate in him?—nature sends him a troop of pretty sons and daughters who are getting along in the dame's classes at the village school, and love and fear for them smooths his grim scowl to courtesy. Thus she contrives to soften the granite and feldspar, takes the boar out and puts the lamb in, and keeps the balance true. The farmer imagines power and place are fine things. But the President has paid dear for his White House. It has commonly cost him all his peace, and the best of his manly attributes. To preserve for so short a time so conspicuous an appearance before the world, he is content to eat dust before the real masters who stand erect behind the throne.
>
> Or do men desire the more substantial and permanent grandeur of genius? Neither has this an immunity. He who by force of will or of thought is great and overlooks thousands, has the responsibility of overlooking. With every influx of light comes new danger. Has he light? He must bear witness to the light, and always outrun that sympathy which gives him such keen satisfaction, by his fidelity to new revelations of the incessant soul. He must hate father and mother, wife and child. Has he all that the world loves and admires and covets?—he must cast behind him their admiration and afflict them by faithfulness to his truth, and become a byword and a hissing.

As we have mentioned already, the greater the capacity for joy, the greater the capacity for pain. The swing of the pendulum of vibration between the two poles of the opposite polarities measures our relative happiness and unhappiness—comparative satisfaction or dissatisfaction. The capacity for pain is the symbol of advancement. The tramp has nothing and desires nothing beyond his immediate wants. His arc is small. Another will have much, but desires still more. His arc is large. Each, and both, fall a little short of what would constitute happiness for them. Query: which of the two is the happiest, or the most miserable? The answer of compensation is: "They are equal in their degree of happiness and unhappiness—in satisfaction and misery. They are twin brothers of equal heritage."

A financial panic that makes the millionaire writhe in terror, passes entirely over the tramp. The more one has, the more afraid of losing it is he; and the harder the blow if the loss occurs. Many ancient philosophical writers insisted that the measure of pain and pleasure is equally distributed between persons—although the degrees of each vary greatly. The man who makes two dollars a day and is able to save a half-dollar out of it, is possibly happier and better satisfied than he who makes a hundred and spends half as much more. What would bring happiness to a savage would bring misery to a college professor. Happiness is comparative, and so is unhappiness. We find happiness where we least expect it—and unhappiness where it surprises us. Just as "to know all, is to forgive all"; so, to know all, is to understand the relativity of satisfaction and happiness. It is said that the "back is always made strong enough to bear the burden"—we do not assert this as a fact, but we feel that the back gets used to the burden, and feels it not more than other backs feel lesser burdens. While the proverb that "God tempers the wind to the shorn lamb" may not be scientifically correct, still it is true that the shorn lamb becomes tempered to the wind, and "gets used to it."

Clodd says: "The simplicity of the simplest forms has been their salvation. A high organization brings with it many disadvantages, for the more complex the structure the more liable is it to get out of gear. We cannot have highly convoluted brains and at the same time digestive organs simple and renewable like those of the sea-cucumber. Death is the price paid for complexity." Pain is the natural consequence of complexity in life, knowledge, and possessions.

Each one has his troubles and his joys, each his pains and his pleasures. If we knew all the inside facts concerned with others' lives we would not be willing to exchange with them, providing we had to live exactly their same lives. Who would wish to exchange his personal life with that of another—taking all that goes with the other's, and giving up, completely, all that composes his own? Each man's "cross" is fitted exactly to his particular shoulders—and each man's "crown" is adjusted nicely upon his particular brow. It takes a philosophical mind to realize this—the tendency is to consider one's own lot the very worst of all, and the other man's lot much the better. The other man is probably thinking the same about yours. Neither would exchange, if he knew the full facts of the case—all the counterbalances and counterchecks. Each has his own "character," and all that goes with it. Each has his own arc of happiness and satisfaction, with their opposite poles. As the old Egyptian proverb ran: "'What will you have?' said the gods to man. 'Take it, and pay for it!'"

Triad V.

Three aspects of the Law of Polarity: the interrelation of opposites, the mutual defining of opposites, and the transmutation of opposites.

The Law of Polarity teaches that everything in the Cosmos—every quality, attribute or condition—has its opposite. Every thing, quality, attribute or condition is one of a pair of opposites and on further analysis, contains within itself a pair of opposites. Everything has its two poles; and also is itself one pole of something else. The pairs of opposites—the two opposing poles—are phases or modification of one thing, and therefore it is in the union of opposites that is to be found the essential nature and reality of a thing. There is thus always a reconciliation and agreement between opposites—always a synthesis that emerges from the play of thesis and antithesis. Every thing "is" and "is not" at the same time, in its qualities, attributes and conditions, and the reconciliation of the opposites reveals a new "is," a new thesis. In this way, in turn, the reconciliation of one pair of opposites is itself one of a pair of opposites, of a new and higher polarity, and this proceeds to infinity. In this realization is contained a secret understanding of all things in the Cosmos.

Thus, while every thing has its opposite, still the two opposites together form the reality of the thing. Every truth is but a half truth. Everything is a paradox. There is another side to everything. There are two extremes to everything. In this great Cosmic Law is found the fact that diametrically opposed things, on the physical, mental, and spiritual planes, are in reality but the different poles of the same thing. In this Law is found the explanation of all physical phenomena—of all mental activities and states—the secret of generation and regeneration—and many other important facts and laws of Cosmic Activity.

When one has had his attention directed to the existence of the Law of Opposites, he will see evidence of its presence and operation in all the phenomena of the Cosmos. He will soon see that no matter what may be the quality of a thing, another quality diametrically opposed to the first one will always be found in that same thing. Sometimes it is difficult to discover the opposing quality, but the Law is invariable and constant, and a careful search will always reveal the opposite. Thus you will always find an up and a down; a high and a low; a right and a left; a hard and a soft; a heavy and a light; an abstract and a concrete; a positive and a negative; a male and a female; a good and a bad; a love and a hate; a courage and a fear; a truth and an untruth; and so on until you will find that, the moment you notice a quality of a thing, at that same moment you will recognize an opposite quality within the same thing.

The uninitiated think of these pairs of opposites as composed of things entirely different from each other, and far from being "the same thing." Examine a little closer, and what do you see? Where do you draw the line between up and down? You may say that one thing is "up" and another "down," in comparison with each other, or in relation to some other thing. But, in the abstract, apart from any particular comparison, where is your dividing line which causes one direction in space to be "up" and another to be "down?" There is no such absolute division, and your "up" and "down" are but relative and comparative terms, depending upon some arbitrary decision. Astronomers recognize this fact, and one of the first things they teach their students is: "There is no 'up' nor 'down' in Space!" The same is of course true with with the cardinal points, which consist of pairs of opposites. Travel north as far as you can go, and reaching the North Pole you find yourself in a position in which whatever direction you travel your next step will lead you south. Travel east as far as you can and you will find yourself returning to your starting point from the west. What is west to us is east to others. China and India, which most people think of as eastern nations, are west of America. We can reach them by traveling either east or west.

The point can be made more clearly by a consideration of heat and cold. At first thought no two things seem further removed from one another than these two—they seem to have nothing in common. But let us see. We find that science assumes the existence of a certain quality called "temperature." The word is derived from a Latin word meaning "measure; proportion; degree." Science uses it to indicate the "intensity of radiant heat." And heat is held to be simply a "state or condition of matter, resulting from vibration." Temperature then is merely a term used to indicate varying degrees of vibration in matter. Therefore we see that heat and cold have no real existence as things in themselves, but are merely degrees in the scale of heat, the latter being but a term indicating certain kinds of vibrations. Therefore heat and cold are but degrees of the same thing, in the end—and that "same thing" is but a quality of something else—a quality of motion, having its own opposite in a higher scale.

Moreover, even on the lower plane heat and cold are but relative and comparative. At what point on the thermometer would you draw a line dividing hot from cold? Everything is a little hotter than something else, and a little colder than a third thing. It is quite relative and comparative. Come from a cold hallway, into a warmer room, and you feel quite warm, even though those in the room be shivering. Dip one hand into ice-water, and the other into very hot water, at the same time—and then plunge both hands into a basin of lukewarm water, at the same moment. What is the result? To one hand the water seems quite warm, while to the other it seems quite cool—and yet the temperature of the water is fixed. Where is your hot and cold, then? You say that today is warm, meaning that it is warmer than it has been. A month from now, you may call the same temperature cool.

In the end you will find that heat and cold are but names designating degrees of vibration. You know very well what you mean by each term—you recognize them as opposites—and yet you are unable to fix a dividing line between them or to separate things into two distinct classes labeled "hot" and "cold" respectively. You find that they blend into each other, and that the shades of differences between close degrees are almost indistinguishable in sensation. You see that they are but a pair of opposites, and together form two poles of the same thing—heat. The very cold thing is as much a degree of heat as is the very hot thing—the distinction is merely one of degree.

The same law may be applied as well to good and bad. Here we do not refer to right and wrong in the moral or religious sense, although even that comes under the Law of Polarity, and is a matter of degrees upon a standard erected by some particular school, religion, or custom—the standard varying greatly among the schools, sects, or localities. It is often very difficult to determine between right and wrong in any particular standard or scale, so closely do the degrees shade into each other.

We refer, rather, to good in the sense of "desirable, conducive to satisfaction and happiness"; and to bad in the sense of "undesirable; conducive to dissatisfaction and unhappiness." We find, upon analysis and examination, that these two terms are but another pair of opposites, which represent degrees of something which we may call "satisfaction" or "happiness." A good thing is one which causes happiness and satisfaction; a bad thing, one which produces unhappiness and dissatisfaction. We readily distinguish between these two in the abstract!

When it comes to drawing a fixed line between them in practice, however, we find it impossible. Some things are better than others; some things are worse than others; but these degrees are comparative, and relative. A dirty crust of dry bread tastes very good to a starving man while the same thing would be very bad to the taste of a well-fed person. And so it is with everything good and bad.

Moreover, the same thing may be both good and bad at the same time—that is, good for some purposes and bad for others. So we must always inquire "good for what?" "Bad for what?" And, likewise, the same thing may be both good and bad, at the same time, for the same purpose, for two different people. A good day's fishing is a bad day for the fish. "Good!" says one man when wheat advances on the Board of Trade, and yet that advance may be exceedingly bad for another. A writer on Natural History once pointed to the long legs and long beak of the crane, so well adapted to catching fish, as a "mark of the goodness of Providence." The fish probably thought it an exceedingly bad provision.

Let us consider the positive pole of emotional energy, which we call "love." We find here a high degree of one emotional quality. On the extreme opposite of the scale—the negative pole—we find the quality which we call "hate." These two emotional states seem as different as any two things can be, do they not? It seems almost impossible to conceive that they are but the opposite poles of what we may call "emotional connection"—and yet such is their real relation. Returning once more to the pole of love, let us descend the scale. Moving down a little on the scale we find states of less regard or less attraction. Then still further down, we find states in which the regard or attraction is very greatly reduced. Finally we come to a point at which there appears to be no regard or attraction, and still no repulsion or dislike. This is the neutral point of balance which is always to be found somewhere in the consideration of every pair of opposites, and yet which is not a fixed or absolute point, but varies according to circumstances and a wide range of influences. Passing down the scale further we find manifested a slight repulsion or dislike; this increases as we move down the scale. Finally we notice degrees of intense dislike and repulsion, until finally we find the negative pole of hate. You will understand this readily—you have noticed the different degrees of love and hate, and have also noticed how these degrees rise and fall according to circumstances and conditions. But have you ever noticed that extreme love often is suddenly transmuted into extreme hate, and vice versa, under extreme emotion or exciting cause. Who has not seen instances where a woman's intense love has been transformed into burning hate, by the influence of some new cause? In some cases the emotion moves rapidly backward and forward, to and fro, between these two poles, until the person does not know whether he or she loves or hates. In one of Kipling's poems a woman says:

> "I *'ate* you, grinnin' there. . . . Ah, Gawd, I *love* you so!"

It will be seen that all these transmutations of emotional states from one pole to the other—from love to hate—from fear to courage—are but changes of polarity, or a shifting of position on the emotional scale. But these changes are always along the scale of the emotion which has the two poles—and not from one emotion to another. Emotions of different scales cannot be transmuted one to another—they must belong to the same scale. Water may be transformed into steam, and wood into smoke; but water cannot be transformed into smoke, nor wood into steam. So it is with the emotional states—the transmutation must be along the degrees of, or between the poles of, the same scale.

Here we arrive at the point of the Druid teaching in which are revealed the processes of Mental Alchemy in its phase of change of polarity. By the application of the trained will, it is possible for the student to *transmute one emotional state to its opposite*, by changing the polarity. Thus, one may change his love into hate, or his hate into love, simply by concentrating the attention and will upon the opposite pole of the state or quality. In Mental Alchemy, the student is never told to "fight" or "kill out" an undesirable emotional quality by opposing sheer will to it—this is a waste of energy, and rarely has useful results. Nor is it necessarily useful to swing from one pole to the other. The proper method is to use the opposite pole to change the vibrations and shift the emotional center of balance, so that it becomes possible to choose one side or the other, and one degree or another, instead of being subject to uncontrolled passions.

In the same way, and under the same law, the emotional states of others may be influenced by polarizing their minds on the opposite pole of the scale of the emotion in question. Hate is not to be combatted by hate—this only adds fuel to the fire. The proper way is to form the mental image of liking and attraction, in your mind, and then concentrate its effects upon the other person. Just as you may change you own emotional states, so may you change his, under the proper conditions and by the proper methods. It is the principle taught in the old fable, in which the Sun and the North Wind dispute their power to tear away a man's cloak from him. The harder the North Wind blew, the closer the man hugged the cloak around him. But when the Sun tried the effect of its heated rays, the man soon dropped the cloak because he found it uncomfortable.

This process does not consist in the sentimental, negative attitude of mind that many outward religions preach—it does not consist in "turning the other cheek" to be smitten. Far from it, this process is purely volitional and not emotional. It is the bringing into play of the scientific principles of Mentalism—not emotional sentimentalism. The initiates of the mysteries are not sentimentalists, nor emotional weaklings. On the contrary, they dwell on the plane of the individuality and recognize that the emotions are on a lower plane, not to be neglected or ignored, but not to be allowed to run uncontrolled.

If you are strong enough to hear the full truth, listen to these words: the initiate regards both love and hate, in the ordinary sense of these words, as emotions of the personality, the "Me" side of the self. Therefore he rises above both. He thinks that the slave to love is as miserable as the slave to hate—and he avoids both extremes. He finds that the one thing, of which love and hate are phases or manifestations, is in itself but one pole of something else—and he moves up higher to that something. That "something" is not indifference, which is the opposite pole of that of which love and hate are themselves subsidiary forms; the point of balance between indifference and submission of the tides of the emotions is a state of its own—and is itself one pole of yet another polarity. Step by step, as he gains mastery over these polarities, the initiate becomes able to choose how he relates to others on the emotional plane—and then, for the first time, becomes capable of love in the deeper and fuller sense of the word.

Triad VI.

Three aspects of the Law of Balance: regularity, harmony, and limitation.

The Law of Balance arises from the existence and operation of the Law of Polarity. Everything in the Cosmos is dual. There is always something opposed to, counterbalancing and checking something else. The manifest Cosmos could not exist and remain operative without this law. Just as the watch or clock requires a nicely adjusted system of counterweights, counterprings, and counterbalances, in order that their opposing action may render the movement of the timepiece uniform and regular, so does the Cosmos require, and possess, a far more infinitely balanced and counterbalanced system, in order that its activities may be uniform and regular.

The regular and uniform movement of the planets around the sun is made possible only through the operation of the counterbalancing forces of centrifugal force and gravity, the former manifesting in the tendency of the planet to fly from the central point, the sun; and the latter manifesting in the tendency of the planet to move toward the central point, the sun. The counterbalance of these two opposing tendencies produces regular and constant movement in the elliptic orbit.

In the same way the two phases of force or energy oppose and counterbalance each other—one tending to build up, and the other tending to tear down. Some authorities have adopted the use of the term "force" to designate that form of motion which tends to bind together two or more particles of matter, and which retards or resists motions tending to separate such particles; for instance, gravitation, cohesion, chemical affinity, etc. The same authorities use the term "energy" to designate that form of motion which tends to separate two or more particles of ponderable matter, or of the ethereal medium, or which resists or retards the force tending to bind them together.[24] Clodd says:

> If Force had unresisted play, all the atoms in the universe would gravitate to a common center, and ultimately form a perfect sphere in which no life would exist, and in which no work could be done. If Energy had unresisted play, the atoms in the universe would be driven asunder and remain forever separated, with the like result of changeless powerlessness. But with these two powers in conflict . . . the universe is the theatre of ceaseless redistributions of its contents.

All through living Nature this same law of counterbalance is in force. Plant life nourishes animal life, and the latter by means of its waste matter and its disintegrating forms nourishes the former. Moreover, the very breathing of the two great forms of life tend to support life in each other. Animals breathe in oxygen in order to support life, and breathe out carbon dioxide, the latter being poisonous to animal life. At the same time the plants, under the action of the sun's rays, break up the carbon dioxide, absorbing the carbon which nourishes plant-life, and releasing the oxygen needed by animal life. Thus the refuse element of the plant is the life-giving element of the animal; and the refuse element of the animal is the life-giving element of the plant. As Emerson says:

> Whilst the world is thus dual, so is every one of its parts. The entire system of things gets represented in every particle. There is somewhat that resembles the ebb and flow of the sea, day and night, man and woman, in a single

---

24. This distinction between force and energy is no longer used by scientists, but it may still be useful for students of this course to consider.

needle of the pine, in a kernel of corn, in every individual of every animal tribe. There action, so grand in the elements, is repeated within these small boundaries. For example, in the animal kingdom the physiologist has observed that no creatures are favorites, but a certain compensation balances every gift and every defect.

Each life-form is kept in check by some other life-form. If this were not so, particular life-forms would overrun the earth. Darwin says: "There is no exception to the rule that every organic being naturally increases at so high a rate, that, if not destroyed, the earth would soon be covered by the progeny of a single pair." Clodd adds:

> If all the offspring of the elephant, the slowest breeder known, survived, there would be in seven hundred and fifty years nearly nineteen million elephants alive, descended from the first pair. If the eight or nine million eggs, which the roe of a cod is said to contain, developed into adult cod-fishes, the sea would quickly become a solid mass of them. So prolific is its progeny after progeny that the common housefly is computed to produce twenty-one millions in a season; while so enormous is the laying power of the aphid, or plant-louse, that the tenth brood of one parent, without adding the products of all the generations which precede the tenth, would contain more ponderable[25] matter than all the population of China, estimating this at five hundred millions.

It is the same in plant life. If any single species were to expand unchecked, the entire globe would be covered with it inside of less than twenty years. The fungi, and other lower organisms, multiply so rapidly (some a billion-fold in an hour) that they would cover the earth in a year, if not counterchecked by nature. But the countercheck is always there. Each animal, plant or fungus has its natural enemy which preys upon it for food. Every living thing lives upon other living things—each according to its kind. This is one of the forms of Nature's counterchecks. This law is brought forcibly to mind when certain plants or animals are transported to other regions, without their natural enemies accompanying them, the result being that they speedily become a danger to the land, and their natural enemies have to be brought to the new region to keep them in check. Students of evolution see in natural selection, and other laws of evolution, many phases of Counterbalance in the Cosmos—the working out of the law that everything is set off and offset by other things.

---

25. Ponderable: having measurable weight, thus "ponderable matter" is physical matter.

Triad VII.

Three aspects of the Law of Unity: the unity of the Seven Cosmic Laws, the unity of the circle and the circumference, and the unity of the Self and the Cosmos.

In the commentaries on the first six triads of this lecture, you have seen how the Seven Cosmic Laws form a progressive series of instructions in the art of Mental Alchemy. You have been taught that you have the capacity to turn the circular movement of the emotions into a creative spiral; you have been shown how correspondence influences the emotional life; you have been instructed in the importance of varying the rate of vibration; you have been guided toward a grasp of the role of cause and effect; you have caught something of the secret of balance; you have received the keys to the attainment of poise. All these are aspects of a single process, or better still, a single teaching, which is the secret of poise—and in this secret all the lessons of the Seven Cosmic Laws enter into unity.

Poise is power. Poise results from balance. Balance is secured by adjusting and maintaining the center between the poles of the pairs of opposites. By balanced poise the initiate neutralizes polarity and rhythm, by resolving them into unity. The one place of peace in a hurricane is at its center; in the same way, the place of peace in any process is the place of balanced poise where the two extremes meet and are one.

Simple as this concept is, it is of crucial importance, for the attainment of poise between the opposites is the secret of mastery. In all things there is a center, a point of balance, but the center exists only because of the existence of the circumference. There is always a point of poise between the poles of every pair of opposites, but that point exists only because the extremes exist. In the central point is always found the power of the whole. In the center of gravity of the Earth, one would be able to remain in a position of perfect poise, unsupported except by the concentrated gravity of the whole Earth—so precisely poised that a mere effort of the will would exert sufficient energy to propel him in any desired direction. The power of the opposites is concentrated at the central point. There, and there only, is all power to be found.

The axiom that "for every action there is an equal and opposite reaction" indicates the existence of a central point which functions as a lever which will move the whole. At the center one is able to use action and reaction without being subject to either. The initiate strives to attain this state of equilibrium. Pitting the opposites against each other—neutralizing pole by pole—balancing law by law—the master traverses the slender thread which separates the world of desire and personality from the world of will and individuality. This, in turn, you yourself shall do. In the center of life shall you indeed find poise and power. In the heart of the storm shall you find peace. In the center of the Cosmos shall you find yourself. He who finds the center of himself, finds the center of the Cosmos—for these two, in the last analysis, are one.

After these seven triads come two that deal with the Seven Cosmic Laws all together:

Triad VIII.

Three approaches to the Seven Cosmic Laws: from the last to the first, from the first to the last, and from each to every other.

Triad IX.

Three realms of labor to which the Seven Cosmic Laws apply: the realm within oneself, where the labor of initiation is done; the realm within another, where the labor of healing is done; the realm surrounding both, where the labor of enchantment is done.

Triad VIII.

Three approaches to the Seven Cosmic Laws: from the last to the first, from the first to the last, and from each to every other.

In the discourses just given, you have witnessed one way of unfolding the potentials within the Seven Cosmic Laws. The principles of Mental Alchemy extracted from the laws in those discourses will be of great practical advantage to you, provided always that you strive to understand them, contemplate them in meditation, and apply them to the circumstances of your daily life. It is in this way that any of the teachings of any of the mystery schools may be turned from mere words, first into ideas thoroughly comprehended, then into opportunities clearly recognized, and finally into achievements firmly manifested.

These same discourses have a second lesson to teach, and a greater one. The art of Mental Alchemy is only one of many teachings that can be drawn from the Seven Cosmic Laws. The value of such laws is precisely that they may be unfolded into practice. They are not provided to you that you may have a handful of abstract notions to think about in your spare time, or that you may believe that you know the truth and, knowing it, are freed from any obligation to put it into practice—common as these habits of thought are, there is but little in all the worlds that is of less value. No! The importance of the Seven Cosmic Laws is found in their application to every plane of existence, including that of your own everyday life. The ability to extract practical applications of the kind here suggested from the seemingly abstract Laws, in turn, is the mark of the initiate of the Greater Mysteries.

As you consider in your meditations the triads already given, follow the way that each Law becomes the starting point from which practical applications are unfolded, and then observe how each Law becomes the foundation upon which the next unfolds its own potentials, following the normal course of the Cycle of the Cantrefs. This may be understood and used in three ways. The first, as you have already been shown, is to begin with the seventh Law and proceed in reverse order up to the first. In their normal order, the Seven Cosmic Laws follow the sequence by which the Cosmos itself is created, the sequence of the Cycle that you have been taught in this grade. The seventh Law, by this principle, represents the last stage in the emergence of the Cosmos, and it is therefore in a sense closest to us; it most clearly reflects our own experience of the Cosmos and of ourselves; and may more easily be applied directly to that experience.

Take, then, some particular situation in your own life or some general condition of existence in the circle of Abred, and apply to it the Law of Circularity, the seventh of the laws. The traditions of the Druids hold that it is wise to seek a triad in this work, just as was done in the discourses just given. Find, then, three ways in which the Law of Circularity applies to the situation or condition, and commit them to memory or, should your skill at the memory work taught in this course not yet be sufficient, write them down. Proceed to the sixth of the laws, the Law of Correspondence, repeating the process, and go on from there to the remaining laws. As you proceed, you will find that ideas brought to the surface in the consideration of one law will cast light on another, and when you arrive at the Law of Unity, the first of the laws, you will be able to draw your reflections together into a clear understanding of how the cosmic process as a whole relates to the situation or condition. On the basis of this understanding, the options available to you for practical action will become clear to you.

Working with the laws in the other direction, from first to last, is best done starting with an abstract concept or principle, the manifestations of which on the plane of everyday life you wish to understand. In this manner of working, begin with the Law of Unity, and find three unities that are present in or part of the concept or principle you seek to understand. Go on to the Law of Polarity, and find three polarities at work in the concept or principle; and proceed from there through the remainder of the Cosmic Laws.

The third approach, from each law to every other, is the most demanding of these meditations, for it presents the student of the Greater Mysteries with the task of finding the relationships between all of the laws. The results of this work, if successfully accomplished, however, are incomparable, for it is in the unity, harmony, and mutual relationship of the laws that their innermost secrets and most important practical applications are found. The scientist learns a single law of Nature; it is simply a curiosity. He learns two laws; in the interplay between them, practical applications emerge. He learns a set of laws, all dealing with the same aspect or dimension of Nature, and a new science is born, bearing in itself the potential of countless new insights into the secrets of Nature and an equally great number of inventions and discoveries in the field of everyday life.

The same principle holds with the Seven Cosmic Laws, but on an even vaster scale, for these Laws govern not one part of Nature, but the process by which the Cosmos itself comes into being out of the interplay between Awen and Annwn. Understand one of the laws, and you know something interesting about the Cosmos. Understand two, and know how they relate to each other, and certain secrets and applications become available to you. Understand all seven, and trace out the ways that each of them interrelate with the others, and you have the keys to unlock the doors of cosmic knowledge and power.

Triad IX.

Three realms of labor to which the Seven Cosmic Laws apply: the realm within oneself, where the labor of initiation is done; the realm within another, where the labor of healing is done; the realm surrounding both, where the labor of enchantment is done.

This triad brings the work of this lesson in Druid philosophy full circle, for it applies the Seven Cosmic Laws directly to the three privileges of the Druid initiate, the arts of healing, enchantment and initiation. Each of the Seven Cosmic Laws may usefully be understood as a principle in each of these arts. Indeed, you will learn through the practice of the initiate's privileges that the more closely your work in each of these fields follows the guidance offered by the Seven Cosmic Laws, the more powerful and effective your results will be.

It would be possible to append a detailed commentary explaining how each of the Laws may be applied to the three privileges of the initiate. At this point in your studies, however, you have the knowledge and capacity to create such a commentary for yourself, through sustained meditation on the Laws and their relevance to the practices you have already studied. You are encouraged to begin this work in this grade, though it is only fair to say you will not complete it within the time you spend as a Gwyddon y Cylch. Rather, if you approach the work as it should and ultimately must be done, you will be continuing to explore the relevance of the Seven Cosmic Laws, and of all the teachings of Druid philosophy, to every aspect of your practices and your life more generally, not only in the life in Abred, but up through the immeasurable circles of Gwynfydd itself. Even as your course of study in these lessons draws toward its end, the greater course of studies in the mysteries of yourself and the Cosmos have just begun.

THE MAGICAL MEMORY: THE LAWS OF MEMORY

THOSE WHO HAVE MADE a careful study of the subject of memory training, and who have no pet theories to promote, generally agree that cumulative training is the necessary foundation for developing the power of memory. It depends upon no set of tricks or catchwords, but proceeds on the theory that the development of memory must be gradual, and by easy stages. It seeks to develop the memory in much the same way that lifting barbells develops the muscles. Its underlying theory, indeed, is that the memory may be developed just as one would develop a muscle or part of the body—gradually, and by easy exercises constantly repeated. Upon this system of developing and training the memory until it can readily recall things, any more elaborate method of memorization may and indeed must be built. It is Nature's own way of doing things—of developing from the seed to the plant. At the same time it affords the best possible plan of committing to memory anything of great length.

There is nothing new about this form of cumulative training. It is merely the oldest system revived. It is the system used by all ancient people in training the mind to carry without mistake their sacred teaching and philosophies. You may wonder concerning the reason why this old system was discontinued; the answer is plain to see. In the old days before printing was discovered, very few people could write, and the writings themselves were apt to be lost or destroyed, and the custodians of many ancient traditions recognized the value of memory training—the ancient Druids were far from alone in this awareness. So teachers trained the minds of their pupils until they could commit to memory immense quantities of material, such as texts longer than the modern Bible. The philosophies, religious books, and even the laws of many nations were thus transmitted and perpetuated for many centuries, without ever being committed to writing at all. Even in our own days, the rituals of secret societies are transmitted in this way, as the rules of these societies prohibit the writing or printing of certain parts of their ritual, or in some cases of any of it.[26]

With the dawn of printing, when it became apparent that thousands of copies of a book might be printed, and the chance of loss reduced, the necessity for the oral transmission of the teachings faded, and the old art of memorizing almost entirely passed away. Men no longer found it worthwhile to memorize things which they could find in the books on their shelves. They overlooked the fact that in allowing the old system to pass out of use, they not only lost the art of memorizing matters of great length, but they also lost the art of training the memory to remember ordinary things, and the result is seen in our condition today, when a person of good memory is looked upon as a curiosity. Moreover, many have grown to believe that a good memory is almost an abnormal thing and that the natural condition of man is to have a poor memory. They do not realize that everyone has the power to develop his memory very far beyond its present condition. Of course, some naturally remember better than others, but a person with a poor memory may so develop it by proper training that he can remember better than can one with a good memory without training.

There are a great many systems of memory training that teach the student to remember a thing by its association with another thing which is perhaps more easily remembered, or with some thing already fixed in the memory. These can be useful indeed, but they do not take the place of the fundamental training of the mind—the use of exercises to so develop, strengthen and train the mind that it is enabled to easily commit to memory anything which it desires, and is also able to easily recall the thing memorized, by will.

One of the beauties of this system is that while you are practicing you are committing to memory valuable information and knowledge, and while you are committing interesting and useful things to memory, you are developing the memory itself. It must be remembered, however, by the student that the great importance of the system lies not in the mere ability to memorize long poems, speeches, or the like, but in the developing and strengthening of the memory itself. And not only does it develop in one the power of storing away impressions in the mind, but also trains one in the faculty of recollection—in recalling

---

26. This is still the case among Freemasons, for example.

readily that which has been memorized. The result of an earnest study and application of this system is that

1. the special thing studied will be easily memorized, long remembered and readily recalled;
2. there will be a marked and steady increase in the power of memorizing anything; and
3. a marked increase and growth of the power of recalling anything by an effort of the will.

Cumulative memory training is based upon the proven theory that the power of memorizing and recollection, like any other power of body or mind, may be enormously increased by a system of progressive exercises and by frequent reviews.

The student should begin by selecting something to commit to memory that interests him, and the subject of which is pleasing to him. Those students of this course that have found its teachings interesting and useful may wish to consider the tales of the Mabinogion, the lessons on Druid philosophy, or any other material in the course as a potential subject for memory training. Alternatively, some other text may be chosen, it matters not which.

Begin the training by committing to memory one sentence from the text you have chosen. Learn this sentence well, until you can repeat it readily, and understand it in all its parts. Learn not only its sound when read aloud, but also its appearance in print, its leading words, its arrangement, its meaning. This will be enough for the first day.

On the second day the sentence of yesterday should be reviewed and repeated aloud. Then another sentence should be learned in the same way, and then joined to the first sentence and the two reviewed together.

On the third day the two sentences previously learned should be reviewed, and a third sentence thoroughly learned, and then joined to the previous ones, and then reviewed as a whole.

Continue this exercise for a month, learning and adding one sentence each day, and reviewing as a whole frequently. We cannot impress upon you too often the necessity of frequent reviewing. The gist of the whole matter is in the reviewing, so do not shirk this part of the work in the slightest. The continual addition of verses memorized tends to develop the faculty of memorizing, whereas the constant reviewing is for the purpose of developing and strengthening you in the direction of easy recollection. It is not sufficient merely to obtain good clear mental impressions, but it is of vital importance for you to be able to locate and bring out the things stored away in your mental storehouse. You not only get acquainted with the particular articles you are bringing out every day, but are also developing the "knack" of finding things in the mental storehouse, and of bringing them to view when wanted.

At the beginning you will probably find that it is often necessary to refer back to the lesson to supply a missing word or phrase. Do not let this discourage you, for you will soon overcome it. And do not unduly strain the memory by a forced effort to recall the elusive word or phrase, but take up the lesson packet and learn that particular sentence over again. If necessary refer to the lesson a dozen times rather than to go on omitting words or remain in a state of uncertainty about their correctness. Do not go on in a slipshod manner, but insist upon exactness. By insisting upon this from the start, the mind will soon take on that quality.

Do not miss a day's exercise. You will find it far better to learn a single sentence each and every day than a greater number every few days. The will and the memory are both strengthened by regular exercise and practice. The entire series of exercise will be found to strengthen and develop the willpower of the student, and the strength thus gained will be found most useful in other forms of Druid practice, to say nothing of daily life.

At the beginning of the second month, learn two sentences a day instead of one. Keep this up during the second month, learning two sentences each day, and reviewing those previously memorized—both those of the first month and those learned after the two-verse plan has been adopted. You will find that the second month's work is no more difficult than that of the first month. The two-sentence task will be as easy as the one-sentence exercise. You will find that your memory has anticipated the increase, and that you can easily learn three or even four sentences each day, but stick to two, and do not attempt to get ahead of your lesson. The efficacy of this system lies largely in the fact that it leads the student gradually, and develops him in Nature's own way. And remember that in the reviewing lies the secret of increased powers of recollection.

At the beginning of the third month, commence with three sentences, and proceed as before, adding each day to your store, and reviewing each day that which you have previously learned. When the fourth month comes adopt the four-sentence plan, and so on. Of course there is a limit to this constant increase, of which we will speak a little later on. This limit will be found to vary with the individual but the most backward student will be able to attain wonderful proficiency with very little effort, by following the gradual and progressive method.

If the reviewing after a few months takes up more time than you have to spare, drop the new verses and devote the entire time to reviewing. And later on if you cannot review the whole thing in the time at your disposal in one day, divide it in two and review the first half today and the rest tomorrow.

If, after a time, the task of committing additional sentences to memory seems tiresome, it will be as well to discontinue this part of the work for a short time, but keep up the reviewing, devoting all the time usually devoted to the exercise to the review work alone. Sometimes that part of the mind which attends to the work of receiving impressions will rebel at its daily task, but the other part of the mind which we use to recall things already impressed there will prove to be bright and perfectly willing to work.

The student will find that certain ways of doing this work best suited to his particular temperament will suggest themselves to him. He may vary and improve on the plan we have given here, providing always that he does not slight the review work, which must not be omitted or cut down. Cut down the memorizing if you must, but hold fast to the review work. The increased strength of the memory lies in the work of frequently calling back the remembered material to mind. This review work, although somewhat tedious at first, will soon grow to be a pleasant occupation, and then the pleasure of the conscious increase in mental power will render the task most interesting.

If you have not the time to devote to the full carrying out of this system, as herein laid down, you may vary it by learning short poems by this method, and after thoroughly mastering one, so that it may easily be reviewed at any time, pass on to another, devoting all your time and attention to the new one when learned. But when the second one is learned, go back to the first one and recall it. Continue reviewing the ones you have learned, at odd times, or occasionally, and devote your daily review work to the one on hand until it too is thoroughly learned. Exercise the faculty of recollection by frequently recalling things which you have learned in the past, as each time you give yourself this exercise you strengthen the faculty.

If you lose interest in the particular thing you are memorizing, lay it aside for a while, and take something of a different character by way of a change, not forgetting to occasionally review the one laid aside.

You will probably find that some passages in a lecture are more easily remembered than others. Do not slight the difficult ones, in fact you should bestow upon them more time and attention than upon the favorite ones. There is some reason for the trouble with the difficult parts, and by keeping at the work until you conquer, you will be strengthening some weak spot in the faculty of memorizing or recollection, and will be gaining additional willpower besides.

After you have been practicing this system for a number of months, you will find that you will be able to retain any particular thing in your memory with less frequent reviews, and you may vary your plan to accommodate yourself to your increased powers, and review well-learned subjects only once in a while. But it is well to review a little of something every day in order to give the faculty something upon which to work.

You will also come to a point, sometime, where you will realize that you have reached your limit in the matter of the number of sentences to be memorized at any one time. You cannot go on forever increasing your limit at the rate of one additional daily sentence each month. When this time is reached, stop the monthly increase, and rest on your oars so far as the increase of the daily work is concerned. Keep on with the work of memorizing and reviewing, but limit your lines or verses to the highest easily memorized number. Remember that the main purpose of the exercises is not to see how much you can do, but simply to give you training and development. After stopping for a time, without making any attempt to increase, you may find, all of a sudden, that you are able to master a much heavier daily memory task. But whether you do or do not, matters little. And in any event you will find that your power of recollecting steadily increases, apparently having no limit.

Learn a thing thoroughly before going to the next. It is better to know one thing thoroughly, than ten things partially. Do not pass on to another sentence or verse until you have mastered the one upon which you have been working.

Do not attempt to "rush" matters. Take your time, and do not attempt too much at first. The average student is too eager. He starts off with a rush, and is apt to tire before he has gone very far. Better hold yourself in a little, and develop naturally as does the plant which grows from seed to shoot, from shoot to stalk, from stalk to leaves, from leaves to flower.

Do not attempt to do this work when you are tired or worn out. In such condition you will fail to receive clear impressions or to recall clearly and distinctly. Many find the morning the best time in which to practice.

The Value of Analysis

While you are studying a sentence in order to commit it to memory, following the cumulative method outlined above, it is a great help to memorization to dissect the sentence—to subject it to thorough analysis, so that you first examine the parts in detail and then gain a comprehensive idea of it as a whole. This process of mental analysis will arouse the faculties to activity, and will cause the memory to receive intense impressions which will be readily recalled.

It has been found that by a little analytical work of this kind, the meaning of a thing is brought out so plainly that the mind will readily grasp it and hold on to it. The best way to investigate a thing is to ask questions about it. The best way to bring out your knowledge of a subject is to ask yourself questions about it. The best way to fix a thing in your mind is to ask yourself questions calculated to bring out its full meaning.

To illustrate this idea, let us take the first line from the First Branch of the Mabinogion, and analyze it as just suggested:

> Pwyll, Prince of Dyfed, was lord of the seven Cantrefs of Dyfed, and once upon a time he was at Arberth his chief palace, and he was minded to go and hunt, and the part of his dominions in which it pleased him to hunt was Glyn Cuch.

Who is the person being discussed? Pwyll. *What* did he rule? Seven Cantrefs. *Which* seven Cantrefs? The seven Cantrefs of Dyfed. *When* does the tale start? Once upon a time. *Where* was he at that time? At Arberth. *What* was Arberth? His chief palace. *What* was Pwyll minded to do? To go and hunt. *Where* did it please him to hunt? Glyn Cuch. *What* was Glyn Cuch? Part of his dominions. If you have gone over the above questions and answers in earnest, you will never forget this line. It will stand out clearly in your mind.

The attention, as a rule, is attracted by a moving thing more readily than by something at rest, and if the *action* of the verb is impressed on the mind, the rest of the sentence will be connected with it by the law of association. It helps the memory to picture the verb's meaning in the mind. In committing a thing to memory, find out what it all means by this analytical method, and you will have simplified matters very materially.

The Sevenfold Wheel of Thought Revisited

Among the most useful tools that may be used in the analytical approach to memory just outlined is one that you have already learnt in another context—the Sevenfold Wheel of Thought, one of the tools of meditation, which was introduced to you many months ago in the Gradd yr Ymarferiwr and was recalled to your mind in the Game of the Cantrefs introduced earlier in the present lesson packet. You may find it useful to review the paper on that subject in the third lesson packet you received before continuing with this lecture.

Every person has in his subconscious storehouse a vast assortment of general information or knowledge. He knows something about every object or subject which has ever attracted his attention or interest in the faintest degree. The character and amount of such knowledge of course depends largely upon the degree of attention he has bestowed upon it, and upon the opportunities for observation he may have had in the past. But even a person of the most limited opportunities and the most careless observation has stored away much valuable material of whose existence he is normally almost unaware. The information has been stored away mechanically, and no attempt to resurrect it has been made, as no demand for the stored knowledge has been apparent in the man's everyday life.

If we would by intelligent practice occasionally bring forth to the light of day the stored-away knowledge we would give our minds beneficial practice, increase our powers of recollection, broaden our field of available knowledge, develop our powers of reasoning, and make ourselves better informed regarding a great variety of subjects. Bringing forth these stored-up memories will compel us to classify them, arrange them in their proper order, make comparisons, note associations, draw conclusions, and make use of a variety of our mental faculties, which will result in mental development and culture. Many of us are like misers who have hoarded away precious metal, which we never again see or make use of.

Many of us have heard of prisoners, and men compelled to live away from congenial companions, compelled to look to themselves for company, who turned their vision inward and extracted from the storehouse of the mind the knowledge which had been laid up there, and directed their mental processes to this work, with the result that when they emerged from their seclusion they had attained a degree of mental development far in advance of that which they possessed when they entered it. There are cases of record where political prisoners have written the most interesting books during their confinement, without having a single reference book, their information being drawn from that great storehouse, the subconscious memory. People sometimes go about taking casual notice regarding the people and things around them, with no special object in view. Years afterward, these people have become writers, and draw upon their old, almost forgotten, impressions of the past, and putting them on paper give to the world a vivid picture of the life of the town or city of their former abode. Dumas[27] has given us an example of this subsequent use of stored-up knowledge in his well-known novel *The Count of Monte Cristo*. He shows us the old political prisoner, the Abbe Faria, who has been shut out from the sight of men for years, resurrecting his old fund of information for the benefit and instruction of his fellow prisoner, Edmond Dantes, and exciting the interest and concentrated attention of the latter, he develops him from a bright but uneducated fisherman-sailor into a well-informed and educated man of the world. The old Abbe has stored away in his mind the learning of a lifetime, and draws from it for the benefit of Dantes. The story is, of course, pure fiction, but given the circumstances and the men, there is no reason why the result could not be obtained.

This resurrecting of stored-away impressions has another good result. It awakens in one an interest in the theme under consideration, and the mind thereafter will be awake to impressions concerning that theme, and one's fund of information regarding it, and things associated with it, will be greatly augmented. The mere directing of the attention upon the theme, after placing oneself where he will not be distracted by outside impressions, or after shutting out impressions if he has the power, will bring into the field of consciousness many interesting impressions and important information. If one pursues a systematic plan for bringing out the impressions, his power of recollection will be greatly increased, and at the same time his mind will be developed along the lines of systematic thinking.

This is where the Sevenfold Wheel of Thought comes into play as a tool for the training of the memory. It is simple but wonderfully effective, and its continued use will repay many times the value of the time and labor expended upon it. Here as in the practice of meditation, a set of Seven Conceptions or basic categories of being, and set of Seven Questions that relate to the Conceptions, work together to form the Sevenfold Wheel. When the Wheel is applied to the theme under consideration, and each Question is asked and answered concerning each Conception by bringing into the field of consciousness all the stored impressions to be found in the mind, it will be found to have brought into play all the information concerning that particular thing possessed by the student.

The Seven Conceptions, for the student's convenience, are repeated here:

- Being,
- Becoming,

---

27. Alexandre Dumas, the famous French novelist of the nineteenth century.

- Source,
- Substance,
- Power,
- Purpose,
- Value.

The Seven Questions, in turn, are these:

- Whether?
- What?
- How?
- Who?
- Where?
- When?
- Why?

You will find that this system of Conceptions and Questions will bring to light all of your previous impressions regarding the thing under consideration, and also will cause you to classify, arrange, consider, and determine its various features. It will educate you in recollecting, thinking, studying and observing. Each question will suggest something to you, and when you are through with the subject you will find that you know much more about it than you thought possible. Provided that you have already committed the Conceptions and Questions to memory, or are willing to do so hereafter, you may also use the same system to guide your study of any other subject, and thus provide yourself with more impressions to use in future practice and learning.

As you work with the cumulative method of memory training, in particular, you will find it a great help in memorization to ask at least a few Questions about a few Conceptions relating to the sentence you are memorizing, along the lines of the method of analysis already described. With practice you will find that you can quickly ask and answer all Seven Questions of each of the Seven Conceptions relating to any sentence you wish to commit to memory, and the impressions stored within the mind by this exercise will be far more vivid and complete, leading to the prompt and easy recall of the sentence and much that is connected with it.

Let us demonstrate this by applying part of the Sevenfold Wheel of Thought to the passage from the First Branch of the Mabinogion already quoted:

> Pwyll, Prince of Dyfed, was lord of the seven Cantrefs of Dyfed, and once upon a time he was at Arberth his chief palace, and he was minded to go and hunt, and the part of his dominions in which it pleased him to hunt was Glyn Cuch.

Let us start with the First Conception, Being. According to this sentence, does something exist? Yes. What exists? Pwyll, the seven Cantrefs of Dyfed, his chief palace of Arberth, his desire to hunt, and Glyn Cuch. How or in what manner do these things exist? As people, places, and plot elements in a legend. Who exists—that is, which of the existing things are people? Pwyll. Where do they exist? In Dyfed, which is in the southwestern corner of Wales. When do they exist? In the "once upon a time" of legend and myth. Why do they exist? To communicate something to the listener or reader that may only be communicated through a story of this kind.

The Second Conception is Becoming, which may also be described as change. According to this sentence, does something change? Yes. What changes? Pwyll's mind. How does it change? Toward the desire to hunt. Who changes? Pwyll. Where does the change take place? At Arberth, Pwyll's chief palace. When and why does the change take place? The story does not yet say. The lack of information is as important in this practice as its presence, for it points to what is not yet known, and alerts the mind to watch for new information to fill in the gaps.

Most of the remaining Conceptions are left unanswered by the sentence just given. It is very common for a sentence to provide answers to the Questions about only a few Conceptions, or perhaps only one, leaving for later sentences the task of filling in the remaining details. The first sentence of the First Branch, in this way, provides answers to questions about the First, Second, and Sixth Conceptions.

Exercise 1

In the manner just shown, ask the Seven Questions about the Sixth Conception, Purpose, with relation to the first sentence of the First Branch of the Mabinogion, and answer them. (You will find this easiest if you ask them about Pwyll's purpose, rather than the purpose of the unknown author of the First Branch.) When you have done so, notice how much easier it is to remember the sentence; you may find, in fact, that you have memorized it.

Exercise 2

Choose three more sentences from one or more of the tales of the Mabinogion you have studied so far. With each sentence, ask the Seven Questions about each of the Seven Conceptions, noting whether the sentence answers the question or not. When an answer is provided by the sentence, state it.

Exercise 3

The next time you have reason to commit something to memory, apply to it the Seven Conceptions and Seven Questions and analyze it thoroughly. See how this affects the speed and accuracy with which you are able to memorize it.

COMPLETION EXERCISE: MASTERING THE OPPOSITES

THE MANIFESTATION OF INDIVIDUALITY by the initiate who has understood the nature of intentionality, evidences itself in a variety of forms and phases. It is in the mastery of the opposites, however, that we find one of its most important phases, and one which influences the greater part of life. The student who wishes to shape his mind by his awakening consciousness, and thus acquire poise and balance, must first learn the art of mastering the opposites in his own bywyd and nwyd—the instinctive and emotional aspects of his being. In acquiring this art he also does much in the direction of gaining poise and balance, and in neutralizing rhythm.

We have learned that in Druid teaching, every quality, attribute, or condition has its opposite. We have seen how these pairs of opposites are in reality, but the contrasting poles of the same thing. Just as heat and cold are the poles of temperature—just as hard and soft are the poles of texture—so love and hate are seen to be but the contrasting poles of the attachment of the passions between persons. In the same way, and for the same reason, all contrasting emotions, states and feelings are but the opposed poles of a fundamental emotion which both depends upon the will for its expression and outward activities, and influences the will when the latter is not governed by the individuality.

All activity proceeds from and through the bryd, or will, under the direction of intentionality. The will is involved in all action; thus there can be no action without will, and therefore without intentionality. In the life of one in whom the individuality has not yet awakened, however, will does little of itself; it is through the stimulus of emotion, and chiefly of desire and fear, that the will is called and directed into activity. Awakening begins the moment that the will is no longer identified with the desire or fear which inspires it to action. Just as the water in a glass may be colored by a chemical dissolved in it, and yet in itself remain water as it was in the beginning, so is the will colored and apparently changed by the influence of the emotion that brings it into play. The will, to extend the metaphor, is clear and colorless like the water—its emotional coloring is of a character remote from its own. To use another metaphor perhaps more revealing, emotion is the body, while will is the nwyfre that indwells it and gives it life; intentionality in this metaphor is in turn the soul that shapes and directs.

To the unawakened person, it is impossible to divorce the will from the emotional influences that bring it into play, or to grasp the nature of intentionality in any real sense. Without desire and fear, or the other emotions that now and again excite the will, nothing brings the will into manifestation at all. To those for whom the personality is the highest expression of self yet achieved, will is merely a name, corresponding to nothing in their experience. This is because in such persons the will is effectively unconscious. When the first stirrings of the consciousness of the individuality are attained—when the "I" begins to know itself and experiences the will as its natural expression, then the will begins to become conscious. In this latter state, instead of remaining centred on the emotional plane of the mind, the will is raised up to its rightful seat, as part of the hunan, the conscious self, and it assumes the sceptre of power and authority which naturally and innately belong to it; it then becomes possible for intentionality to be understood and used in the manner we have discussed heretofore.

When the consciousness of individuality is acquired to a certain degree, the "I" sees that the opposites of the emotional life are things that are external to its essence. It comes to know them as forms by which it has expressed itself or, better still, as leading strings that supported it when it was as yet too young and inexperienced to walk without aid.[28] From the moment that this realization comes to the student, even in the faintest degree, then he has begun to move toward the freedom of the individuality, and has started on the road to the mastery of the opposites.

Contrast the condition of the man who is still hypnotized by the belief that his emotions and feelings are himself—that he is the character he is playing, with its emotions and feelings and incidents of personality, on the one hand; and on the other hand, the individual who realizes that he, himself, is will in his

---

28. At the time this course was written, children who were learning to walk had cords—"leading strings"—fastened to their clothing, so that the child's nurse or mother could keep it upright while it took its first unsteady steps.

real nature, and that the personality assumed by him in this lifetime, together with its incidental qualities, character and emotions, is an outer reality which he may change, and which he will eventually put off as a man puts off a suit of old clothes. You will see that one is the master of the opposites, and the other their slave.

The initiate in whom the individuality has begun to awaken knows his real nature, knows that he is no emotional creature bent now this way and then that by the power of inherited or acquired feeling—knows that he is the master of his emotional life, capable of using emotion as a means of expression when it suits itself, and likewise dispelling it when it is best to do so. Nay, more than this—he is capable of changing any emotion from one of its poles to the other—changing hatred to love, desire to aversion, pain to pleasure, sorrow to joy—backward and forward, at will, and solely because he wills to do it, and it suits his will so to do. When the individuality realizes that it is the lord of itself, instead of a subordinate and slave to its feelings and emotions, or personal traits and characteristics, then alone is it free.

The following exercise will tend to bring about a heightened realization in consciousness of the mastery of the opposites. It should be performed, as previous Completion Exercises have been performed, between the time you finish the other studies of this grade and your beginning of the work of the final grade of this system of Druid teaching—the Grade of *Gwyddon Rhydd* or Free Loremaster.

Completion Exercise 1

Let the student place himself in the ordinary position of meditation and pass through the usual preliminaries. Let him meditate upon the real nature of the "I." Let him cast off the illusion of the personal self, and its attributes, as indicated in previous exercises. Then let him imagine himself as rising above the lower planes of personality toward the higher planes of individuality—as in a balloon which is rising above the surface of the earth into the higher regions of purer and more rarefied air. Let him then imagine himself throwing overboard from his mental balloon all the likes and dislikes, loves and hates, prejudices for and against anything and everything whatsoever, either good or bad; in short the entire collection of inherited or acquired emotions which have formed the garment or body of his personality for so long. Let him consider each of these emotions as he prepares to throw it over the side, feel its distinctive tone, and reflect on how it has influenced his life up to this point; let him recognize the role that it has played in teaching and guiding him, and acknowledge his indebtedness to it; and when that consideration is finished, let him throw it overboard and watch it drop out of sight, conscious that it is no longer with him.

As the mental balloon rises higher and higher let him throw off even the more subtle emotions, with the same process of consideration and recollection, until finally he finds himself divested of the whole of his personality, and his individuality is as naked as a newborn babe. Then, after a few trials of this exercise, will come to him a new sense of power and insight—a new realization of his real nature. Then will he realize more fully that the pairs of opposites of the personality are but masks and clothing of the character he has been playing. Then will he feel like Blaedud when his memory of his life as a prince returned to him and he discarded the clothing and habits of his years as a swineherd. Thereafter he may return to the earth and resume the garments of personality he has thrown off, but as their master, not as a slave to them as heretofore. This exercise will quicken the perception of individuality, and will aid in attaining the mastery of the opposites. This exercise should be repeated frequently during the time between this and the next grade

The following exercise will also be found useful in the same direction.

Completion Exercise 2

Let the student place himself again in the posture of meditation and pass through the usual preliminaries, and then meditate upon the fact that opposing emotions are in reality but the opposite poles of the same thing. Let him, in imagination, try the experiment of changing the polarity of some emotion—of inducing the state of love where hate has been dominant, or vice versa. Let him shift the polarity of his feelings and emotions at will, backward and forward. He will thus discover that the feelings and emotions are far from being fixed and constant, as he had supposed, but are capable of being shifted about at will. This exercise will result in giving the student a wonderful power over his feelings and emotion, and preventing them from dominating or ruling him. By shifting the polarity one may change a painful feeling or emotion into its opposite. Distressing feelings may be changed in polarity, or balanced with their opposites, and much pain be obviated.

Once the practice is mastered, it is not necessary always to shift entirely to the opposite pole of the emotion or feeling—many Druids merely change the polarity to the opposite in a sufficient degree to establish a balance and thus create a condition and state of poise and equilibrium, which results in peace of mind and which quiets the stormy sea of passion, emotion or feeling. This condition of poise and balance is the normal state of the advanced initiate. Equally balanced between the pairs of opposites one finds a peace unknown to those who polarize in either extreme. When one fully realizes that he is master of the opposites, and may shift the polarity of emotion and feeling at will, then he himself is able to establish the condition most conducive to his satisfaction and happiness. Such a one is well on the road to mastery.

Gradd
y Gwyddon
Rhydd

The Grade of the Free Loremaster

INTRODUCTION TO THE GRADE

CONGRATULATIONS AND WELCOME to the last and highest of the grades of this course, the *Gradd y Gwyddon Rhydd!* It has been a very long journey since the day you read the first lesson packet of the Dolmen Arch course and began your studies in the Gradd y Newyddian. Over the two or more years it has taken you to reach this point, you have studied a wealth of philosophy and symbolism, exercised your mind with meditations and memory training, learned to draw on the subtle energies of the Cosmos with rituals and energy workings, and taken up the initiate's privileges of healing, enchantment, and initiation. At times it has probably not been an easy road for you, but you have persevered where many others have fallen by the wayside.

Therefore I am delighted to be able to say to you what the ancient Druids, according to legend, said to their initiates at the completion of the highest degree of their initiations:

Welcome and thrice welcome, brother or sister of the Dolmen Arch!

The material in this lesson packet covers a great deal of ground. Most of it relates either to the work that lies before you as a teacher and initiator, or to certain practical dimensions of the work you have already learned. To the former category belong the papers on initiation in the Dolmen Arch tradition, the initiatory version of the Game of the Cantrefs, and the tale of Taliesin, which resumes the initiatory material in earlier branches of the Mabinogion in a simpler form reshaped by the needs of a more recent age. To the latter belongs the papers on the cycle of the Cantrefs; on initiation, healing and enchantment; and on the magical memory.

The lecture on Druid philosophy, and more particularly its addendum, belong to a third category; these cover practical methods of esoteric work, once central to the traditions that were ancestral to the Dolmen Arch tradition and now supplanted as primary techniques of practice by the material you have learned in the previous lessons of this course. These techniques are placed in your hands so that you may use them in your own practice, and teach them to your students, if this seems appropriate to you in the future.

It bears mentioning at this point that the completion of the Dolmen Arch lessons does not mean the end of your work in the Dolmen Arch system. Over the last two or more years, as you have worked your way through the teachings and practices assigned to the different grades, you have been introduced to a great deal of material, not all of which will have been appropriate or relevant to your work at the moment when you received it. It will be your privilege as well as your responsibility to go back over the lessons, not once but many times, in the years to come; you may do this to be better able to instruct students of your own, but it will also benefit and greatly enrich your own work to do so. The more you study the material you have been given, and the more you practice the exercises and rituals you have been taught, the further they will take you.

This lesson packet, like the ones that precede it, contains nine instructional papers:

    The Cycle of the Cantrefs in History and Initiation .... p. 191
    A Guide to Initiation in the Dolmen Arch Tradition......... p. 201
    The Secret Work of the Grail.. p. 205
    The Initiatory Game of the Cantrefs .... p. 211
    The Mabinogion: The Tale of Taliesin .... p. 217
    Druid Philosophy: The Powers of Mind................................. p. 231
    Addendum to Druid Philosophy: Practical Mentalism...... p. 253
    The Magical Memory: Practical Memory...............................p. 265
    Completion Exercises: The Way of the Dolmen Arch....... p. 277

Like the lessons of the preceding grades, these are to be worked through at your own pace, with the Completion Exercises reserved for last. The practical work given in this lesson, like that of the two previous grades, is more advanced than the work of the Lesser Mysteries and will therefore require more time; a minimum of four months should be spent on this work, and as much more as you feel is appropriate. Nothing will be gained, and much may be lost, by rushing through these lessons at a pace faster than your mind can absorb the concepts taught, and your whole self absorb the effects of the practices.

Wishing you all the best in your continuing journey on the Path of the Druid Mysteries,

 *John Michael Greer*

THE CYCLE OF THE CANTREFS IN HISTORY AND INITIATION

IN THE PREVIOUS LESSON PACKET, that for the grade of Loremaster of the Circle, you were introduced to the Cycle of the Cantrefs, which manifest the Seven Cantrefs as an order in time as well as a pattern in space. This sequence or temporal pattern is one of two principal keys to the Greater Mysteries, the other being the Seven Cosmic Laws you have also been taught. Central to both is the transition from a static concept of spiritual realities to an awareness of progression or change through time, and the process of change through time, as suggested in earlier grades, may be grasped in one of two forms: as a circular movement repeating itself in time, or as a creative spiral unfolding itself toward new possibilities while maintaining its own circular movement.

Differing from both of these is the common belief that time moves ahead in a straight line. The believer in conventional religion traces this line from the Creation to the Last Judgment and the New Jerusalem, the believer in progress and evolution, from the days of the cave men to some Utopian future not noticeably different from the New Jerusalem of the religionist; suggest to either one that the two ends of his line bend around to meet at a common point, or at best trace the same curve in a slightly different position defined by the forward movement of the center, and the indignation of the one will be matched by that of the other.

Yet history, that impartial judge of all our fancies, teaches that their indignation is as misplaced as their faith in the linear progress of time. Look back through the centuries, and what do we behold? Nations are born, grow into their strength, put that strength in the service of greed and the craving for power, and perish, and new nations rise in their place. The small and struggling settlement of one age is the proud and wealthy city of a later age, and later still, nothing remains of it but silent ruins half buried in sand or overgrown by the jungle. Consider great Rome itself—in the days of Romulus, little more than a camp in the wilderness where a band of outlaws slept and cooked their meals; thereafter, a town no different from a hundred others in Italy alone, ruled by its own petty kings; then a republic, vying with scores of others for primacy; then an empire—and then a cluster of hovels whose tenants pastured their goats upon what had once been the Forum. Now it is a great city again, and once more vies for empire;[1] who knows but what, five hundred or a thousand years from now, the Forum will again be goat pasture?

The course of history is a circle; the history of a family, a town, a social movement, a style of art or literature, a government, a nation, a dynasty, a civilization or a continent—possibly of the human race as a whole—follows a too-familiar course of rise and fall. The ambition of reformers, who seek to change the circle into a straight line leading to perfection, simply measures a certain portion of the circle, one through which every nation passes as the wheel of its destiny turns; so, too, the arc of decline and fall is never total, but simply traces another part of the circumference. The Cycle of the Cantrefs measures out the whole.

Awyr in History

Awyr as the first stage in the cycle is the phase in which things begin to come into being. In history, this is the first stirring of a new historical existence on any scale, from the smallest town to the greatest empire. That first stirring is always in the realm of mind and spirit, not on the plane of matter; long before a nation is born, for example, the ideas that will define and guide it are already in the thoughts of the multitude, from there they find voice through poets and thinkers, and finally are taken up by those who become the first leaders of the new nation. It is hard to define the beginning of historical epochs of this kind, but they end with a sudden transformation: the birth of the new historical existence.

Fig. 13. The Cantref Awyr

---

1. The reference is to Mussolini's regime in Italy, which imagined itself to be a "new Roman empire."

Dŵr in History

Dŵr as the second stage in the cycle is the phase of growth, enlargement and learning. In history, this is the formative period, when what has been started at the conclusion of the phase of Awyr elaborates itself in concrete forms. Institutions are founded, structures concrete or abstract rise up, and on a subtler level the distinctive character of the new historical existence takes shape. Historical epochs of this kind are relatively peaceful, and any struggles that take place are soon settled and wreak little change. Under the surface calm, however, conflicts are building, which break out into the open in the next phase.

Fig. 14. The Cantref Dŵr

Ufel in History

Ufel as the third stage in the cycle is the phase of choice and conflict, in which alternatives and obstacles must be met and contended with. In history, this is the age of struggle, internal, external, or both, as the new existence measures itself against its environment and confronts the discords within itself. It is only in the confrontation with these difficulties that a person, a nation, or any other historical existence can complete the process of coming fully into existence, and it will be seen that historical epochs of this kind in the life of a nation are those in which its historical identity and destiny are sealed.

Fig. 15. The Cantref Ufel

Daear in History

Daear as the fourth stage in the cycle completes the descent of spirit into manifestation. In history, this is at once the period of greatest apparent energy and the fullest manifestation of the original impulse that will be achieved within the cycle. Its most visible keynote is outward expansion, but the essential inner nature or guiding idea, having achieved as much expression as it is capable of having, no longer has the motive force to bring about further development. Historical epochs of this kind

Fig. 16. The Cantref Daear

display great power, repeated triumph, immense wealth, and the beginning of the trends that will destroy all of these.

Maen in History

Maen as the fifth stage in the cycle represents the effects and consequences of the descent into manifestation. In history, this is the period in which expansion runs up against insuperable limits of one kind or another, or that in which the action made manifest in the previous phase evokes its equal and opposite reaction. If, as often happens, Daear marks the zenith of a historical existence, Maen represents the beginning of decline, most often in the form of apparent consolidation and all those sensible, reasonable, practical steps that, once taken, drain what remains of the life and vigor out of a once vital phenomenon. Historical epochs of this kind thus are characterized by the growth of structure and form at the expense of life.

Fig. 17. The Cantref Maen

Nef in History

Nef as the sixth stage in the cycle represents the fading out of the initial impetus or guiding idea, and its replacement by a habitual "going through the motions" or the maintenance of forms that have passed beyond their useful life. In history, this is the period of disintegration and visible decline, as forms from which the spirit has long since passed away fall apart of their own weight, or crumple under the impact of some new and more vital movement in history. Even as forms dissolve, however, the original force in the realms of mind and spirit that brought the historical existence into being attains its final definition. Historical epochs of this kind combine outward disintegration ending in death with, very often, a final and unexpected burst of intellectual and cultural achievement before the end comes.

Fig. 18. The Cantref Nef

Byw in History

Byw as the seventh and last stage in the cycle represents the summing-up and final accounting of all that has gone before it. In history, this represents the aftermath and legacy of that which has passed away, moving outwards through the world like ripples from a stone that has already vanished from sight. What once was becomes part of the background, as much spiritual as physical, from which new existences will draw as they come into being in their turn. Byw therefore does not denote a historical epoch so much as what remains after history has finished its work and moved on.

Fig. 19. *The Cantref Byw*

While history presents perhaps the clearest picture of the Cycle of the Cantrefs in its purely circular mode, the attentive student of this lore will find little difficulty in thinking of other examples. One that deserves particular attention here is the cycle of the ordinary physical life of a human being. Here Awyr is the time from conception to birth, Dŵr infancy and childhood, Ufel adolescence and young manhood or womanhood, Daear adulthood, Maen middle age, Nef old age, and Byw death and that which comes after. Compare this to the sequence just described and it will not be hard to work out the parallels.

All this relates to the Cycle of the Cantrefs as it traces out the circle, rather than the creative spiral, and it must be admitted that most things in human life follow the circle, or at most a spiral whose center moves so slowly that it resembles a circle to any but the closest observation. The spiral, it bears remembering, does not occur of itself, but only when the will is directed toward the movement of the circle, as you have learned. In most circumstances, therefore, the analysis of the Cycle of the Cantrefs given above is more than adequate.

It is in those rare but important situations where the development of the will becomes a real factor, and this development is then directed to the transformation of the individual and his surroundings, that the circle can be transformed, by the movement of the center, into the creative spiral. The most important such situation, at least in the present context, is that in which you have been engaged over the last two years or more—the work of initiation into a school of the mysteries. In the work of initiation, the Cycle of the Cantrefs takes on a slightly different form:

Awyr in Initiation

Awyr as the first stage in the work of initiation again represents the initial inspiration or motive force in the realms of mind and spirit, but here it takes the form of the initiatory teaching and, glimpsed beyond or through it, the possibility of a life that is not simply a circular movement following existing ruts, but an ongoing movement toward something higher and greater. In some cases the teaching is encountered first, and the aspirant glimpses in it what he has the capacity to become; in others, the glimpse of the higher life comes first, and the aspirant seeks out the teaching in an attempt to grasp what he has glimpsed.

Fig. 20. The Cantref Awyr

Dŵr in Initiation

Dŵr as the second stage in the work of initiation is as always the phase of growth, learning, and enlargement, and in any system of training in the mysteries, these work out primarily as practice. Here the aspirant must learn to apply himself patiently to the studies and exercises required of him, with understanding if possible, by rote if necessary, so that the inner capacities that are needed to accomplish the work of awakening the individuality and traversing the path that leads from Abred to Gwynfydd can be obtained.

Fig. 21. The Cantref Dŵr

Ufel in Initiation

Ufel as the third stage in the work of initiation has its usual meaning of conflict and confrontation with obstacles; here it has the specific meaning of the struggle of the aspirant with the ingrained habits of thought and action that have been established through the course of his previous life, and indeed his previous lives along the winding ways of Abred.

Fig. 22. The Cantref Ufel

The ideas introduced by the mystery teachings, and the actions proposed by them, are inevitably at variance with the aspirant's own habitual ways of thinking and doing, and conflict results. It is a mistake to suppose that this conflict may be foregone by replacing existing habits with new ones, or that anything would be gained by doing so; it is precisely the experience of conflict leading to the awakening of self-knowledge that is essential here.

Daear in Initiation

Daear as the fourth stage in the work of initiation indicates, as always, the completion of the process of manifestation and the earthing out of the initial impulse. Here it stands for that stage in the initiatory process at which the work assigned to the aspirant has had its effect, and what was to be learned has been learned. The aspirant, having encountered, practiced,

Fig. 23. *The Cantref Daear*

and contended with the teachings of the mystery school with which he is affiliated, now understands those teachings and is in a position to begin to communicate them to others; he is an initiate and, at least potentially, an initiator. Still, the spiral has not yet completed its full movement.

Maen in Initiation

Maen as the fifth stage in the work of initiation stands for the consequences of the manifestation in Daear, and in the mystery teachings it is specifically the result of continued study and practice of teachings and exercises already mastered. Here the forward movement of the spiral begins to become apparent, for the initiate discovers that there are depths within

Fig. 24. *The Cantref Maen*

depths within even the simplest teachings and practices. As he explores these, he begins, not merely to know and understand the mystery teachings, but to embody them in his own actions and life.

Nef in Initiation

Nef as the sixth stage in the work of initiation may be understood, as always, as the response of the Cosmos to what has been set in motion by the stages already traversed. Here the initiate begins to discover his circumstances changing in unexpected and ultimately positive ways, as patterns he has unwittingly held in place through his own mistaken ideas and unwise actions dissolve and are replaced by new patterns

Fig. 25. *The Cantref Nef*

that mirror the new ways of thought and action he has come to embody. These changes are not things he brings about deliberately, but neither are they done to him by some external force; they unfold from the central, unhidden secret of the mysteries, which is the mutual mirroring of the individual self and the Cosmos.

Byw in Initiation

Byw as the seventh stage in the work of initiation brings the initiatory process and the initiate himself full circle, and allows him finally to measure the gap opened up between where he was and where he now is, on account of the forward movement of the center that has transformed the circle into the spiral. The coming of this realization gives the initiate his freedom; having learned, practiced, contended with, understood, embodied, and been transformed by the teaching, he has now made it fully his own, and may proceed onward.

Fig. 26. The Cantref Byw

It is this last point that is most important, for the cycle of initiation is not followed once only. It is in fact followed on many different levels and over many different periods of time. The encounter with each concept of the mystery teachings passes through the seven stages just named—first, the concept is encountered; second, the student thinks it over; third, he faces the conflict between the new concept and his previous ways of thinking; fourth, he understands it; fifth, that understanding affects his thoughts and actions; sixth, the concept's influence on his thoughts and actions have their own affects on his life; and seventh, he notices these relations, and grasps the concept on a deeper level, not as knowledge but as a tool for the transformation of the self. Each of the grades of the Dolmen Arch is experienced in the same way, and so is the Dolmen Arch course as a whole.

As you complete your formal studies in this course, and reflect on the work you have done and the inner changes you have undergone during the two years or more you have spent working through these lessons, you may find yourself at any of the seven stages just outlined with regard to each lesson, each grade, each sequence of teachings or practices, and the course as a whole. This is as it should be, for each student comes to these lessons with a different background, different potentials, and different resources. The goal of a study course such as this one is not to bring every student to the self-same point, but to provide a set of working tools and useful ideas with which each student may make progress along the spiral at his own pace.

If you come to the end of these lessons convinced that you have failed because you have not yet attained the complete awakening of your individuality, a little realism might be in order. You are engaged in an effort to rise above the level of ordinary humanity and achieve the goal for which your soul has been striving, knowingly or unknowingly, for countless lives. You are close enough to the goal that your own conscious effort is now required to complete the work—otherwise you would not have been drawn to these lessons—but two years or so of work with a course of lessons such as this will not, by itself, bring you to the heart's desire of the ages.

If you do reach that attainment in this life, as you may do, and as many students of the mysteries have done before you, what stands before you then is another turn of the spiral, leading further upwards into realms of light and freedom. This is among the essential teachings of the mystery schools: the achievement of that which is just above the level of ordinary humanity—call it Gwynfydd, enlightenment, the Kingdom of Heaven, or any of a thousand other names—is not an end, but a single step up the grand stairway that rises up endlessly from the deeps of time and primeval matter into a realm hidden in infinite radiance. Upon that stairway, as a living soul, you have climbed through the ages to your present state; now, conscious of your origin and destiny, you may raise your eyes to the stairway's course above you and climb consciously—an initiate of the mysteries.

A GUIDE TO INITIATION IN THE DOLMEN ARCH TRADITION

WHEN YOU FINISH THIS LESSON PACKET, provided that you have done the work of this and all the previous grades faithfully and systematically, you will be prepared to teach and initiate students of your own. It is therefore appropriate to say a few words about the structure of the course through which you have passed over the last two years or more, and to discuss the ways in which the material you have learned may be adapted in your future work as a free instructor in the Dolmen Arch system.

The heart of the entire course of study you have pursued, as you have probably intuited long since, is the method of meditation given in the Newyddian grade, and the Sphere of Protection exercise introduced in stages over the course of the grades. A student who learns and practices nothing but these two things, provided that he makes these into daily practices and perseveres with them over a period of some years, will gain all the most important benefits to be had from this course, or for that matter, any other course of mystery school training.

Does this mean that all the other material you have learned is valueless? Not at all. The worth of these additional studies and practices may be secondary to the core practices just named, but may be measured nonetheless along three dimensions.

First, the core practices of the Dolmen Arch system foster the clarification and expansion of consciousness and the awakening of the individuality; that is their purpose. They do not, by themselves, provide the student with an explanation of the changes he is experiencing, some of which may be troubling if no such explanation is offered; nor do they put those changes, and the new insights and experiences they provide, into a context that gives them meaning. A great deal of the material covered in the lesson packets of the Dolmen Arch grades has for its purpose the provision of explanations and a sense of context for the results of the core training. The lectures on Druid philosophy and the tales of the Mabinogion have this function principally.

Second, the new abilities, insights, and experiences that open up as the student pursues the core practices of the system may usefully be enriched by additional practices which, while not strictly necessary, provide additional benefits to the student and others. Memory training, for example, is valuable in many ways even when pursued apart from a system of mystery school teaching, but when combined with core practices of the sort already described, it leads to a greatly improved ability to learn, remember, and apply not only the mystery teachings, but every other kind of knowledge as well. In the same way, the solar plexus exercises in the third lesson packet, the nwyfre exercises in the fourth, and the self-healing practice in the fifth are not strictly necessary to training in the mysteries, but provide a wide range of benefits that will be of value to the student, both in his studies and in his life during and after the course of study.

Third, and perhaps most simply, very few students—even those who possess the inner resources of desire and determination necessary to complete the course of study before them—will easily tolerate a course consisting only of two fundamental practices, one of which is very slowly developed and expanded during the process of study, and the other of which remains exactly the same, differing only in themes for meditation, from the beginning of the course to its end. Training in a mystery school is challenging enough without adding in the additional difficulty of an ordeal by boredom! Thus the additional material brought into the course serves the important function of making the course more interesting, and rendering the content of each lesson packet at least a small surprise to the student.

These lessons are copyrighted, and if you choose to teach this material in the form given in them, each of your students should purchase their own copy of the book. Alternatively, you may choose to use these lessons as a resource for your teaching, and present the material contained in them to your students in your own words, in a sequence and at a pace that may vary somewhat from the one used in this course. If you choose this latter option, the following notes may be helpful.

First, the core practices—meditation and the first stage in the Sphere of Protection exercise—should be given to each student at the very beginning of training, and the additional elements of the Sphere of Protection added in one at a time in the order they are presented in this course. Do not be in too great a hurry to give students the further developments of the Sphere of Protection; nothing is gained by rushing this work.

Second, the lectures on Druid philosophy and the tales from the Mabinogion should be given in the order in which they are presented in this course, and adequate time should be given to each student to get as much as possible from these resources. In particular, their role as sources of themes for meditation should not be neglected; a student who is working seriously with the meditative work will need a steady supply of new themes for practice, and will benefit from using themes that have been central to Dolmen Arch practice since the early days of the tradition.

Third, the practices of healing, enchantment, and initiation should be reserved to the grades of the Greater Mysteries, since they depend on acquiring a certain degree of experience with the core practices, and cannot be done effectively without this.

Fourth, some of the supplementary practices depend on other, previous practices, and this may or may not be apparent at first glance. It will be obvious, for example, that the Game of the Cantrefs depends on a prior mastery of the Sevenfold Wheel of Thought, which in turn depends on having at least some understanding of the seven Cantrefs. You can, if you wish, introduce the Wheel of Thought as soon as your student has worked through the Cantrefs in study and meditation, and introduce the basic form of the Game of the Cantrefs as soon as your student has shown adequate facility with the Wheel of Thought, but trying to teach the Game to someone who has not yet learned how to use the Wheel of Thought will prove unproductive. In the same way, the different stages of memory training are best given in the order in which they are presented in the course, though the pace may be varied depending on the ability of the individual student, because each lesson builds on the ones that come before it.

Fifth, many of the other supplementary practices may be given in whatever order seems appropriate, given the aptitude and needs of the individual student and the preferences of the teacher. The color breathing introduced in the second lesson packet, the solar plexus exercise given in the third, and the nwyfre exercises presented in the fourth belong to this category of practices; it is important that the student learn them before he proceeds to the Greater Mysteries, but the specific order in which they are learned need not be identical to the one used in the lesson packets you have received.

As a teacher in this tradition, you will constantly have to deal with the need to adjust the teachings you have received for individual students, and for broader changes in society and culture, without losing the benefits to be gained from the various practices. Your best guides in doing so are to reflect on your own learning experience, on the one hand, and to maintain and expand your own work with the practices you have received, on the other. Just as you reviewed the work of the first four grades of the course as a preliminary step to being advanced to the Loremaster of the Path grade, you will find it essential to review the entire course before you begin teaching students of your own, and to read back through your practice journal, remembering what the teachings and practices felt like to you when you first encountered them. This work is discussed in more length in the Completion Exercise for this grade, in the final paper in this lesson packet.

At the same time, it is of the highest importance that you should not allow your own training to come to a halt once you complete these lessons. When you have finished the work in this lesson packet, you will be an initiate of the Dolmen Arch—but it is vital to recall at this stage of your training that this word "initiation" means nothing more than "beginning." You have, indeed, made a solid beginning at the work of awakening your individuality and rising from Abred to Gwynfydd, but a solid beginning is only the first step in the work as a whole, or the first turn of a spiral that has many turns ahead, and you will find—if you continue to work with the practices and teachings you have already received and learned—that the benefits you have received already are but small compared to those you may expect to receive as you proceed.

In a sense, in the work you have done so far, you have merely completed your apprenticeship. Now, as a craftsman or craftswoman, greater, more challenging, and more splendid work awaits you. You can, if you stop here, transmit what you have received to students of your own—but if you go on, continuing to practice what you have learned and continuing to deepen and enrich your own mastery of the tradition, you will not only benefit yourself, but you will become a much better teacher, able to share the riches of a broader and deeper experience in the mysteries.

THE SECRET WORK OF THE GRAIL

OVER THE COURSE of the six previous grades in the Dolmen Arch system, you have been taught step by step the various stages of the Sphere of Protection ceremony, from its most basic form to the complexities and power of the Grail Working. In addition to this core system of ritualized work with nwyfre, you have been introduced to a series of other exercises that direct nwyfre, in particular for the purpose of healing yourself and others. It has already been shown to you, in the lecture on enchantment in the Grade of Loremaster of the Circle, that some of these practices may be combined with one another to produce unexpected effects.

This was partly done to provide you with an effective method for practical enchantment, but it also had a second and deeper purpose, which was to provide you with a hint concerning the intimate relationship among all the ways of working with nwyfre you have learned in this course. You may well, in the course of your meditations in the Gradd y Gwyddon y Cylch, have grasped what this hint was meant to suggest to you—that all the nwyfre exercises you have been taught, and all the different parts of the Sphere of Protection ceremony, may be combined, recombined, reordered and redirected in a nearly limitless number of ways in order to accomplish the Druid initiate's three privileges of healing, enchantment, and initiation.

You are free, in the months and years to come, to create and experiment with any such combination of techniques that appeals to you and furthers your work as an initiate. One such combination of the practices you have learned, however, deserves your close attention and your regular practice. This is the union of the complete Sphere of Protection working with all its parts, including the Grail Working, with the method of directing nwyfre through the palm centers that you have used primarily for the purpose of healing, and also for the purpose of enchantment. Due to its importance, it is given in detail in this paper.

The importance of this method of practice lies partly in that it is an extremely potent method of healing and enchantment—the most potent, in fact, that is taught in this course, or in the tradition from which this course derives—but partly also because it is the basis for a method of initiation, the one form of initiation in the Dolmen Arch system in which a spiritual influence is communicated from a human initiator to an initiate.

It is not necessary to have received this initiation in order to transmit it to another. The basis for this form of initiatory practice is the transformation of the enaid, or body of nwyfre, which takes place in the student of the Dolmen Arch system through the regular practice of the Sphere of Protection; its transmission is made possible by the specific effects on the enaid of regular work with the method of charging the palm centers that was communicated in the Gradd yr Athroniwr and developed as a method of healing in the first two grades of the Greater Mysteries. Anyone who has performed this work has the capacity to use it in an initiatory manner, while a person who attempts to use it without performing the requisite work beforehand, even though he himself may have been initiated by a Free Loremaster using the method about to be described, has but an empty form devoid of power.

The working in question is called the Secret Work of the Grail. It is performed as follows:

1. Perform the Sphere of Protection working as you have learned it in the first five lessons of this course: the Elemental Cross, the Calling of the Cantrefs, the Three Cauldrons working, the Awakening of the Dragons, and the Tree of Light. Leave the Circulation of Light for later.

2. Trace the symbols of the first four Cantrefs on your palms in the usual way.

3. Now perform the Grail Working, formulating your intention according to the purpose of your working. When you invoke Spirit Within and awaken the lunar current, however, instead of allowing the white light to radiate outwards in all directions from your solar plexus, bring it in two currents up and out from your solar plexus to your shoulders, and down both arms to the palms.

4. The next step depends on the nature of your intention, and more generally on which of the three privileges of the Druid initiate you are exercising.

If your intention is one of healing, your palms are now charged with nwyfre in a far more potent manner than the ordinary way of working will accomplish; you may proceed with the usual healing passes or, if your intention focuses on the removal or amelioration of a specific condition, you may simply direct your palms toward whatever part of your own or another's body is affected by the condition, and allow the white light to flow directly into that body part.

If your intention is one of enchantment, you may now project the lunar current, charged with your intention, into a pebble prepared in the way discussed in the previous grade, or into any other appropriate object.

If your intention is one of initiation, you will proceed in the manner described below.

5. When you have finished healing, enchanting or initiating, perform the Circulation of Light, but centered upon whoever or whatever you have healed, enchanted, or initiated. That is, instead of expanding the sphere of light from your own solar plexus, imagine the sphere of light expanding from the solar plexus of the other person, or from the center of the object, out to the edge of the room or other space where you are working, and spinning around itself in three ways. This seals the intention in place, and also banishes any hostile or disturbing influences from the person or object. You will then close as usual.

You will find it useful to experiment with the Secret Working of the Grail as a means of healing and enchantment, and observe its effects. As a means of initiation, however, it may be used in two different ways, a lesser and a greater form, and these should only be conferred upon a student who has already reached the appropriate stage in the study of the Dolmen Arch system of Druid mystery teachings.

The Lesser Form of Initiation

This first form of initiation may be conferred by you upon any student who has successfully completed the Gradd y Newyddian, the first of the seven grades of the Dolmen Arch, and is qualified to begin the work if the Gradd y Damcaniwr. On average, fewer than half of those who begin any course of study of this kind complete the first grade, and those who do not do so will likely not complete any course of mystery training during this lifetime; it is therefore a mistake to burden them with initiatory influences which will bring them no benefit and may expose them to experiences for which they are not prepared. Those who do complete the work of the first lesson packet, on the other hand, have at the very least set their feet on the path, and will therefore benefit from a working that will assist them in making progress on it.

In conferring the lesser form, after you have completed steps 1-3 above, and formulated the intention to initiate your student more deeply into the work of the Dolmen Arch, you will stand on the right side of the student, who may stand or sit, as necessity or convenience determines. You will place your right hand in front of the student's solar plexus, perhaps six inches in front of his body, and your left hand an equivalent distance behind his back at a point directly behind the solar plexus. Having done this, you will allow the lunar current to stream inwards from your hands into the solar plexus, where it forms a sphere of white light, intense and luminous as a star. Continue this as long as seems appropriate to you.

Then move your hands up until the right hand is in front of the student's forehead and the left hand behind the back of the student's skull, again about six inches out. Repeat the same process, visualizing a sphere of brilliant white light in the center of his head. Again, continue this as long as seems appropriate to you. When you are finished, perform the circulation of light as described above, visualizing the sphere of light expanding from your student's solar plexus rather than from your own. This concludes the working.

This lesser form of initiation will be found to enhance and deepen the student's ability to concentrate his thoughts and to direct nwyfre. The solar plexus center and the center at the middle of the head, where the Moon Cauldron will be formulated, are the first two centers of nwyfre awakened by the Dolmen Arch practices, and the stimulus provided them by this initiation will make most of the work of this study course ripen and bear fruit more promptly.

The Greater Form of Initiation

This second form may be conferred by you only upon a student who has successfully completed all four grades of the Lesser Mysteries, has passed the examination at the conclusion of the Gradd yr Athroniwr, and is qualified to begin work on the Gradd y Gwyddon y Ffordd, the first of the Greater Mystery grades. Fewer than one in ten of the students who begin a course of this kind will persevere in it long enough to reach the threshold of the Greater Mysteries; the great majority of those who do so will complete their course of study, and it is for these latter in particular that this form of initiation is intended. Those who do not progress at least as far as the Greater Mysteries will receive no benefit from the connection to the symbolic patterns of the Dolmen Arch tradition that this working confers.

In conferring the greater form, after you have completed steps 1-3 above, and formulated the intention to initiate your student into the inner contacts and powers of the Dolmen Arch, you will stand in front of the student, who may stand or sit as necessity or convenience determines. You will ask him to hold out his hands, palm up, and you will then draw the symbols of water and earth on the palm of his left hand with the first finger of your right hand, projecting the lunar current into the symbols as you draw them. Next, you will draw the symbols of fire and air on the palm of his right hand with the first finger of your left hand, again projecting the lunar current into the symbols.

Next, with the first finger of your left hand, you will draw a circle with a cross beneath it over the student's abdomen, and charge this with the lunar current. With the first finger of your right hand, draw a circle with a cross above it over the student's heart, and charge this with the lunar current. Then, joining your two index fingers together, draw with them a circle with a cross inside it over the student's forehead, and charge this with the lunar current. (These are the symbols of the last three Cantrefs, Maen, Nef, and Byw.) As you finish, visualize all the symbols you have drawn blazing with the white fire of the lunar current, and perform the Circulation of Light with the solar plexus of the student as the center of the sphere, as before. This concludes the working.

This greater form of initiation, when combined with individual practice, will activate the palm centers and the Three Cauldrons more quickly and fully, and enable the initiate to achieve better results in practicing the three privileges of initiation, healing, and enchantment.

A Final Note

While it is inappropriate to confer either of these initiations on any person who is not properly prepared for the experience by attaining the grades already mentioned through their own work, you are not required to perform these initiations for any person if you do not feel, for whatever reason, that this would be appropriate. Furthermore, should you wish to, you may confer them on a student of the Dolmen Arch system who has passed beyond the specific point at which they become appropriate; for example, should you meet another Free Loremaster who wishes to receive the benefit of both initiations, you may confer them upon him.

It is normally wise, however, to wait at least three months between conferring the lesser form of initiation and conferring the greater; the changes induced in the enaid of the initiate by either form of the working are complex enough that they should be given time to work themselves out, with only such additional stimulus as may be provided by the initiate's own daily practices.

THE INITIATORY GAME OF THE CANTREFS

THE BASIC AND INTERMEDIATE FORMS of the Game of the Cantrefs are distinguished by the fact that they are played by a single initiate; they are, so to speak, "solitaire games." Beginning in this manner, the initiate learns to relate the number of dots on each half of each domino piece to their corresponding conceptions and questions from the Sevenfold Wheel of Thought, and to adjust the questions and conceptions as needed to fit the subject of the game.

Once these details have been learned, the Game of the Cantrefs—in either of the forms you have already learned, basic or intermediate—becomes a form of meditation. The dominoes provide a helpful nonlogical element that takes the mind out of its habitual motions and leads it to consider questions it might otherwise never have asked. As you have already learned by now, if you have practiced the Game with any frequency, the sequence of questions and the chains of thought set in motion thereby will very reliably point you toward whatever aspects of the theme or subject of each game you most need to understand.

All this is valuable in its own right, and it is also valuable as a foundation for the more advanced form of the Game of the Cantrefs. This differs from the more basic forms of the Game in that it is not a "solitaire game." It is played by two or occasionally more players, and ordinarily has an initiatory function. There are two modes of this more advanced form of the Game: one in which one player asks the questions and the other provides the answers, the other in which the two players take turns questioning and answering each other.

The First Mode:
One Questioner, One Answerer

In the first of these two modes, the play is precisely the same as in the intermediate form of the Game that you have already learned, except that a second person takes part. A theme or subject for the Game is chosen, and then seven dominoes are selected, face down. The player who will be asking the questions—the questioner, as he will be called hereafter—chooses them, and sets them on end in a line so that he can see their faces but the other player—the answerer—cannot. The questioner then selects one domino, places it face up so that the answerer can see it, and asks the question about the subject or theme of the game that is specified by the chosen domino. The answerer then must answer that question to the best of his ability.

This mode of the advanced game is traditionally much used in personal instruction of a student by a teacher of the Druid mysteries. Either the teacher or the student will suggest a theme, and the teacher will then draw seven dominoes and, following their guidance, ask the student seven questions about the theme, which the student must then attempt to answer one at a time. This obviously provides a good test of the student's mastery of the teachings he has studied, and of his ability to understand, apply, and reason with those teachings; less obviously, perhaps, it allows the perceptive teacher to gauge how the student's training is progressing by noting the strengths and weaknesses, the points of clarity and obscurity, in his answers.

The same mode of the advanced game, it may be worth noting, also allows for the practice of a kind of divination that differs from conventional fortune-telling in an important way. One of the reasons the mystery schools have so often disapproved of fortune-telling of the ordinary sort is that in nearly all cases, the latter treats the future as foreordained.[2] The fortune-teller is expected to tell the client what will happen, as though the client's choices and actions have no influence on the outcome of the question at all; "a tall, dark stranger," perhaps, is to appear at such and such a time, and romance or some other outcome follows as mechanically as the ringing of the bell in a clock follows the movement of the hour hand.

The mystery teachings hold, as you have learned, that the individual will always has a part to play in the unfolding of the future, and very often the de-

---

2. This is fortunately less true of divination as it is usually practiced today; more than a century of popularizations of occult teachings have had some positive effect.

ciding part. Even when coming events are already on their way and cannot be turned aside, the individual always has the power to choose how he will respond to them, and thus to set different causes in motion for times further away in the future; should the "tall, dark stranger" appear, the client still chooses how to respond to his appearance. That ordinary fortune-telling tends to obscure the role of the individual will has caused a great many teachers of the mysteries to consider the professional palmist, tea leaf reader, or the like as a factor leading away from Gwynfydd.

Still, it is possible to turn a consultation not far different from the one a palmist has with her clients into a path to wisdom and even initiation, and the first mode of the advanced Game of the Cantrefs is one tool that may be put to work in this way. In this application of the Game, the answerer provides the theme—it may be a problem he is having in his daily affairs, for example. The questioner draws seven dominoes and then, as in any other game following this mode of play, chooses one and asks the answerer the corresponding question. The play proceeds as before, with the questioner asking seven questions and the answerer answering them.

By the time the game is complete, if the questioner is skillful enough, the answerer will either have figured out his own best response to the problem, or at least the questioner will have gained enough insight into the matter to be able to offer useful advice. Regular practice of the intermediate form of the Game, using personal problems as themes, will quickly teach the initiate how to do this.

The Second Mode:
Both Players Questioning and Answering

The Game can also be played between two people, with each one asking and answering questions alternately. This is a more challenging form of the Game, and can only be played effectively when both participants have studied and practiced the Sevenfold Wheel of Thought and the solitaire forms of the Game of the Cantrefs. In earlier times, games in this mode enlivened those occasional meetings when Free Loremasters of the Dolmen Arch tradition met with one another and with students of lower grades; serious questions were discussed and settled using the Game of the Cantrefs to guide meditation and consideration of the issues involved, and games were also played for the instruction and, it is only fair to say, the entertainment of all those present.

Until such time as the Dolmen Arch tradition again becomes relatively widespread in Druid circles, this is unlikely to happen with any frequency. Yet the Game played in this most advanced of its modes was also used, and may still be used, as a help in the training of advanced students of the Dolmen Arch study course. As you have already learned, some elements of the training you have received may be introduced earlier to personal students than is optimal in a correspondence course, and if you have chosen to teach the simpler forms of the Game of the Cantrefs to your own students immediately after they have learned the Sevenfold Wheel of Thought, as is your right, you may proceed with them to the more advanced forms in due order, and use games of the sort we are discussing as a teaching exercise. There are few better ways to foster keenness of mind and encourage careful study of the tradition's mind and memory training than the repeated experience of being challenged in a game of this kind.

In this mode, the Game begins with one player stating a theme or subject for the game. Each player then draws seven dominoes at random, face down, and sets them on end in such a position that he can see them but the other player cannot. (The standard way to do this for the two players to face each other across a table; each player then sets his dominoes on end in a line, with the backs of the dominoes toward the other player and the faces toward himself.) The player who states the theme, let us say, is player A; player B then makes the first move, laying down a single domino in the middle of the table and asking a question about a conception concerning the theme that takes its lead from the domino played. Player A must then answer this question.

When player A has finished answering the question, he plays a domino of his own. As with the intermediate game discussed in the previous lesson packet, one of the two ends of the newly played domino must have the same number of points as one end of the domino already played, and the two matching ends are placed in contact with each other. Player A then asks a question about a conception concerning the theme; either the question or the conception will be the same that player B used, depending on which end of the domino first played is matched by the second. Player B must then answer the question, and follows his answer by playing another of his dominos and asking a question in turn.

If either of the players is unable to play a domino, because none of the ones already played have an end with a number of points equal to any domino remaining to him from the seven he chose, he says "Pass" and the other player may immediately play another domino and ask another question. If one player has played all his dominoes and the other still has dominoes that can be played, as a result of having to pass earlier on in the game, the player with dominoes remaining can play them one after another and ask a question for each one, which the other player must answer. The game ends when all dominoes that can be played have been played.

There are, properly speaking, no winners or losers in the Game of the Cantrefs, in any of its modes, though differences in skill, knowledge, and insight between players will of course be apparent. The point of the play is not in displaying these differences, however; it is found in the interplay of question and answer, which leads the awakening mind closer to the Great Question of the meaning, purpose and goal of existence in Abred—and closer, in turn, to the Great Answer.

THE MABINOGION: THE STORY OF TALIESIN

The last of the seven tales of the Mabinogion set in the time before the coming of Arthur—and thus reflecting the older traditions of the Druid mysteries, before the redefinition of those mysteries in Christian form that took place in the early Middle Ages and provided the inner meaning and power to the Arthurian legends and certain traditional mystery initiations based on them—is the Story of Taliesin.[3] It is among the very strangest of these ancient tales, a narrative full of transformations and magic, and it has long been recognized even among uninitiated scholars that its central theme is that of an initiation into a mystery school.

Reflection on the themes of this story will reveal many parallels with the more detailed and richly embroidered story of initiation that makes up the Four Branches of the Mabinogion. Like the main character of the Four Branches, who begins the story named Pryderi and ends it named Llew, the main character of the Story of Taliesin begins it bearing the name of Gwion Bach, "little Gwion," and ends it bearing the new name of Taliesin. The cauldron of the Second Branch and the animal transformations of the Fourth Branch have echoes here, and the role of Arianrhod in the Fourth Branch is in some ways echoed by that of Ceridwen in the Story of Taliesin.

Still, the two sequences are by no means identical. The central reason for the difference between them is expressed neatly at the end of the first paragraph

---

3. This story does not appear in most modern collections of the Mabinogion stories, but was included in the collection of translations by Lady Charlotte Guest.

in the Story of Taliesin: Taliesin's initiation takes place "in the beginning of Arthur's time and of the Round Table"—that is, at the time that Christianity was spreading through Britain, and the initiates of the mysteries were facing the need to adapt their teachings to the new religious climate that was taking shape around them. Taliesin's initiation thus represents the final form of the older, Pagan mystery tradition, condensed and simplified as, over time, mystery traditions always are, while the Four Branches echo the more expansive customs of an earlier time and symbolize the extended course of training and initiation through which students passed in the mystery schools of that age.

Pryderi passed through many stages and grades in the course of his initiation; he was caused to reflect not only on his past life, but on what he could guess, intuit, or perceive of his previous incarnations; he underwent repeated tests and challenges of his patience, perseverance, and virtue; upon passing these, he underwent a complex process of training and initiatory ritual before finally emerging from his lattermost trial as king of himself, inheritor of the wondrous realm that is within every human being. Taliesin's initiation, as you will see, takes place over a much shorter time and covers the same ground in a much more compressed fashion. Time was short, and it was no longer easy to support aspirants to the Druid mysteries for years at a time while they pursued their studies; when they finished those studies, in turn, initiates had to support themselves as bards, making poetry and song for noble patrons.

The initiation of Taliesin thus outlines the process as it proceeded in those later and more restricted circumstances. He spent a year and a day laboring in a menial capacity, as a test of his willingness to humble himself and persevere; then followed a ceremonial initiation condensing the symbolism of the cauldron of Annwn and the journey through Abred's animal forms; then nine months' intensive study in the seclusion of the mystery school. Finally, reborn and with a new name, the initiate went to serve a noble family as a household bard, and exercised his magical as well as his poetic talents on their behalf. The whole of this process may be traced in the story that follows.

The Story of Taliesin

In times past there lived in Penllyn[4] a man of gentle lineage, named Tegid Foel,[5] and his dwelling was in the midst of the lake Tegid, and his wife was called Ceridwen.[6] And there was born to him of his wife a son named Morfran[7] son of Tegid, and also a daughter named Creirwy,[8] the fairest maiden in the world was she; and they had a brother, the most ill-favoured man in the world, Afagddu.[9] Now Ceridwen his mother thought that he was not likely to be admitted among men of noble birth, by reason of his ugliness, unless he had some exalted merits or knowledge. For this was in the beginning of Arthur's time and of the Round Table.

So she resolved according to the arts of the books of the Fferyllt[10] to boil a cauldron of Awen and knowledge for her son, that his reception might be honourable because of his knowledge of the mysteries of the future state of the world.

Then she began to boil the cauldron, which from the beginning of its boiling might not cease to boil for a year and a day, until three blessed drops were obtained of the grace of Awen.

And she put Gwion Bach[11] the son of Gwreang[12] of Llanfair in Caereinion,[13] in Powys, to stir the cauldron, and a blind man named Morda[14] to kindle the fire beneath it, and she charged them that they should not suffer it to cease boiling for the space of a year and a day. And she herself, according to the books of the astronomers, and in planetary hours, gathered every day of all charm-bearing

---

4. *Penllyn*: "Head of the Lake."
5. *Tegid Foel*: "Beautiful, the Bald." This is traditionally said to be a title of the Moon.
6. *Ceridwen*: "Bright Correction" or "Bright Chastisement." Notice that since she lives with her husband in the midst of the lake Tegid, she is a Lady of the Lake.
7. *Morfran*: "Black Raven." A reference to Bran and the second branch is implied.
8. *Creirwy*: "Heron's Egg." Creyr the heron was a symbol of the Creator in Welsh legend.
9. *Afagddu*: "Complete Darkness."
10. That is, the alchemists. According to traditional accounts, the ancient Druids had a college of *Fferyllt* or alchemists who dwelt in a city on Mount Snowdon.
11. *Gwion Bach*: "Little Elf."
12. *Gwreang*: "Vast Hero."
13. *Llanfair in Caereinion:* a town in southwestern Wales. *Llanfair* is "the Chapel of Mary," and *Caereinion* is "the City of the Anvil" or "the City of the Just."
14. *Morda*: "Ruler of the Sea."

herbs. And one day, towards the end of the year, as Ceridwen was culling plants and making incantations, it chanced that three drops of the charmed liquor flew out of the cauldron and fell upon the finger of Gwion Bach. And by reason of their great heat he put his finger to his mouth, and the instant he put those marvel-working drops into his mouth, he foresaw everything that was to come, and perceived that his chief care must be to guard against the wiles of Ceridwen, for vast was her skill. And in very great fear he fled towards his own land. And the cauldron burst in two, because all the liquor within it except the three charm-bearing drops was poisonous, so that the horses of Gwyddno Garanhir[15] were poisoned by the water of the stream into which the liquor of the cauldron ran, and the confluence of that stream was called the Poison of the Horses of Gwyddno from that time forth.

Thereupon came in Ceridwen and saw all the toil of the whole year lost. And she seized a billet of wood and struck the blind Morda on the head until one of his eyes fell out upon his cheek.

And he said, "Wrongfully hast thou disfigured me, for I am innocent. Thy loss was not because of me."

"Thou speakest truth," said Ceridwen, "it was Gwion Bach who robbed me."

And she went forth after him, running. And he saw her, and changed himself into a hare and fled. But she changed herself into a greyhound and turned him. And he ran towards a river, and became a fish. And she in the form of an otter-bitch chased him under the water, until he was fain to turn himself into a bird of the air. She, as a hawk, followed him and gave him no rest in the sky. And just as she was about to stoop upon him, and he was in fear of death, he espied a heap of winnowed wheat on the floor of a barn, and he dropped among the wheat, and turned himself into one of the grains. Then she transformed herself into a high-crested black hen, and went to the wheat and scratched it with her feet, and found him out and swallowed him. And, as the story says, she bore him nine months, and when she was delivered of him, she could not find it in her heart to kill him, by reason of his beauty. So she wrapped him in a leathern bag, and cast him into the sea to the mercy of God, on the twenty-ninth day of April.[16]

And at that time the weir of Gwyddno was on the strand between Dyfi and Aberystwyth, near to his own castle, and the value of an hundred pounds was

---

15. *Gwyddno Garanhir*: "Loremaster Tall Heron."
16. Once again, as in the First Branch, the birth of a magical child is associated with May Eve.

Fig. 27. The Mabinogion • *Gwion Bach receives the Three Blessed Drops from the Cauldron*

taken in that weir every May eve. And in those days Gwyddno had an only son named Elphin, the most hapless of youths, and the most needy. And it grieved his father sore, for he thought that he was born in an evil hour. And by the advice of his council, his father had granted him the drawing of the weir that year, to see if good luck would ever befall him, and to give him something wherewith to begin the world.

And the next day when Elphin went to look, there was nothing in the weir. But as he turned back he perceived the leathern bag upon a pole of the weir. Then said one of the weirwards unto Elphin, "Thou wast never unlucky until tonight, and now thou hast destroyed the virtues of the weir, which always yielded the value of an hundred pounds every May eve, and tonight there is nothing but this leathern skin within it."

"How now," said Elphin, "there may be therein the value of an hundred pounds."

Well, they took up the leathern bag, and he who opened it saw the forehead of the boy, and said to Elphin, "Behold a radiant brow!"

"Taliesin be he called,"[17] said Elphin. And he lifted the boy in his arms, and lamenting his mischance, he placed him sorrowfully behind him. And he made his horse amble gently, that before had been trotting, and he carried him as softly as if he had been sitting in the easiest chair in the world. And presently the boy made a poem of consolation and praise to Elphin, and foretold honour to Elphin; and this was the first poem that Taliesin ever sang, being to console Elphin in his grief for that the produce of the weir was lost, and, what was worse, that all the world would consider that it was through his fault and ill-luck. And then Elphin asked him what he was, whether man or spirit. Whereupon he sang this tale, and said,—

"First, I have been formed a comely person,
In the court of Ceridwen I have done penance;
Though little I was seen, placidly received,
I was great on the floor of the place to where I was led;
I have been a prized defence, the sweet muse the cause,
And by law without speech, I have been liberated
By a smiling black old hag, when irritated,
Dreadful her claim when pursued:
I have fled with vigour, I have fled as a frog,

---

17. *Tal iesin* in Welsh means "Radiant Brow."

I have fled in the semblance of a crow, scarcely finding rest,
I have fled vehemently, I have fled as a chain,
I have fled as a roe into an entangled thicket,
I have fled as a wolf cub, I have fled as a wolf in a wilderness,
I have fled as a thrush of portending language,
I have fled as a fox, used to concurrent bounds of quirks,
I have fled as a martin, which did not avail,
I have fled as a squirrel, that vainly hides,
I have fled as a stag's antler, of ruddy course,
I have fled as iron in a glowing fire,
I have fled as a spear-head, of woe to such as has a wish for it,
I have fled as a fierce bull bitterly fighting,
I have fled as a bristly boar seen in a ravine,
I have fled as a white grain of pure wheat,
On the skirt of a hempen sheet entangled,
That seemed of the size of a mare's foal,
That is filling like a ship on the waters,
Into a dark leathern bag I was thrown,
And on a boundless sea I was sent adrift;
Which was to me an omen of being tenderly nursed,
And the Lord God then set me at liberty."

Then came Elphin to the house or court of Gwyddno his father, and Taliesin with him. And Gwyddno asked him if he had had a good haul at the weir, and he told him that he had got that which was better than fish.

"What was that?" said Gwyddno.

"A Bard," answered Elphin.

Then said Gwyddno, "Alas, what will he profit thee?"

And Taliesin himself replied and said, "He will profit him more than the weir ever profited thee."

Asked Gwyddno, "Art thou able to speak, and thou so little?"

And Taliesin answered him, "I am better able to speak than thou to question me."

And forthwith Elphin gave his haul to his wife, and she nursed him tenderly and lovingly. Thenceforward Elphin increased in riches more and more day after day, and in love and favour with the king, and there abode Taliesin until he was thirteen years old, when Elphin son of Gwyddno went by a Christmas invitation to his uncle, Maelgwn Gwynedd,[18] who sometime after this held open court at Christmas-tide in the castle of Dyganwy, for all the number of his lords of both degrees, both spiritual and temporal, with a vast and thronged host of knights and squires. And amongst them there arose a discourse and discussion. And thus was it said: "Is there in the whole world a king so great as Maelgwn, or one on whom Heaven has bestowed so many spiritual gifts as upon him? First, form, and beauty, and meekness, and strength, besides all the powers of the soul!" And together with these they said that Heaven had given one gift that exceeded all the others, which was the beauty, and comeliness, and grace, and wisdom, and modesty of his queen; whose virtues surpassed those of all the ladies and noble maidens throughout the whole kingdom. And with this they put questions one to another amongst themselves, "Who had braver men? Who had fairer or swifter horses or greyhounds? Who had more skillful or wiser bards than Maelgwn?"

Now at that time the bards were in great favour with the exalted of the kingdom; and then none performed the office of those who are now called heralds, unless they were learned men, not only expert in the service of kings and princes, but studious and well versed in the lineage, and arms, and exploits of princes and kings, and in discussions concerning foreign kingdoms, and the ancient things of this kingdom, and chiefly in the annals of the first nobles; and also were prepared always with their answers in various languages, Latin, French, Welsh, and English. And together with this they were great chroniclers, and recorders, and skillful in framing verses, and ready in making englyns in every one of those languages. Now of these there were at that feast within the palace of Maelgwn as many as four-and-twenty, and chief of them all, was one named Heinin the Bard.

When they had all made an end of thus praising the king and his gifts, it befell that Elphin spoke in this wise. "Of a truth none but a king may vie with a king; but were he not a king, I would say that my wife was as virtuous as any lady in the kingdom, and also that I have a bard who is more skillful than all the king's bards." In a short space some of his fellows showed the king all the boastings of Elphin; and the king ordered him to be thrown into a strong prison, until he might know the truth as to the virtues of his wife, and the wisdom of his bard.

---

18. *Maelgwn Gwynedd*: a historical figure, the king of north Wales in the early sixth century and thus a contemporary of the historical King Arthur.

Now when Elphin had been put in a tower of the castle, with a thick chain about his feet (it is said that it was a silver chain, because he was of royal blood); the king, as the story relates, sent his son Rhun to inquire into the demeanour of Elphin's wife. Now Rhun was the most graceless man in the world, and there was neither wife nor maiden with whom he had held converse, but was evil spoken of. While Rhun went in haste towards Elphin's dwelling, being fully minded to bring disgrace upon his wife, Taliesin told his mistress how that the king had placed his master in durance in prison, and how that Rhun was coming in haste to strive to bring disgrace upon her. Wherefore he caused his mistress to array one of the maids of her kitchen in her apparel; which the noble lady gladly did; and she loaded her hands with the best rings that she and her husband possessed.

In this guise Taliesin caused his mistress to put the maiden to sit at the board in her room at supper, and he made her to seem as her mistress, and the mistress to seem as the maid. And when they were in due time seated at their supper in the manner that has been said, Rhun suddenly arrived at Elphin's dwelling, and was received with joy, for all the servants knew him plainly; and they brought him in haste to the room of their mistress, in the semblance of whom the maid rose up from supper and welcomed him gladly. And afterwards she sat down to supper again the second time, and Rhun with her. Then Rhun began jesting with the maid, who still kept the semblance of her mistress. And verily this story shows that the maiden became so intoxicated, that she fell asleep; and the story relates that it was a powder that Rhun put into the drink, that made her sleep so soundly that she never felt it when he cut from off her hand her little finger, whereupon was the signet ring of Elphin, which he had sent to his wife as a token, a short time before. And Rhun returned to the king with the finger and the ring as a proof, to show that he had cut it from off her hand, without her awaking from her sleep of intemperance.

The king rejoiced greatly at these tidings, and he sent for his councillors to whom he told the whole story from the beginning. And he caused Elphin to be brought out of his prison, and he chided him because of his boast. And he spake unto Elphin on this wise.

"Elphin, be it known to thee beyond a doubt that it is but folly for a man to trust in the virtues of his wife further than he can see her; and that thou mayest be certain of thy wife's vileness, behold her finger, with thy signet ring upon it, which was cut from her hand last night, while she slept the sleep of intoxication."

Then thus spake Elphin. "With thy leave, mighty king, I cannot deny my ring, for it is known of many; but verily I assert strongly that the finger around which it is, was never attached to the hand of my wife, for in truth and certainty there are three notable things pertaining to it, none of which ever belonged to any of my wife's fingers. The first of the three is, that it is certain, by your grace's leave, that wheresoever my wife is at this present hour, whether sitting, or standing, or lying down, this ring would never remain upon her thumb, whereas you can plainly see that it was hard to draw it over the joint of the little finger of the hand whence this was cut; the second thing is, that my wife has never let pass one Saturday since I have known her without paring her nails before going to bed, and you can see fully that the nail of this little finger has not been pared for a month. The third is, truly, that the hand whence this finger came was kneading rye dough within three days before the finger was out therefrom, and I can assure your goodness that my wife has never kneaded rye dough since my wife she has been."

Then the king was mightily wroth with Elphin for so stoutly withstanding him, respecting the goodness of his wife, wherefore he ordered him to his prison a second time, saying that he should not be loosed thence until he had proved the truth of his boast, as well concerning the wisdom of his bard as the virtues of his wife.

In the meantime his wife and Taliesin remained joyful at Elphin's dwelling. And Taliesin showed his mistress how that Elphin was in prison because of them, but he bade her be glad for that he would go to Maelgwn's court to free his master.

After this he took leave of his mistress and came at last to the Court of Maelgwn, who was going to sit in his hall and dine in his royal state, as it was the custom in those days for kings and princes to do at every chief feast. And as soon as Taliesin entered the hall, he placed himself in a quiet corner, near the place where the bards and the minstrels were wont to come in doing their service and duty to the king, as is the custom at the high festivals when the bounty is proclaimed. And so, when the bards and the heralds came to cry largess, and to proclaim the power of the king and his strength, at the moment that they passed by the corner wherein he was crouching, Taliesin pouted out his lips after them, and played " Blerwm, blerwm," with his finger upon his lips. Neither took they much notice of him as they went by, but proceeded forward till they came before the king, unto whom they made their obeisance with their bodies, as they were wont, without speaking a single word, but pouting out their lips, and making mouths at the king, playing "Blerwm, blerwm," upon their lips with their fingers, as they had seen the boy do elsewhere. This sight caused the king to wonder and to deem within himself that they were drunk with many liquors. Wherefore he commanded one of his lords, who served at the board, to go to them and desire them to collect their wits, and to consider where they stood, and what it was fitting for them to do. And this lord did so gladly. But they ceased not from their folly any more than before. Whereupon he sent to them a second time, and a third, desiring them to go forth from the hall. At the last the king ordered one of his squires to give a blow to the chief of them named Heinin the Bard; and the squire took a broom and struck him on the head, so that he fell back in his seat. Then he arose and went on his knees, and besought leave of the king's grace to show that this their fault was not through want of knowledge, neither through drunkenness, but by the influence of some spirit that was in the hall. And after this Heinin spoke on this wise.

"Oh, honourable king, be it known to your grace that not from the strength of drink, or of too much liquor, are we dumb, without power of speech like drunken men, but through the influence of a spirit that sits in the corner yonder in the form of a child."

Forthwith the king commanded the squire to fetch him; and he went to the nook where Taliesin sat, and brought him before the king, who asked him what he was, and whence he came. And he answered the king in verse.

"Primary chief bard am I to Elphin,
  And my original country is the region of the summer stars;
  Idno and Heinin called me Myrddin,
  At length every king will call me Taliesin.
  I was with my Lord in the highest sphere,
  On the fall of Lucifer into the depth of hell:
  I have borne a banner before Alexander;
  I know the names of the stars from north to south;
  I have been on the galaxy at the throne of the Distributor;
  I was in Canaan when Absalom was slain;
  I conveyed the Divine Spirit to the level of the vale of Hebron;
  I was in the court of Don before the birth of Gwydion.
  I was instructor to Eli and Enoch;
  I have been winged by the genius of the splendid crosier;
  I have been loquacious prior to being gifted with speech;
  I was at the place of the crucifixion of the merciful Son of God;

I have been three periods in the prison of Arianrhod;
I have been the chief director of the work of the tower of Nimrod;
I am a wonder whose origin is not known.
I have been in Asia with Noah in the ark,
I have seen the destruction of Sodom and Gomorrah;
I have been in India when Roma was built,
I am now come here to the remnant of Troia.
I have been with my Lord in the manger of the ass;
I strengthened Moses through the water of Jordan;
I have been in the firmament with Mary Magdalene;
I have obtained the muse from the cauldron of Ceridwen;
I have been bard of the harp to Lleon of Lochlin.
I have been on the White Hill, in the court of Cynfelyn,
For a day end a year in stocks and fetters,
I have suffered hunger for the Son of the Virgin.
I have been fostered in the land of the Deity,
I have been teacher to all intelligences,
I am able to instruct the whole universe.
I shall be until the day of doom on the face of the earth;
And it is not known whether my body is flesh or fish.
Then I was for nine months
In the womb of the hag Ceridwen.
I was originally little Gwion,
And at length I am Taliesin."

And when the king and his nobles had heard the song, they wondered much, for they had never heard the like from a boy so young as he. And when the king knew that he was the bard of Elphin, he bade Heinin, his first and wisest bard, to answer Taliesin and to strive with him. But when he came, he could do no other, but play "blerwm" on his lips; and when he sent for the others of the four-and-twenty bards, they all did likewise, and could do no other. And Maelgwn asked the boy Taliesin what was his errand, and he answered him in song.

And while he was thus singing his verse near the door, there arose a mighty storm of wind, so that the king and all his nobles thought that the castle would fall on their heads. And the king caused them to fetch Elphin in haste from his dungeon, and placed him before Taliesin. And it is said that immediately he sang a verse, so that the chains opened from about his feet.

Taliesin having set his master free from prison, and having protected the innocence of his wife, and silenced the Bards, so that not one of them dared to say a word, now brought Elphin's wife before them, and showed that she had not one finger wanting. Right glad was Elphin, right glad was Taliesin.

Then he bade Elphin wager the king, that he had a horse both better and swifter than the king's horses. And this Elphin did, and the day, and the time, and the place were fixed, and the place was that which at this day is called Morfa Rhiannedd;[19] and thither the king went with all his people, and four-and-twenty of the swiftest horses he possessed. And after a long process the course was marked, and the horses were placed for running. Then came Taliesin with four-and-twenty twigs of holly, which he had burnt black, and he caused the youth who was to ride his master's horse to place them in his belt, and he gave him orders to let all the king's horses get before him, and as he should overtake one horse after the other, to take one of the twigs and strike the horse with it over the crupper, and then let that twig fall; and after that to take another twig, and do in like manner to every one of the horses, as he should overtake them, enjoining the horseman strictly to watch when his own horse should stumble, and to throw down his cap on the spot. All these things did the youth fulfil, giving a blow to every one of the king's horses, and throwing down his cap on the spot where his horse stumbled. And to this spot Taliesin brought his master after his horse had won the race. And he caused Elphin to put workmen to dig a hole there; and when they had dug the ground deep enough, they found a large cauldron full of gold.

And then said Taliesin, "Elphin, behold a payment and reward unto thee, for having taken me out of the weir, and for having reared me from that time until now." And on this spot stands a pool of water, which is to this time called Pwllbair.[20]

---

19. *Morfa Rhiannedd*: "Moor of the Maidens."
20. *Pwllbair*: "Pool of the Cauldron."

Druid Philosophy: The Powers of Mind

WITH THIS LECTURE on Druid philosophy, the journey from first principles to practical application discussed earlier in this course is complete. The concepts introduced in previous grades each have their applications in the work of the Druid initiate, and those applications are as many and various as the understanding and effort of the Druids of past generations have been able to make them; only a certain portion of the whole can be discussed in the space available to us here. Still, careful attention to this sample of practical applications, combined with meditation on the principles discussed earlier in this course, will open many doors, some of which may not be visible to the student at first glance.

You have learned, in the grades already completed, of Awen and Annwn, of nwyfre, of the rising spiral of evolution, of the nature of a Cosmos governed by law, of the many beings that inhabit the Cosmos alongside humanity, and of the manifestations of the seven laws or spiritual principles of the Druid teaching. Within a Cosmos of the kind we have described—brought into being by a transcendent spiritual principle; permeated by a single current of life, of which all lives are expressions; unfolding according to a process of physical and spiritual evolution; subject to laws that unfold in an orderly progression from the spiritual principle that shapes all things; full of lives and intelligences on every imaginable level and mode of existence—certain possibilities naturally unfold, and certain opportunities for creative action present themselves to those who have risen to the requisite level of awareness.

This simple fact is the basis for most of the powers exercised by the initiates of the mystery schools in every land and age. To those whose mental horizons do not extend beyond the limits of physical matter, such powers are unthinkable, and anyone claiming to exercise them must therefore be shouted down as a liar or a fool; to those whose horizons reach a little further, to the limited but real vistas unfolded by outward religion, such powers can only come as a gift of some supernatural being, whether that being be a god or angel in the case of a person recognized as holy, or a devil in the case of a person considered unholy— or simply belonging to some other faith. To the initiate, by contrast, the powers of mind are both real and natural, the inevitable unfolding of evolutionary potential within the individual who has begun the great adventure of our level of the Path of Ascent, the awakening of individuality.

At the time when the materials in this course were first assembled, it was a little less difficult to discuss such things in a reasoned and reasonable manner, for the powers of mind, their awakening, and their deliberate cultivation were subjects of widespread interest in the popular culture of the time. The field of psychical research, as it was then called, had not yet been stigmatized by the devotees of a materialist science, and respected scientists engaged in its study. The word "psychism" was commonly used in those days for the entire field of study embracing the subtle powers of the mind, and will be used here; the word "mentalism," in turn, was used at that time as a term for the more active dimensions of psychism, and will be used as well. Though both terms have nearly vanished from the collective imagination of our own age, they carry less of a freight of misunderstanding and confusion than most of the possible synonyms in use today.

Under the heading of mentalism may be grouped all occult phenomena which have been described as mental influence, mind power, thought force, mental magic, suggestion, and so on, the distinguishing feature of which is the communication of influence from mind to mind. This phase of occult phenomena was well known to the general public when these lessons were first compiled, by reason of the great interest which was manifested in those years regarding the influence of the mind over physical states, and the resulting activities surrounding what is commonly termed "psychical research." Yet this power, and the knowledge thereof, is by no means a new thing. We find traces of it in the history of every one of the ancient peoples, as well as in the records of the nations of more modern times. The hierophants of ancient Egypt, Chaldea, and Greece were adepts in all of the various branches of mentalism and understood the underlying principles far better than do the majority of the teachers and writers upon the subjects today. It thus should come as no surprise that the same principles and practices may be traced in what remains of the legacy of the ancient Druids.

The following three triads outline the foundations of practical mentalism:

Triad I.

Three false sayings concerning mental influence: that it is nonexistent, that it is supernatural, and that it is mediated by physical matter.

Triad II.

Three true sayings concerning mental influence: that it is mediated by nwyfre, that it emanates from every mind, and that it influences every mind.

Triad III.

Three secret sayings concerning mental influence: that it functions by means of the polarity of sex, that it functions by means of the presence of mind in all things, and that it functions by means of the laws of nature.

Triad I.

Three false sayings concerning mental influence: that it is nonexistent, that it is supernatural, and that it is mediated by physical matter.

To understand mentalism, one must understand the nature of mental influence, or the transference of mental states from one mind to another. We hear much of telepathy and psychic phenomena these days; there are many books and magazines devoted to the subject, as well as scholarly and public conferences, and the teachings of the various metaphysical movements which have risen into prominence rarely fail to discuss these subjects.[21] Many are the theories advanced to account for the phenomena. First, we hear the old guard of materialism insisting in stentorian tones that mental influence does not happen because it cannot happen; that is to say, the theories to which these gentlemen give assent do

---

21. The early twentieth century was the heyday of American occultism, and there were hundreds if not thousands of secret societies and correspondence schools teaching such things at that time.

not leave room for mental influence, and therefore the abundant evidence for mental influence must be discarded because it conflicts with their theories. One may be forgiven wondering whether, by the same logic, these same gentlemen believe that the discovery of Copernicus that the Earth moves around the Sun ought to have been disregarded, since the theory of astronomy accepted by all in the great Polish astronomer's day made no provision for such a thing to happen.

Second, we hear many theories derived from religious teachings which seek to account for the phenomena of mental influence on supernatural grounds— the desirable forms being considered evidences of divine power, and the undesirable being regarded as arising from diabolical sources. Here the problems are, first, that no one has yet been able to provide a definition of the word "supernatural" that is more, in practice, than a confession of ignorance, and second, that what is considered desirable by the followers of one religion is as often as not considered undesirable by the followers of another, leading to reasonable doubt concerning which power is divine and which diabolical.

Third, we hear much of theories of "the ether waves" which carry "thought vibrations," both being likened to, and held as but higher forms of, the other vibrations of the ether, such as radio waves, light waves, and the like.[22] The steady expansion of the known range of ether waves, such as that accomplished by Roentgen the discoverer of X-rays, has however shown no trace of such a "higher form" that might communicate thought and other mental phenomena from mind to mind; nor have other material bases, such as have occasionally been proposed by theorists of the subject. Thus, in conclusion, none of these three approaches provides a helpful way to understand the phenomena of mentalism.

Triad II.

Three true sayings concerning mental influence: that it is mediated by nwyfre, that it emanates from every mind, and that it influences every mind.

The correct explanation is that age-old and world-old concept of a Life Force, which the Druid mysteries call by the name of nwyfre, the principles and pos-

---

22. Until Einstein's theory of relativity was generally accepted, physicists believed that a substance called "ether" provided the medium through which radio waves, light waves, and all other electromagnetic phenomena functioned.

sibilities of which you have explored since the beginning of your studies in the Dolmen Arch tradition.

You have learned in the first grade of your studies that three principles of manifestation pervade all of the Cosmos, and one of those principles is consciousness. It is worth your while to consider just what this means. All the space there is, or can be, is occupied by the mind principle of the Cosmos. Pervading all space there is a great cosmic ocean of consciousness, living, pulsating with life and energy, in the depths of which there lies the quietude of eternal calm and peace—on the surface of which are ripples, eddies, waves, currents and whirlpools—upon which and in which is manifested the fiercest tempests and the most absolute rest. In this great ocean of mind—in the principle of consciousness—occur all the manifestations of consciousness that are known on the lower planes of life—on the human plane—and on planes that extend far beyond our ability to conceive.

Those theorists of today who believe that thought is carried from mind to mind by way of the undulations of the ether, or by some other material means, have wandered nearly as far from the teachings of the mysteries as those who dismiss the mind as "a secretion of the brain"[23]—and in the same direction. The notion that mind is dependent on physical matter, common though it is at the present time, grasps the matter entirely from the wrong end, for as you have already learned, the first principle of manifestation—*calas* or substance—comes into being from nwyfre, the principle of consciousness which is also the One Life pervading all things. Thus mind does not depend on matter; matter depends on mind; and while every manifested existence in the whole of the Cosmos possesses substance, motion, and consciousness, not every substance is of the dense form we call matter, just as not every motion or consciousness is of the kind today's humanity perceives, or is capable of perceiving.

Mind requires substance in order to manifest itself, but it travels in its own medium, which is the universal nwyfre. Its waves are waves of mind—its currents are currents of mind—its vibrations are vibrations of mind. Activities in a center of consciousness—that is, a created being of any kind—are not confined to that particular focus of manifestation, but extend in all directions in rapidly widening circles, unless the sender deliberately concentrates his thought force in a special and particular direction, either by conscious intent, or else by reason

---

23. A claim made by scientific materialists at the time that these lessons were originally composed. The same claim, phrased in slightly less crude terms, is still made by scientific materialists today.

of intense desire. The force of any thought or feeling flows out in currents and waves, exerting more or less influence upon all minds with which it comes in contact.

The degree of influence depends upon the power with which it is projected, and the degree of harmony to the patterns of thought and feeling that are present or habitual in the receptive minds. Still, all minds in the Cosmos—that is to say, all things whatsoever, for every manifestation has some form of mental life, be it ever so small or ever so vast—are influenced, at least to a minute degree, by every thought, every feeling, and every perception of every being in the Cosmos. It has indeed been truly said that we live one life—or, more precisely, the One Life lives in us.

Triad III.

Three secret sayings concerning mental influence: that it functions by means of the polarity of sex, that it functions by means of the presence of mind in all things, and that it functions by means of the laws of nature.

One of the core practical secrets of mental influence lies in the fact that the mind is subject to the Law of Polarity, and the working of mind in many ways may best be understood in comparison with that form of polarity that human beings ordinarily call sex. Not mind alone, but all polar phenomena may be understood in this way—even the atoms, in their attractions and repulsions. In electricity and magnetism the polarity manifested corresponds closely to sex. On the mental plane, will is the equivalent of the masculine principle—that which projects outwards from itself. Desire is the equivalent of the feminine principle—that which draws inwards toward itself. Most of the activities of the mind result from the union of the two principles. Desire, the female principle of mind, arouses and attracts the will, the male principle, and draws it into action. Yet the action of will is the inciting cause of the activities of desire. The will can create only by its action upon the feminine principle—it cannot create by itself. On the other hand, desire cannot bring forth without union with the will.

This takes place within the individual. Both the feminine desire and the masculine will of a person, however, may also be incited into activity by the will or desire, as the case may be, of another person. The will of another person may incite and arouse the activities of one's desire, and render it so active that it will drag into action its own mate, the will of the person affected. And, in the same way, a strong desire in the mind of a person may act to arouse into activity the will of another, taking the latter away from its lawful mate—the desire of the person affected. In the same way, two wills (that of the person affected and that of the person affecting) may struggle for the control, mastery and possession of the desires of the first mentioned person. Likewise, there is often found the struggle between the feminine principle of desire in two persons, each wishing to maintain and exert influence over the will of one of the persons. In this statement is contained the secret of the mental influence of one person upon another. It is the secret underlying hypnotism, personal magnetism, psychic influence, and all the other forms of mental influence.

The feminine principle of mind acts always in the direction of exerting an attracting, drawing influence upon the will; and also in the direction of creating and conceiving ideas, mental images and other forms of mental creative activity. The masculine principle of mind always acts in the direction of inciting activity within the feminine principle of mind. The will is free and in theory may act without restraint from within, but in reality it never does act unless aroused by desire. It can "act as it pleases," but the "pleases" depends upon desire, the feminine principle.

The men and women of strong will, who dominate all around them, emanate strong currents charged with will which, coming in contact with the feminine principle in the minds of others, arouse the latter and cause the desires of those persons to be in accord with the will of the strong individual. The rulers and masters of humanity possess this power to a great degree, and then "work their will" upon others in this way. Their influence is felt far and near, and they make people do as they like by making them "want to" do a thing that way, or else by causing them to fear, which is but a negative form of desire. In the same way, men of strong desire may and do exert powerful influence over the minds and wills of others, and lead them their way.

The "magnetic" persons attract, allure, and seduce the wills of other people.[24] They are emotional, and capture the will of others, and at the same time produce a consequent reaction on the emotional natures of the others, by sympathetic vibration. The "electric" persons manifest the masculine principle and cause others to "want to" do as the person wishes. They are "motional" and not only arouse the desire in others, but also overawe and terrorize the will of

---

24. The terms "magnetic" and "electric" were common in the literature of early twentieth-century occultism. "Magnetism" was used to refer to the passive, desire pole of energy, while "electricity" referred to the active, will pole.

others. The men and women of greatest power are those who manifest both the masculine and the feminine principles and consequently affect others on the lines of both poles of their mentality. One moment they exert the power of will; the next the attracting, drawing, charming power of desire. If you will test all the phenomena of mentalism by this principle of sex polarity, you will see that it affords an explanation and a reason for them all.

This explains the influence of mind over mind, but what of the influence of mind over things? The answer to this question is very simple: there is mind in everything, ready to respond to the influence of other minds. With a Cosmos that is mental in its nature, with energy and substance; matter and motion; all receptive and responsive to mind—what cannot be accomplished by those who understand the laws of mentalism? With will as the great creative power in the Cosmos—what is not possible to one who understands the art of willing? With desire as the great creative energy, can we not see why desire can be understood, directed, and employed in our lives, careers and destinies?

These manifestations, and the force which produces them have been called "occult" because of the fact that they belong to the less understood phases of natural forces and phenomena. The word "occult" means: "secret or hidden from the eye or understanding; not seen or understood; mysterious, invisible, unknown, undetected." To many persons, occultism is considered to be concerned with supernatural forces, things, and manifestations. This is erroneous, for there is nothing supernatural—nothing outside of or over nature, of which we can ever have any knowledge. Every thing in the Cosmos is natural, and under natural laws. Awen is the only supernatural reality that there is or can be—and we can know nothing of its inner nature, for it is not a "thing" with attributes, qualities, or limitations, as we understand those terms. Everything in the Cosmos is natural—the unknown as well as the commonly known. Therefore, when we say "occult" we mean merely some natural thing, force, or manifestation, not commonly known or recognized by men. When a thing, force, or manifestation becomes commonly known, it ceases to be regarded as "occult." Electricity was once regarded as an "occult" force—but today it is commonly known and employed, although its real nature is still a mystery. To the trained and advanced occultist the so-called occult forces are just as familiar and natural as are the manifestations of force common to the knowledge of everyone. The occult forces are simply finer forces of nature which are not recognized, known, or understood by the average person of the race today. This must be thoroughly understood. There are no supernatural forces, things, or manifestations—all are natural, and under natural laws.

The following three triads introduce some of the basic concepts of that application of mentalism known as psychism, or the use of psychic powers:

Triad IV.

Three kinds of psychism: that of knowledge, that of power, and that of communion.

Triad V.

Three kinds of psychic knowledge: clairvoyance, psychometry, and telepathy.

Triad VI.

Three kinds of clairvoyance: of the past, of the present, and of the future.

Triad IV.

Three kinds of psychism: that of knowledge, that of power, and that of communion.

The traditional division of the phenomena of occult forces operative in the Cosmos, divides the same into three general classes, as follows:

1. that form of psychism that obtains knowledge, consisting of what are generally known as clairvoyance, psychometry, and telepathy, the distinguishing feature of which is the attainment of knowledge by some route other than the ordinary senses;
2. that form which obtains power, consisting of mentalism in all its aspects and applications;
3. that form which obtains communion with other intelligent minds in the Cosmos, or the arts of invocation and evocation—literally, the "calling in" (*in-vocare*) of beings greater than human, or the "calling forth" (*e-vocare*) of beings equal to or lesser than human. Thus mentalism is only one part

of that wider realm of theory and practice that is presently known by the name of psychism.

Each of these may be practiced by the initiate, and a variety of formulæ for practice of this kind have already been provided you in symbolic form. Some practices of mentalism that will be found useful on a day-to-day basis are included as an appendix to this lecture, and may be practiced safely by the initiate who has progressed this far in the training. Still, it has generally been considered wisest in the mystery schools to concentrate, in the training of students, on those disciplines that will ripen the potentials for psychism that are present in every human soul, and do so at a natural rather than a forced pace.

Many occultists have been led into mental imbalance of various kinds by practices that force open the psychic perceptions before the individual is ready to exercise them. For this reason, this course provides only theoretical knowledge of psychism, outside of the simple, practical methods of mentalism already mentioned. The daily practice of meditation and the Sphere of Protection with its additions will open your psychic potentials at a rate appropriate to you. Since, however, you have at this point been studying and practicing in the work of this system of mystery training for nearly two years at minimum, and possibly longer than this, it is entirely possible that some at least of your own natural capacities will already be awakening; this is the reason why a detailed account of the powers of mind is included at this point.

Triad V.

Three kinds of psychic knowledge: clairvoyance, psychometry, and telepathy.

The receptive forms of psychism, as distinct from the active forms that are comprised in the word "mentalism," all make use of the same principles we have already discussed in the first three triads of this lecture, but it will be helpful to explore them in more detail here. You learned early on in your studies that there are three principles of manifestation in the Cosmos, *calas* or substance, *gwyar* or motion, and *nwyfre* or consciousness. In each of these three principles, there are manifested correspondences which we may call "vibrations," "waves," "currents," and the like. On the plane of calas or substance, we have vibrations and waves of matter, which result in the various forms, shapes, and actions of material objects.

All these are caused by the principle of motion acting upon the principle of substance. Much that we call energy is but the appearance of fine degrees of substance energized by motion. The light-bearing ether itself is but a fine form of substance. There are also vibrations and waves of pure motion, which may be considered as independent of substance. There is a plane of pure motion, which is unimaginable except to minds which have been specially trained to grasp the subject. Likewise, there are vibrations, waves, and currents in nwyfre, the principle of consciousness, produced by the action of motion upon that principle. It is to this plane that the vibrations, waves, and currents concerned with psychism properly belong.

While it would not be useful at this point to go into the matter in great detail, your attention to one fact should serve to give you a plain mental picture of the phenomenon, into which you can fill the details as you proceed in the study and experimental work along these lines. This general statement is as follows: The Cosmos, as you have already learned, may be understood as a vast mind, in which thoughts become things, taking on substantial form as they are thought into being. With a Cosmos mental in nature, there must be a circulation of consciousness, or currents of thought, just as there is a circulation of water by the currents of the ocean; or as there is a circulation of air by reason of the winds; or as there is a circulation of electricity, and all other forms of what we call energy. Consciousness is a principle, just as are substance and motion, and what is true of one principle is in some sense true of the other two, according to the law of analogy. Therefore, we can speak of vibrations, waves, and currents of consciousness, just as truly as there are corresponding manifestations on the material plane.

In clairvoyance, psychometry, and telepathy, we have several expressions of these mental waves and currents. In clairvoyance, the waves and currents bring the mind knowledge about events that have happened, are happening, or will happen in some other place or time, to which the ordinary, physical senses cannot penetrate. In psychometry, impressions left by the mental waves and currents in the mental dimension of some physical object may be read by the sensitive mind. In telepathy, the action of one mind is immediately made apparent to another.

But how does the mind of the person receive and register the impressions received through these three forms of psychism? No mind can receive impressions without the medium of some form of organ, though that organ may or may not be material in nature. This rule holds true in the case of the phenomena which we are now considering. Organs for the perception of psychic stimuli do exist, and are called the organs of astral sensation. You have already learned of the existence of the enaid or body of nwyfre; this body is endowed with counterparts of the physical senses, which it may use in sensing the objects and impressions of the astral plane.

The average person has not developed the capacities of the enaid sufficiently well to use them consciously, and merely picks up the occasional psychic sensation. Development of these senses, however, is possible to those who have sufficient interest and patience to undertake the task. Here and there are found persons whose astral senses manifest their existence in an unusual degree. These persons become very sensitive to the impressions of the astral plane, and although, as a rule, they are untrained and do not comprehend the nature of the phenomena, still they afford conclusive proof of the existence of the faculties in question.

I shall not attempt to "prove" the existence of psychic phenomena in this lecture. Evidence sufficient to convince any unprejudiced person may be found in many books on the subject, notably the reports of the English Society for Psychical Research. Moreover many persons have experienced these facts in their own lives.

Triad VI.

Three kinds of clairvoyance: of the past, of the present, and of the future.

The power generally called clairvoyance may be defined as a faculty or power by which the clairvoyant is able to see mentally things concealed from physical sight. With the exception of cases in which a person travels in a detached portion of his enaid—the so-called "astral body"—to some other place, and there witnesses the events actually occurring there, clairvoyance results from one general cause, and in the same general way. Let us suppose an event occurring at a distant place. In the manifestation of that event there occurs a constant, regular, and continuous series of mental states on the part of all things affected by the event, not only on the part of all those things conventional thought describes as living things, but in those things generally considered inanimate.

A central teaching of the mysteries is the existence of mind and consciousness in so-called inanimate objects, even down to the level of individual atoms, and in nwyfre itself, for everything in the Cosmos has some degree of consciousness. This being so, it follows that the consciousness in every created thing must follow the natural law, and transmit waves or currents of consciousness, which radiate upon the astral plane where they may be sensed by those astral organs attuned to receive them. Just as radio waves may be received only by instruments tuned to the proper frequency, so may these currents be received only by those who are in tune with them.

One whose astral senses are sufficiently sensitive and attuned may receive and register these currents, just as the physical eye registers light waves, or the ear registers sound waves. The astral body need not travel to the scene of the event, for the astral senses can perceive the currents set in motion by events at a great distance. Those who may doubt the reasonableness of sensing things and events over thousands of miles, may wish to consider the fact that by the unaided human eye impressions are received from distant stars, across distances so vast that it requires centuries for the light waves to travel from their source to the watching eye. It is no more wonderful that a skilled clairvoyant may perceive events going on at several hundred miles of distance—as the famous Swedenborg did on more than one occasion[25]—than it is that a skilled astronomer may perceive the seasonal changes on the planet Mars.

Clairvoyance of past events, which also happens upon occasion, has a slightly different explanation. Nwyfre, the substance of consciousness, receives impressions from the mental states undergone by everything in the Cosmos, and these leave their records and impressions, just as the events of the experience of a man leave records and impressions in his brain. It is under some circumstances possible for a mind naturally suited to such experiences, or powerfully affected by some particular circumstance, to experience the recorded impressions left behind by some event in the past. Some of those phenomena commonly described as "ghosts" or "hauntings" are in fact a manifestation of this effect. Some event perceived by one or more minds with great intensity leaves impressions of unusual strength, which are then perceived by another person, perhaps hundreds of years in the future. The suicide is again seen to leap from the window, the adulterous lovers to meet in the garden; they and all who knew them are dead and gone, but the impressions remain, and are mistaken for spirits.

---

25. Emmanuel Swedenborg, the Swedish clairvoyant and mystical author, was well known for having described accurately a fire in Stockholm, while it was happening, while with friends hundreds of miles away.

Clairvoyance of the future, strictly speaking, is a misnomer, for the future itself does not yet exist to be observed. Nwyfre itself, even when it is understood as Cosmic Mind, cannot be said to know before the manifestation—for the knowing is the manifestation. Yet the phenomena which are called clairvoyance of the future do exist. Occasionally individuals seem able to foretell with more or less accuracy, the events which afterward come true at least partially. The secret to such glimpses of the future consists in the fact that since the Law of Causation is always operative, there must always be in existence the "shadows cast by approaching events"—that is to say, active causes moving to bring about certain effects. Among these active causes, desires and mental imagery in the minds of living human beings play an important part.

The clairvoyant, perceiving the evidences of these active causes in the astral, is often able to make very good guesses or intuitive conjectures of the events which will follow, in the same way that one may predict something that will happen tomorrow, from something that is happening today. There is no absolute certainty about the prediction, in either case, for there may be other causes which will play their part at the time of action, and thus render the prediction false. Clairvoyance of the future perceives probable effects of existent causes and no more.

Beyond the functions of mentalism already discussed—the influence of mind on circumstances and the subtle perceptions of psychism—are a set of higher functions, discussed in theoretical terms in an earlier grade. The following three triads explain the higher reaches of mentalism as a means of mental alchemy, or the transformation of personality through the influence of individuality.

Triad VII.

Three stages of the Law of Vibration in mentalism: the recognition of rhythm, the attainment of central poise, and the application of emotional energy.

Triad VIII.

Three stages of the Law of Circularity in mentalism: the recognition of circularity, the direction of will, and the transition from the circle to the spiral.

Triad IX.

Three stages of the Law of Balance in mentalism: the recognition of balance, the deliberate control of the opposites, and the awakening of the individuality.

Triad VII.

Three stages of the Law of Vibration in mentalism: the recognition of rhythm, the attainment of central poise, and the application of emotional energy.

In the teaching previously offered in this course you have encountered some discussion of the universality of the Seven Cosmic or Creative Principles. Each of these laws has its influence on the art of mentalism, and more particularly on that higher dimension of mentalism that we term mental alchemy. In the inner world as in the outer world, it is essential to master and apply these laws, instead of assuming a passive attitude toward them. Instead of meekly bowing and yielding to these laws, the initiate either neutralizes their effects when these work to his disadvantage, or else applies the laws to his own advantage. Instead of allowing himself to be overwhelmed by the laws, as by a great wave, he rises on the crest of the wave and rides to safety on it. The laws may be harnessed and made to work for the individual, instead of being allowed to overwhelm and master him.

The three Laws of Vibration, Circularity, and Balance are of special importance in this context, and particularly so in the practice of mentalism and other expressions of the higher power of the mind. The principle of resolving or neutralizing the opposites, which has been discussed in numerous forms in these lessons, is the underlying principle governing the mastery of these three laws. Vibration, after all, is a movement to and fro between two poles. Circularity is a movement imparted by the polarity of centre and circumference. In Balance is shown the presence of the two poles or opposites, the weights of each tending to maintain the balance or compensation. Poise, that great attainment, is accomplished by preserving the right relation between the poles or opposites. So you may see that in the mastery of the opposites the initiate acquires the basis for the mastery of Vibration, Circularity, and Balance. The principle of Polarity underlies everything.

On the plane of emotion and feeling the Law of Vibration is constantly in evidence. We find that we swing like a pendulum between the extremes or poles of our feelings or emotions. Today we are sad—tomorrow we are joyful; today we are gloomy—tomorrow we are bright and hopeful; today we are slothful—tomorrow we are active and energetic. A study of our emotions and feelings will reveal to us the fact that these mental states are like the ocean and have their tides, in and out, high and low, flood and ebb. We find action and reaction ever evident in our emotional life.

Moreover we find that when we indulge in an extreme degree of any emotion or feeling we have a tendency to fly to the opposite pole of that feeling or emotion. The law of reaction follows the action. Either we are unable to attain what it is that we desire, and feel a revulsion occasioned by the sense of powerlessness, or else we attain it, and experience a satiety resulting from that attainment and the discovery that it was not what we had expected of it. We need not point to special examples of this, for the experience of everyone who reads these words will supply the necessary examples.

Love, hate, or anger, if carried to an extreme point, have a tendency to fly back to the opposite pole with a startling rapidity. Likewise, extreme elation is very apt to bound back to its opposite and cause us to experience extreme depression. In the same way, many know that fear and courage have a tendency to react into each other, if either be carried to an extreme. Many a man manifesting extreme courage will find himself swung suddenly back to a state of dire fear. In the same way, and from the same law, many have found themselves in a state of extreme fear, and then when they could proceed no further they would experience a sudden bound of desperation carrying them to a state of extreme recklessness and daring. The experiences of soldiers have shown the bravest men suddenly possessed of a pitiful fear—the reaction from the courage; and, likewise, we see the manifestation of occasional bursts and spurts of reckless daring and startling bravery from notorious cowards.

Persons who dwell principally on the plane of the emotions thus live in a state of alternate heaven and hell. Now enjoying to the fullest the upward swing, they revel in the ecstasies of happiness. Then comes the backward swing which plunges them into depression, melancholy, remorse, regret, or a feeling of impotence and uselessness. The more emotional the person, the higher and lower in the scale of feeling does he travel. Those who are willing to pay the price of these extremes—the toll of feeling—are of course free to do so. Yet the individual who begins to experience the awakening of individuality grows impatient and restless under the wild swings of his emotive nature, and takes steps to master and direct that part of his being. Instead of swinging backward and forward between the poles of emotion and feeling, he seeks and acquires the balance and poise of the focused will.

The first step in the direction of neutralizing rhythm lies in the realization of the existence of rhythm itself. When one comes to realize that the hot fit is certain to be followed by the cold—the high by the low—the exaltation by the depression—the courage by the fear—the activity by the slothfulness and vice versa, then does he cease to identify himself so closely with either of the poles, and, on the contrary, grows to regard them as mere natural incidents of his mental nature. He values them at their true worth, and refuses to allow his will to become involved in his emotion and feeling. He knows that his depression will be followed by a stage of reaction, and so he refuses to take his depression seriously. Likewise, knowing the truth, he refuses to allow his exaltation to excite him unduly. In short, he comes to find a place of poise in the midst of the opposites, and from that position he stands aside, as it were, and watches calmly the swing of his feelings and emotions between their two poles. He detaches himself from the swing of the rhythmic emotions, and stands above them, rising to the threshold of the plane of individuality.

The initiate may acquire this immunity from the effect of emotional vibration by using the tools of practical mentalism or magic when the swings of his emotional life become disruptive. With practice he will acquire a mental "knack" of rising above the plane of emotional turmoil, and calmly watching and observing the storm of emotion, without being influenced by it. It is like one sailing in a balloon above the storm clouds which are thundering beneath him. This immunity to the vibratory rhythm of emotion does not come to the student all at once. It is a matter of time, practice, and growth. It is aided by the steady practice of refusing to take the emotional swing too seriously. Refuse to admit it as being yourself. See and think of it always as something connected with your inner life but not in any real sense identical to you yourself. Stand aside and watch the play of your emotional nature, and before long you will be able to laugh at its antics. You will see how essentially unreal it is. Once even partially freed from bondage to emotion, you will never willingly return to the old thralldom.

This does not mean that you should ignore or despise your emotional nature. On the contrary, you will find it useful to remain attentive to it, for the energies aroused by the emotions are strongly motivating, and will enable you to accomplish much if they are properly applied. Remember always, however, never to allow yourself to become enmeshed in the emotional storms. Handle the emotions as a master musician does an instrument; never yield yourself up to your emotions as their instrument, any more than you would yield yourself up to the power and influence of some entity outside of yourself.

You have a part to play in the world—a part which is as arbitrary and formal as that assumed by an actor. In order to play it well, you will find it necessary to put feeling and emotion into it, just as the actor puts these into his part. But the actor always remains aware that he is merely acting, and his emotional activity is the result of previous thought and trained art. Art in the management of the emotion consists in selecting the emotional activity adapted to the accomplishment of the task or work on hand, and redirecting or rising above all other emotions.

Instead of being a blind tool and instrument of the emotional nature, you should use the latter deliberately, selecting that which is desirable and helpful, and restraining the rest. Watch always for the reaction and return swing of the rhythm of emotional vibration. Never attempt to suppress or deny the unwelcome side of the rhythm of the emotions. When your emotional life swings back from a desirable emotion, rise above your feelings to the point of inner poise, and from that vantage view the backward swing and its emotional energies with equanimity.

Triad VIII.

Three stages of the Law of Circularity in mentalism: the recognition of circularity, the direction of will, and the transition from the circle to the spiral.

The vibratory swing of the pendulum, in emotional life as in the physical world, is always at right angles to its central line of suspension—always to-and-fro, backward and forward, from a fixed center of gravity which is directly under its point of suspension. A similar law is evident in the movements of a body revolving in a circle. In its orbit is manifest the power of the central point which holds the body from flying off into space, and also the power which causes the body to continue in cyclic revolution instead of falling toward the center. In fact, the cyclic motion is merely another form of vibration and is dependent on the latter, just as vibration itself is dependent on the existence of the Law of Polarity.

All active movement expresses itself in rhythmic motion, between its two poles or opposites. But this rhythmic motion is rarely in a straight line, as in the case of the pendulum. In fact, the motion of large bodies, and also of history and other great trends, is generally in a circle. This results from the attraction and repulsion of objects and forces outside of the swinging thing, which tends to draw it out of its linear backward and forward swing, and which gradually converts the straight line of the swing into a circle. Consequently, on all sides, and in all things we find the Law of Circularity in full operation.

It is evident to all who will examine the subject that the mental life of the average person is merely the constant traveling around and around in a recurring circle—the circle gradually widening from childhood to the prime of life, and then narrowing from that time to old age and death. The average person is held firmly bound by this Law of Circularity, and while he finds the circle widening or narrowing as the case may be, he never passes beyond the circumference of his circle. It is always a constant swing around the same old central point—a process similar to the travel of the squirrel in the treadmill of his cage—a constant traveling which results in his getting nowhere.

It is only when the individual is able to convert the circle into the spiral, that he is able to experience change. All spiritual transformation is accomplished in this way. Many attain the spiral movement "by accident," as it were, without understanding that this is what they are doing. They find that by the application of will, with or without the use of formal techniques such as those embodied in practical mentalism or magic, they are able to advance the central point of the circle, and so enter into motion. Initiates learn to consciously advance the central point of their lives, and thus do intelligently what the average person does to a lesser degree under the unconscious influence of circumstances.

It is most difficult to make the formula regarding this form of mental alchemy plain to the uninitiated, for it is so bound up with the conscious use of the will that it cannot be understood except by those who have begun to feel the first stirrings of individuality, in the form of that consciousness of will that makes it possible to will to will—to stand aside from the pressures of the outward life and make a relatively free choice to do or not do. The unawakened person under most circumstances merely desires to advance. This desire exerts more or less influence on the will, and can under some circumstances accomplish positive change. When, however, a person has learned to will to will, he is able to accomplish far more than he could by the mere power of ordinary desire.

By his conscious will he is able to project himself a step at a time in advance in the cosmic scale, and thus establish a new center of circular motion.

At first this happens occasionally, at times of great stress or at the peak of a cycle of inner work. As it is repeated, however, the initiate establishes a habit of spiral motion which replaces the old circular movement. By cultivating the habit of constantly willing an advance at each circle, he will find that though his life still maintains its circular movement, at each return to a given point will he advance a little higher in scale and plane. Just as a traveler ascending a mountain must needs go round and round, each time a little nearer the peak, so will the traveler along the Path of Attainment find that at each circling the old paths will be below him.

Triad IX.

Three stages of the Law of Balance in mentalism: the recognition of balance, the deliberate control of the opposites, and the awakening of the individuality.

The distinguishing mark of the advanced initiate, who is well along the path of the awakening of individuality, is poise or balance. This is always a mark of power, just as its opposite is always a mark of weakness. The old mystery teachings were wont to illustrate the balanced life of the initiate by the figure of one crossing a deep chasm on a narrow bridge. They would picture the initiate traversing the narrow bridge of life, balancing himself by the aid of the opposites. Now shifting the weight on one side, and now on the other, he is able to walk the Path in safety. Having the confidence of the initiate he trusts the bridge beneath his feet and the opposites that pull him one way or the other.

The unawakened person attempting the crossing would be pulled over by the pull of one emotion or another, and would be dashed to ruin. But the initiate walks in confidence and safety, because of his mastery of the art of Balance. Pitting one emotion against another he neutralizes the one which threatens to pull him down. By mental alchemy, he is able to transmit a dangerous pull into a part of his balancing process. His axiom is "action and reaction are equal," and this principle he applies in all the emergencies and crises of life. He always manages to have a push or a pull to counteract a push or a pull in a different direction, and thus poise is maintained.

Poise may be attained directly by the awakening of individuality, and the recognition of the unity of the self and the Cosmos. It may also be attained indirectly, by those still laboring to realize the awakening of individuality, by repeated meditation on the real nature of the self—that the personality with its cares and concerns, its emotions and relationships, is merely a projection of the individuality down into the planes of form and manifestation. As this is realized, and the relative unimportance of the personality and its emotions grasped, poise comes naturally.

Balance results from mastery. Mastery results from knowledge and practice. You have been told the way to mastery. Make it your own. Realize what you are. Practice the methods that you have been taught. Then, and then only, will you enter into that consciousness of peace, poise and power, which comes to those who have acquired balance. It is said in an ancient teaching of the mysteries: "In the midst of life shalt thou indeed find poise and power. In the heart of the storm shalt thou find peace. In the center of the Cosmos shalt thou find thyself. He who finds the center of himself, finds the center of the Cosmos. For, in the final analysis, they are ONE!"

ADDENDUM TO DRUID PHILOSOPHY: PRACTICAL MENTALISM

THE FOLLOWING PAPER, as mentioned in the introductory letter to this lesson packet, covers a set of practical methods that were once central to the technical or operative side of the Dolmen Arch system. In the early twentieth century, effective methods of ceremonial magic were rarely to be met with outside the closed doors of magical lodges and occult societies, and many schools of the mysteries that offered their teachings to the public at large instead made use of the simpler art of mentalism—the use of affirmations, visualizations, and similar mental tools to cause change in the self and the Cosmos.

While the methods of ritual working you have already learned are generally more effective than those of mentalism, there is still a place for the latter, partly because they were at one point central to the practical side of the tradition and so deserve to be remembered, partly because they are easier to use in some situations than the formal methods of enchantment. Initiates of the Dolmen Arch are not required or expected to master them, but some familiarity with the methods of mentalism may be found useful, and some initiates may choose to specialize in it. With this in mind, we proceed to the practical art of mentalism.

In the teachings you have already studied, you have learned the fundamental principle of mentalism in all of its forms, which is the fact that the Cosmos itself may be understood as one universal mind. There is mind in everything, and everything is in mind. Consequently, just as thoughts become things in the

Cosmic Mind, so is it possible for a strongly concentrated and focused mind to shape things and conditions on the three planes of manifestation.

Just as the Cosmic Will manifests the cosmic activities and forms, so may the individual will materialize activities and forms on its own plane. The difference between the Cosmic Will and the individual will is in the final analysis a difference in degree, not of kind. All will from the Cosmic Will to the feeblest individual will is identical in nature, although widely differing in degrees of power. In fact, as you have already learned, individual wills are but concentrated centers in the great Cosmic Will, varying greatly in power and manifestation. Thus it follows logically that the same laws and principles are applicable in all manifestations of will, from the highest to the lowest.

The triads presented in the lecture on Druid philosophy you have already studied cover the basic principles of mentalism. In this appendix you are provided with the practical formulae for the demonstration and manifestation of these principles. Each of the formulae here presented could be, and indeed has been, enlarged upon in whole books; but the principles you have learnt already, combined with your own experience and such experiments as you may choose to perform, will readily teach you everything you could learn from many volumes of this kind.

Formula for Positivity

It is a fundamental principle of mentalism that the positive mind always shapes and directs the negative or receptive mind—the negative is always subordinate to the positive. Everything has its keynote of positivity, and that keynote depends upon the strength of will. When one has grasped the nature of will—when he has learned to will to will—he can at any moment choose to be intensely positive to all around him—not only persons but also environment and conditions.

This positivity is, of course, dependent upon the capacity for will that has been developed by the individual. The degree of will that can be manifested by the individual depends entirely upon his degree of orientation toward the Cosmic Will itself. The greater the realization of one's own relation to the Cosmic Will, the greater is his capacity for manifesting will. Consequently all efforts toward developing positivity must be based upon the fundamental realization of the personality's dependence on the individuality, and the individuality's dependence on Awen.

The practical formula for the manifestation of the will's power consists simply in the development of the realization of individuality—of the fact that the individual person is a center of force and will within the great Cosmic Will. The higher the degree and fullness of this realization, the higher degree of positivity will the individual possess. Meditate on this truth until you have grasped it fully in your mind: The will power of the individual person is not something created by him, but is an expression of the power of the Cosmic Will in which he lives and moves and has his being. The personality is a focal point of will, a channel through which the individuality may act. The individuality, in turn, is itself a focal point of will, a channel through which the Cosmic Will may act. In these few words are contained the whole secret of mentalism.

Strengthening the Enaid

The initiate will find it useful to charge his aura, the outermost sphere of the enaid or body of nwyfre, with the energy of positive will, to serve as a protective armor shielding him from adverse influences from outside, and also to amplify the effect of his mind power when it is necessary or desirable to make use of it. The resulting atmosphere of will is a reality—it is a pattern in the ocean of nwyfre with which all the Cosmos is filled, and radiates outward from the aura to influence the regions of that ocean close to the initiate.

The charging of the aura is brought about by an act of will, assisted by the visual imagination. The initiate wishing to do this should first clear and concentrate his mind. Then he should visualize (that is, imagine or see in the mind's eye) the nwyfre in his immediate vicinity becoming charged with the positive power of will. It will aid him to think of himself as surrounded for a distance of about three feet with an egg-shaped aura or atmosphere of golden light, radiating from him and vibrating with an intense energy. As a matter of occult truth, this aura exists once formed, although the ordinary senses cannot perceive it.

The practice of the Sphere of Protection ceremony has the effect of charging the enaid in this way, but it is sometimes of value to perform the practice just described in addition to your daily Sphere of Protection practice. For example, should you be required to spend time in a place, the mental vibrations of which are unwholesome, regular practice of this exercise just before entering into that place will be found helpful in maintaining health and mental positivity; in the same way, should you find yourself in a situation in which great positivity and strength of will are required, this exercise will be of use in achieving and retaining that state. The more clearly you can visualize, or imagine, the existence of this aura or atmosphere, the greater will be your degree of positive personal atmosphere.

The initiate who has carefully attended to the lessons already studied will have learned long since that the imagination is not an unreal, fanciful thing—it is a mental activity of wonderful occult power. Using it in the way just outlined, the initiate will soon discover that he has acquired a new positive personal atmosphere, and that those with whom he comes in contact will feel something distinctive about him, and will tend to become receptive to him, unless they, too, understand the principles involved. As time passes, and practice renders him more perfect, the initiate will move about among ordinary people just as a highly charged magnet or electric wire. It is difficult to describe this, but those who will practice to acquire it will soon become conscious of their newly found strength.

In order to focus the effect more fully, the initiate may hold in his mind the following words while visualizing the egg-shaped aura of golden light: "I am a center of positive will."

Personal Positivity

The Neophyte may occasionally encounter other persons who have had training in mentalism, and attempt to use it to influence his thoughts and actions. Careful attention to his own mental state will alert him to this effect, for a sense of passivity and receptiveness to ordinarily unwelcome ideals and feelings will be perceived; alternately, a quality of mind that might best be described as "murky excitement" may be noted, or a certain peculiar sense of tiredness and chill centered on the back of the neck. Once any of these states are experienced they will not readily be forgotten.

In such cases the initiate should at once determine mentally that the persons in question shall not invultuate him—this is the occult term used in such cases, and means the overriding of one will by another. This is accomplished by at once visualizing the golden egg-shaped aura, radiating force in all directions, and holding the following words in his mind: "The Cosmic Will comes into manifestation through me." While doing this the initiate should concentrate on his own will and consciousness, seeing himself as a focal center of will, and having the Cosmic Will flowing through him. He will soon find that he will rise in the scale of positivity, and the other will be unable to override his will.

If he finds himself oppressed by a sense of negativity while mingling with a crowd, he should assert his individuality in the same way. The greater the realization of one's self as a focal center of will, the greater the degree of positivity will be manifested.

Visualization

Visualization is one of the most important of all the processes used by initiates of the mysteries to formulate patterns that will then manifest on each of the planes of being. Visualization consists in forming and holding a mental image of things and conditions as you wish them to be. The mental image tends to create for itself an objective form and existence—it is the pattern around which mental, astral, and material conditions tend to group themselves. It is thus the seed-form of the thing you wish to bring into being.

The prime factor in visualization is to endeavor to create as clear as possible a mental image of the thing or condition you desire, as if it were actually existent at that moment. Around your visualized ideals, do the material realities form and crystallize.

Affirmation

It is important in any of the practices of mentalism to be able to formulate precisely what you desire in exact words, as well as in exact images. An affirmation is a positive assertion of the existence of the conditions which you wish to bring about. Affirmations aid visualization to a great degree, and additionally have a power of their own. There is an occult power in the spoken word, for it combines the vibrations of sound on the material plane with the vibrations of mind on the mental plane; those who cultivate the gift of astral vision report that the spoken word also sets astral patterns in motion.

Affirmations should always be phrased in the present tense. Do not say to yourself, "Such and such a thing will take place by and by," but boldly assert "Such and such a thing exists or happens now, at this moment." This is because an affirmation in the future tense will put the thing desired forever in the future, never in the present! Make your affirmations earnestly and positively—avoid all half-hearted phrases, for they result in half-hearted results. Also, avoid negative phrasing—"Such and such a thing does not happen" concentrates your intention on the thing you do not desire, which is not helpful at all. Make your affirmations always in positive words—if you wish to remove some condition from your life, determine the opposite of that condition, and affirm that in positive terms.

In making your affirmations, do not use a tone of entreaty, or of asking a favor—speak in a tone of confidence and authority. Never, though, speak your affirmations aloud in the presence of other people. They have the best effect when made in a state of meditation and concentration. Use them in connection with visualization, and you will find that they will tend to energize and vitalize your mental images.

Mental Vibration

In all forms of mentalism there is in evidence the phenomenon of mental vibration. Vibration is not confined to the gross material substance of the universe, but is equally in evidence in the nwyfre with which all space is filled. When anyone thinks, feels, or wills, there is manifest vibration just as truly as in the vibration of the atom or the tuning fork. Each kind of thought, feeling or emotion has its own rate of vibration, or keynote.

When a certain rate of mental vibration is manifested it tends to reproduce similar vibrations, and consequent similar mental states in the minds of those in proximity. Just as a tuning fork will cause similar vibrations in the objects in the room, so will a mind sending forth vibrations tend to reproduce those vibrations in other minds in its vicinity, or under certain circumstances, at long distances.

Thus it follows that if an individual will carry in his mind a positive, persistent idea, backed up with an application of his will, he will be able to impress that idea upon other people and beings, and also on the surrounding space, or rather the nwyfre filling that space. He will be aided in this by the practice of affirmation and visualization, for both of these practices tend to send forth mental vibrations of a high degree of strength and power.

Thought Waves and Currents

There are waves and currents in the great ocean of nwyfre, just as there are waves and currents in the ocean or in the air. Thoughts, feelings and emotions manifested by an individual will tend to create waves or currents in nwyfre, which will flow out in all directions influencing and affecting others who are close by, particularly if those others happen to maintain a degree of mental vibration corresponding to that of the traveling wave or current. Everyone sends forth these thought waves or currents, usually unconsciously and without direct intention, and consequently with comparatively slight effect. Those who understand the laws of mentalism are able to consciously direct, concentrate and focus these waves and currents in accordance with their will, and consequently their thought waves and currents create a much greater effect.

Practical Techniques

Anyone may obtain some degree of success by practicing the techniques given in this lecture, but in order to obtain any marked degree of success with them, it is necessary to have first developed the will through magical practice. The will is the motive power behind all forms of mentalism. It thus follows that one who has awakened his individuality to at least some extent will be able to bring to bear the very highest degree of power in the phenomena of mentalism. Since the previous lessons of this study course will have provided the necessary preparation, in the form of development of the will and at least the first steps toward the awakening of individuality, we may therefore proceed to a consideration of practical methods. These are here expressed in as few words as possible. The student must read every word carefully so that he will achieve a full understanding of the techniques thus described.

Concentration

The art of concentration is essential to every phase of mentalism. The word "concentration" literally means "bringing to a center," and mental concentration may thus be defined usefully as the art of bringing the will into focus by means of attention. Concentration may be developed by practice. Learn to shut out distracting thoughts and ideas for a few moments, holding the mind "one-pointed" upon whatever thing or idea is before you. Next, after an interval, proceed to concentrate upon something else. After you have worked for a certain time at subduing the wandering tendencies of the mind, you will find that you have started to acquire a new power of mind which will enable you to direct and apply a focalized mental power upon whatever idea or thing toward which you may direct it.

We could fill page after page with detailed exercises in concentration, and there are a great many books full of such exercises, but after reading them you would find that the essence of the whole thing consists in directing the attention upon anything, and holding it there. This ability is attained only by practice, and the practice may be had by fixing and holding the attention upon anything, for a few moments at a time, until you grow more and more proficient by practice. Remember, concentration does not mean "staring" at a thing—it consists of fixing and holding the mind, not the eyes. Begin practicing, and you will soon acquire the knack. It is altogether a matter of the use of the Attention, by means of the Will. All the rest is mere detail and "trimmings."

Many of the exercises you have already learned and practiced, as you will doubtless already have recognized, have this effect. In going beyond these practices, it will do you far more good to invent methods for yourself, than to blindly follow some lesson mapped out by others. Use your own mind, and you will gain thereby.

Imagination

The key to practical mentalism may be readily described as the union, in a mind capable of concentrating, of thought, imagination and will. While to the beginner the subject of mentalism may seem a very complicated one, the initiate knows it to be of remarkable simplicity. Mentalism, under whatever name or form it may masquerade, may be found to consist, at the last analysis, of simply *creating strong, clear mental images to represent clearly understood ideas, and projecting the images into the outer world by means of the concentrated will.*

Read over the above italicized words several times, and fix them firmly in your mind. You will find that all the countless books and articles on the subject may be boiled down to the principle stated above. The rest is mere detail. Whatever the circumstances or the particular formulation of the practice may be, the principle is ever the same, i.e., the projection into the Cosmos of the mental image that represents a desired conception, and the materializing of that picture by the operation of the same laws by which every other thing in the Cosmos comes into being.

In ancient times, teachers of many mystery schools used, as a material object-lesson to their pupils, a simple contrivance which has since been developed in more complex form as the "magic lantern." The teachers would take a design or picture which was painted on glass or another clear substance, and pass it in front of a concentrated light—the image being reproduced on a large scale on a plane surface, at a greater or lesser distance.

The teachers would explain to the students that the concentrated light represented the focused will; the glass containing the picture represented the mental image held in the mind; the plane surface represented the world of manifestation. The pupils of the ancient teachers were bidden to fix this metaphor firmly in their minds, and to recall it always when practicing or manifesting any of the phenomena of mentalism, because it provides a clear mental image by which the phenomena of mentalism themselves may readily be understood.

With this image in mind, we see that the power and strength of the projection depends utterly upon the strength and focused force of the light in the lantern. If the light be weak, dim, or flickering, the reflection will be likewise, and if the rays of the light be not properly focused and concentrated, the power of the light will not be properly directed. These same principles may be applied to any process of mentalism, for the strength and concentration of the will is as essential to mentalism as the strength and concentration of light is to the projection of images.

Likewise, if the slide containing the picture be poorly and faintly drawn, the reflection will also be faulty. Indeed, the fault will be more apparent, for it will be magnified to a degree depending on the distance it is projected. Therefore, cultivate the art of imagination, and endeavor to train your mind to form and hold plain, clear pictures of things and conditions, so that you may do this with anything that you wish to bring into being. Upon this one thing depends much of the efficacy and success of the processes of mentalism. If you cannot fill in the details of your mental picture at first, at least draw firm, strong general outlines, and as you proceed with the work you will be able to add the details.

Descending the Planes

The Cosmos, by its very nature, tends to bring down into the densest matter what begins on the most abstract and rarefied plane of mind. The material Cosmos itself is a materialization of the patterns in nwyfre. By the principle of correspondence, the same thing may be known to be true on all the planes of the Cosmos. Everything that is, first existed as an abstract conception, either in the mind of the Cosmos, or in the mind of some conscious being in the Cosmos, and then became an image in consciousness either in the Cosmic Mind or that of a being in the Cosmos. There is always a mental pattern and an astral image behind and in every material form, shape or condition. Once this principle is clearly understood, many of the secrets of mentalism become understandable.

When this has been fully understood, the student learns to avoid making and concentrating upon mental images of the things which he does not wish to bring about, on the one hand; and to make and concentrate upon mental images of the things which he does wish to materialize, on the other hand. When he realizes that mental ideas expressed in clear imagery tend to materialize whenever conditions on the astral and physical planes permit, then he has grasped an important occult truth, and may direct his efforts accordingly. We urge the student to fix this idea firmly in his mind, for until he realizes that the mental, astral, and physical planes are but stages of the one process, he has not grasped the working principle of mentalism. When this fact is grasped, then the rest is merely a matter of practice, development, and application.

Affirmation and Visualization

The careful student doubtless will have recognized by this time that the process of affirmation is simply an aid to mental imaging. When affirmations are used, a mental image is created, consciously or subconsciously, and consequently the intention thus expressed is given an additional urge to materialization. Do not undervalue affirmations—they are powerful factors in mentalism, in the direction of strengthening and vitalizing mental images.

General Applications

Most of the literature on the subject of mentalism proceeds, after covering the above principles to one extent or another, to enter into a detailed description of the various forms of the application of mentalism. There is, however, nothing gained by going on at length, other than the dubious goals of money-making and humoring the popular taste and demand. It would be easy to fill several volumes with detailed description of various forms of application—but to what purpose? The perceptive student would soon discover that what had been done was simply to build various structures around the one vital and underlying principle of mental imaging and projection. It is of more value to encourage students to think and work for themselves, and not be mere blind followers of any teacher or tradition. Mentalism cannot be given or taken in sugar-coated capsules, one before each meal, like quack medicines. It must be thought out, and worked out in actual practice. So, if you wish your mentalism in capsules, tabloids, or sugar-coated pills, you must go elsewhere for it; the field is full of occult nostrums, as many of you have found out.

It is far more useful and practical to provide instead a formula by which you can work out and manifest every form of mentalism for yourself. No matter how complicated the form may be, it may be worked out by this formula. We shall not attempt to prove this to you—you can best prove it by actual practice in your own experiments. Try it for yourself, and see what you can accomplish by it.

The Magic Lantern Formula

The first step in applying this formula is for the student to lay aside all other theories of mentalism, for the time being. Forget all about thought-force, mind-waves, mental currents, and the rest of it—these are mere details, and are of limited value in the real work of mentalism. Forget all about theory, for the time being, and then proceed to get down to actual work.

Then, fix firmly in your mind the image of the magic lantern, with its concentrated light representing the will, and its painted slide the mental image. Regard the outer world of persons, things, and circumstances, as a great screen upon which you wish to project your mental images that they may materialize objectively. Get this picture clearly in your mind. See your individuality as the light in the lantern, with its concentrated will focused directly upon the mental image slide of the lantern. Hold this idea in mind whenever you practice mentalism: always stand behind your images, as the light in the lantern.

Then, having your mental image impressed upon your imaginative lantern slide, direct your lantern tube upon whatever object in the outside world you wish to influence. Places, present or absent, may be "treated" in this way, in order to dispel undesirable conditions or vibrations. The vibrations of places may be entirely changed in this way.

Conditions may be "treated" successfully by turning upon them a strong mental image of the changed conditions you wish to bring about. All the phenomena of mental alchemy may be successfully undertaken by the use and application of this formula. You will find that this formula is applicable to all manner and kinds of conditions. A little analysis of each case will show you how the formula may be applied to it.

Let not the simplicity of this method cause you to discard it in favor of some more complicated or metaphysical theoretical method. This method may be put to work with all the theories of the metaphysical schools—and analysis of the latter, divested of the surrounding theories, will show the underlying principle of this method in full operation in each and every one of them.

Truth, at the last, is always found to be simple. In the case of this formula, the very simplicity of the operation is among its special values, particularly when a little experiment and practice will prove its general usefulness. Analyze all other forms of mental treatment or mentalism, and see whether or not this formula can be applied to them. The beauty of this formula is its simplicity and its capacity for universal application. It may be put to use in a thousand forms or disguises, but the principle remains unchanged.

In conclusion, remember that the essence of mentalism is conveyed by the symbol of the mental magic lantern, with concentrated will as the light; the mental image as the pictured slide; the projected idea as the picture thrown on the screen; and the world of persons, things and conditions as the screen on which the picture is thrown.

THE MAGICAL MEMORY: PRACTICAL MEMORY

IN ADDITION TO the general principles of memory training covered in previous grades, there is a wealth of specific technique having to do with committing specific classes of information to memory. Of these, memory of numbers, places, faces, and names are the most important, as many people find one or more of these things more difficult to remember than other things.

Memory of Numbers

There is a great difference between persons regarding the memory of dates, prices, and numbers of all kinds, the difference being caused by the varying degrees of development of the mental faculty of numeration. Those in whom this faculty is well developed will have little difficulty in gaining a clear and lasting impression of numbers and everything connected with them, while those in whom the faculty is weak will find it difficult to remember anything connected with the subject. The latter class should develop the faculty of numeration by practicing thinking with numbers, in particular by means of mental arithmetic. If you are one of this latter class, buy an elementary text on mental arithmetic, of the sort that is used in the primary grades of schools, and carefully study it, working out every example given. Study one lesson every day, and in a short time you will find that you are developing an interest in numbers, and are beginning to remember them much better. The most satisfactory results may be obtained from practice of this kind. The development thus gained is permanent, and the faculty will continue to develop and register clearer impressions of numbers and all concerning them.

To those who find difficulty in remembering or recalling dates, the plan of forming a mental image of the date attached to the image of some important character or thing connected with the date has proven helpful. For instance, if you wish to remember the year of the discovery of America by Columbus, you will find it easy if you form a mental picture of Columbus standlug on the shores of the newly-discovered land, with the figures 1492 upon his clothing. If you wish to remember the date of the Declaration of Independence, form the picture of the Liberty Bell with 1776 painted on it in bright figures. In the case of the beginning of the Civil War, form the mental picture of Fort Sumter under cannon fire, with 1861 appearing on its sides in large figures. In forming the mental picture it is well to have the date marked on a piece of paper in large figures, upon which the eye should intently gaze while the mental picture is built around the figures. Then close the eyes or turn away the head, and revive the impression. If this is done several times the memory of the figures will be indelibly impressed upon the mind. A strong mental image may be formed by the average person, and when a strong impression of the date accompanying the person or object is stored away, it is likely to prove permanent and the associated impressions will always appear when the subject is recalled.

In the case of students who have many important dates to remember, it is a good plan to connect the name of the person or event with the date, by the law of associated impressions. By always thinking of "Waterloo 1815" or "Yorktown 1781" or "Hastings 1066," the dates of these battles will become inseparably associated with the events themselves, and the two impressions will become fused. Of course, this will require the frequent repetition of the event and associated date to fix the combined impression in the mind. If the date and event had been associated in this way from the beginning, there would have been no more trouble about the association than in the case of the words "Washington" and "George," or "Napoleon" and "Bonaparte." If we had not heard Washington's first name or Napoleon's last name until long after we had formed a clear impression of the other name of each, we would have sometimes forgotten the last learned name, whereas having learned them both together, the two names are practically one so far as our memory is concerned. If teachers would always speak of "Waterloo 1815," the students would never forget the date of that battle, so long as they remembered its name.

This plan of forming a mental image associating the figures with the object is of the greatest importance to clerks, salespeople, and the like, whose work requires them to remember the price of goods. In many cases the clerk may mentally see the prices attached to the goods by reviving the impression several times when looking at the goods in question. A certain young man who was employed in a large retail grocery store would form a mental image of this kind of every new lot of goods placed on the shelves, and always thought of the goods as being plainly marked with the price. If anyone asked him the price of baker's chocolate, he would think of the package with the price marked upon it. He could give the price of hundreds of articles of every description from memory. When the price changed, he would wipe out the old mental figure and replace it with the new price. Today, after the lapse of over twenty years, he is able, by a mental effort, to recall the picture and price of the majority of the goods carried in the old store, the impression coming as a mental picture of the article with the price attached. His faculty of locality is large, and he is able to mentally rebuild the old store shelves, bearing upon them the goods just as they appeared twenty years ago, prices and all. If you will clearly associate the price with the appearance of the goods, the mental picture of the latter will bring with it the recollection of the former, and the figures themselves may appear in the "mind's eye."

Figures other than dates or prices may be associated with any object to which they would naturally be attached. If there is no appropriate object to which to attach the figure, the simple "visualizing" method may be used. This method consists in photographing the figures upon the mind until the mind will recall the details and shape of the figures as it will those of a picture. Imagine the figures painted in large white characters on a black background. Hold the mental picture until you see it plainly in your "mind's eye." The ability to do this increases with practice. It is, however, always better if you can associate the figures with some appropriate object. The theory of this "visualizing" method, either with or without association, is based upon two facts: first, that many minds accept and retain a visual impression more readily than they do a mere abstract idea without a picture; and second, that the law of association makes the mental picture (including the date) come easily into the field of consciousness, when the thought of the object suggests it.

Memory of Places

Some people have the faculty of locality largely developed and are able almost intuitively to find their way in strange places. Such people never get lost, and seem to carry the location of the points of the compass in their minds without any effort. They remember places, directions, position, nature's arrangements as to space and place. Others possess this faculty in a lesser degree, and some seem to be almost without it. The last mentioned class find great difficulty in finding their way; they dare not trust themselves in strange places and are constantly getting lost.

The faculty of locality, like any other faculty, may be greatly developed by exercise and practice. When the sense of locality is but poorly developed, one takes no interest in the subject and pays no attention to it, hence the memory regarding places is deficient, the impressions recorded being but faint and imperfect.

If you possess a poor memory for places, location, direction, and the like, you may improve this by developing your faculty of locality. To do this, you must begin by taking an interest in places and directions. You must pay attention and observe. Without interest you will do neither. You must look about you and notice the landmarks passed, and the direction in which you have traveled, and objects with which you have met on the way. You must look about you and see, not merely pass by, your surroundings. If you are in a city, note the corner buildings and their signs. Stand on the corners for a few minutes and get your bearings. If you put your heart in the task you will find much of interest, and the work will soon become interesting and pleasant. The person with a strong faculty of locality notices these things instinctively, but you must start the habit by giving conscious attention until your mind establishes the correct habit and it becomes "second nature."

Study maps and take imaginary journeys from place to place on the map. Follow rivers from source to mouth. Take imaginary trips on the railroad, tracing the journey with the finger. Get a school geography book and study it when you are indoors. When you are outdoors keep on noticing things, directions, and landmarks.

If you live in a large city, procure a copy of the city map and study it carefully. Start from a given point on the map and proceed to another given point, noticing the names of the streets over which you travel, and also the names of the cross streets you pass, not forgetting to keep track of the direction. Then work your way home on the map over the same route, watching carefully that you turn the right corners and so forth.

Then make the same trip (still on the map) by another route, returning in the same manner. It is astonishing how this practice will brighten up your sense of locality and direction. Once in a while, memorize the names of the streets in the order in which you pass them on the map. One can get well acquainted with the city in which he is living in this way. On holidays or other times when you contemplate a long walk or ride, go to your map before you start and trace out the line of your trip, studying it carefully. When you then go over the same ground in person you will be continually noticing the cross streets and other features because of your previous work on the map. A little practice of this sort will prove quite interesting, particularly if the trip is to some unfamiliar part of town.

In your study of maps, it is well at times to memorize them, wholly or in part. Look at the map and study its parts and details. Then put the map away and endeavor to reproduce it on paper, in the rough, endeavoring to note as many points of interest as possible. Then gradually add the details in their relation to each other. The object of this map drawing, of course, is to fix location and direction in your mind, not to make an artist of you. In this practice you will find that if you lay aside the map after gazing at it a few moments and then close your eyes you will see the picture of the map in your "mind's eye."

The first attempt at forming this mental picture will not prove very satisfactory, but open the eyes again and take another look at the map and fill in what you have missed in your mental picture. Then close your eyes again and fill in the missing parts. After a few trials you will be able to reproduce the picture in the mind with reasonable accuracy, when you may reproduce it on paper. Schoolchildren sometimes form these mental pictures of their geography maps, and thus make their geography lessons much easier. When asked to "bound" a state, they are able to bring up the mental picture and describe it as if the map were actually before them.

This study of maps may seem to have but little connection with keeping you from getting lost or "losing your bearings." You will find, however, that it will so rapidly develop your interest and strengthen your faculty of locality that you will quickly notice the improvement when you are outdoors. Always remember to keep your eyes open and to notice where you are going; this task will now have fresh interest to you, thanks to your journeys on the map.

A story is told of an American traveler who was traveling in Europe with a party. It was soon noticed that he seemed perfectly at home in the strange cities visited, and that he not only knew the names of the principal streets but the location of the points of interest and important buildings as well, and also the direction from one part to another. It appeared as if he had visited the place before, whereas it was his first trip abroad. When asked for an explanation by his puzzled friends, he replied that when he was on the train going to a particular city he would take out his map and guide book and carefully study them, noting carefully the general plan, the points of interest, direction, etc. He would especially note the location of the railroad station and the hotel at which he intended to stay. He would then shut his eyes and recall these points, and make the trips between them, mentally. After about fifteen minutes or half an hour he was sufficiently acquainted with "the lay of the land" to find his way about without difficulty. In this way he learned Cologne, Prague, Old Vienna, Dresden, London, Paris around the Opera House, and other places.

After one has studied maps with interest, they grow very real and a close connection between the actual points and the pictured ones is noticed. Remember, in practicing the exercises herein given you are developing not only the memory but the faculty itself, upon whose ability to record clear impressions the remembrance depends.

Any faculty may be developed by interest and use. Remember this and you have the key to all self-improvement.

Memory of Faces

The faculty of remembering the faces of persons with whom we meet varies greatly in degree among different individuals. Many persons have to meet a stranger several times before they recognize him at sight. Many persons seem to easily forget faces with which they have grown familiar, if the owner happens to pass from their immediate circle for a year or two. On the other hand many persons recognize the face of any person whom they may meet, and the impression once formed seems to remain forever, subject to instant recall. Detectives have this faculty largely developed, and so have many hotel keepers, and others whose business brings them into contact with many people, and to whose interest it is to remember and recognize those with whom they meet. It is a valuable gift, as one's chance acquaintances feel most kindly disposed toward him when he readily recognizes them. On the other hand, the failure to recognize a man may make him dislike you and may result even in gaining his active ill will.

A deficiency in the development of this faculty indicates that the person has not made active use of that portion of the mind that notices the appearance and featnres of those with whom he comes in contact. Such people look at others, but do not really see them. They are not interested in faces, and give but scant attention to them. The rule of "slight interest, slight attention; slight attention, poor memory" applies here. The person who wishes to develop this faculty should begin to study faces, taking an interest in them, and paying attention to them. In this way the power of observation is directed to features and appearance, and a great improvement may he noted in a short time. We recommend to such persons the study of some elementary work on physiognomy, which will give to the study of faces a new interest. This will result in a greatly improved memory along these lines.

To cultivate the power of observation as applied to faces and features (after determining to take an interest in them, of course), you should study the face of every person you meet, taking note of the general shape of the head and face, eyes, nose, mouth, chin, and forehead, at the same time holding the thought, "I'll know you the next time I see you." This thought will cause the will to operate in the direction of recording a clear and distinct impression.

The taking of interest in, and the bestowal of attention upon the study of the human face will repay one for his time and trouble, for he will not only be training his attention and memory, but will be obtaining an education in physiognomy as well, especially if he is using an elementary book on this last mentioned subject, as advised.

There are very few persons who can recall the features of an absent friend, and it is quite amusing to hear some people attempting to describe the appearance of someone with whom they are presumably well acquainted. Try it and be surprised at how little you really can recall, and yet you have no trouble in recognizing the friend when you meet him. Describe the eyes, nose, and mouth of your best friend, if you can, from memory.

Look at the next man you meet. Note whether his forehead is high or low, narrow or broad; whether his eyebrows are light or heavy, straight or arched, and of what color; what kind of nose has he, aquiline, Roman, Grecian, pug, or what not; whether he has a large or small mouth, etc.; whether his teeth are good or bad, large or small; whether he wears a beard or mustache, large or small, shape, etc. And so on with each feature, noting the details just as if you were required to report them at your place of business, and your promotion depended upon a full and correct report. You will not forget a face studied in this way. A little practice of this kind is useful in developing the deficient faculty. You will begin to classify features and observe them naturally, having aroused an interest in the subject. The aroused interest means a clear impression, and the clear impression means an easy recollection.

Then practice recalling the faces of people you meet, making a mental picture of them. After you have acquired the art of recording good impressions of faces, by recalling several times the mental image of the face of anyone whom you have met, you will be able to easily recognize the person after the lapse of considerable time. The repeated reviving of the mental image is almost equivalent to repeated meeting with the person in question.

You may have noticed how easy it is to remember and form a mental picture of a face in a photograph or painting, and how much more difficult it is to carry in mind the face of the same person as it appears when you see him in person. It is all a matter of habit, however, and by a little practice you will be able to remember the living face just as easily as the pictured face.

There is a story of a "hasty sketch" artist, who had classified noses, eyes, ears, mouths, chins, eyebrows, shape of faces, etc., and had given to each class a number. He would take a steady gaze at the face of his sitter to get the expression and air, and the general outline, and would rapidly note, mentally, the class of each feature, thus, "shape of face, eyes, 8-6; eyebrows, nose, 3; mouth, 4; chin, 7," etc. Your study of faces will soon teach you the several classes and varieties of each feature, and if you are studying physiognomy, as advised, you will find that the knowledge of the significance of each class of features will greatly increase the interest and pleasure in the task.

Summing up, we would say that the faculty of remembering faces may be developed just as may be any other faculty of the mind, and that the secret of such development is: Cultivate an interest in faces—study them—attention will follow interest—and memory will attend upon attention.

Memory of Names

The faculty of remembering names also varies greatly among individuals. Many find it difficult to remember the names of even their closest friends, while others manifest a wonderful proficiency in the matter of remembering the names of almost everyone with whom they come in contact. This faculty has been an important factor in the success of many public figures, and almost incredible incidents are related of some who have developed the same to a very great extent.

Nearly every successful politician has been forced by necessity to develop this faculty. James G. Blaine and Henry Clay owed much of their popularity to their ability to recall the names of chance acquaintances, and to call them by their names after having met them but once. Of Thomas Wharton, Macaulay says, "It was impossible to contend against this great man who called the shoemaker by his Christian name." Napoleon's wonderful memory of names and faces endeared him to his soldiers. Aristotle had a remarkably clear memory for names, and Pericles is said to have known the names of all of the citizens of Athens.

The man who readily recalls names has a powerful weapon at his command in gaining the good will of people, and it will be worth the while of anyone to develop this faculty. Memory for names may be developed just as one would develop any other faculty of the mind, or part of the body, i.e., by attention and practice. Many persons content themselves with bewailing the fact that they have a poor memory for any special thing, and make no effort to improve it. When you realize that you can practically make yourself over by gradual improvement and practice, you will have opened the door to great things.

The first requisite for the development of the memory for names, is, of course, the recording of clear and distinct impressions. It is often found that it is a help to repeat aloud the name of a person to whom we have just been introduced, thereby appealing to the auditory memory by a repeated impression of the sound as well as the abstract general impression of the name. The trouble with many people is that they do not think of the names of people they meet. They do not let the name impress itself upon the mind, the entire attention being given either to the apearance or to the general personality of the stranger, his business, motives, etc. Carelessness in this respect will invariably result in the failure to recall the name a little later on. That is not the worst of it—by allowing ourselves to get into a careless habit regarding the names of others, we misplace what little name-memory we have, as nothing will so quickly resent a careless attention as the memory, which seems to act upon the principle that if its owner does not take the trouble to interest himself in a thing, it will not take the trouble to store it away with any degree of care.

If you have found it hard to revive the impressions of names, you may feel assured that it is because you have paid but little attention to people's names. Begin at once to take an interest in names. Analyze names; think about them; notice their peculiarities, their resemblances, their points of difference, and so forth. There are books published giving the origin of surnames, which are read by some people with considerable interest. We venture the assertion that no one who has ever read such a book with interest will ever have any trouble in remembering names. He will remember them because they will mean something to him. He will remember them as he remembers the names of the goods he sells, or the names of anything else possessing an interest for him. Every name has its origin and meaning, and it is quite interesting to trace back a name through all its variations to its origin.

One example worth noting is a family in Pennsylvania, whose ancestors came over from Germany bearing the name of Bichley (pronounced Beekley).

The grandchildren scattered and gradually adopted the spelling of their English neighbors, various changes being undergone by different branches of the family. At the present time the family reunions are composed of Beachleys, Beachlys, Beechlys, Beechleys, Beckleys, Bickleys, Bockleys, Backleys, Buckleys, Beechys, Beachys, Beachleys, Beachlys, Beechlys, Beekleys, Bickles, Buckles, Peachys, Peaches, and Pecks. Given a few more generations and the resemblance will have been entirely lost, the dropping of a letter here and the change of spelling there destroying all connection. The author had much trouble in remembering the original name when he first heard it, but after hearing from an old member of that family a history of his family, he never had the slightest trouble in remembering the name of anyone bearing the original name or any of its variations.

The above instances may help give you an idea of the change wrought by an acquired interest in a particular name. If you will remember something suggestive about a name, you will he very apt to have no trouble in recalling the name itself. A man named Miller may be remembered by thinking of the miller at work. Baker, Painter, Carpenter, etc., may be remembered in the same way. Names derived from those of animals may also be remembered by association, Lyon, Fox, Lamb, etc., being instances. Names derived from the names of trees are also in the rule, Mr. Cherry being associated with the fruit. Black, Brown, Green, Blue, White, and Gray have an easy means of association. Bacon, Clay, Gun, Cannon, Hall, Kane, etc. are easily handled. We knew a woman who could not remember the name of a man called Hawlk, until she fixed in her mind the fondness of that man (a preacher, by the way) for chicken, when the association of Hawk and Chicken occurred to her, and she had no trouble thereafter. A ridiculous association is sometimes the better, particularly if one has a sense of humor.

All of the above plans are, at the best, makeshifts. The better way is to begin to pay attention to the names of people whom you meet, and thus train the mind to take an interest in names, and to store away clear impressions. Force your attention upon the name, and by an act of will impress it upon your memory. Take an interest in the name—think of it and give it your attention. Then endeavor to connect it to your impression of the person's appearance. One man would associate names with noses, his mind seeming to be open to such associations, the result being that when he saw a man's nose he would remember his name; and when he would think of a man's name he would form an involuntary mental image of his nose. After leaving the person, endeavor to recall his appearance always in connection with his name. Form the strongest possible connection between the appearance and the name, so that they will be fused. Bring up a mental picture of Dr. Street, whom you have just met, and repeat the name several times, "Street, Street, Street," forcing the name in upon the image, by an effort of the will. You will find that this practice will soon result in your taking an unusual interest in persons' names, and the consequent attention will give clear impressions The clear impressions once obtained, the remembrance or recollection easily follows.

It is easy to remember the names of writers by forming a mental image of the book or poem, and attaching to it the name of the writer. This plan may be assisted by always associating the name of the writer with the title of the book or poem, in speaking of the latter, thus: "Hawthorne's *Scarlet Letter*," "Poe's *Raven*," or "Tennyson's *In Memoriam*." This association will render it difficult to ever speak or think of the work unless the name of the writer also comes before the mind.

Many find it advisable to also get the benefit of the eye-impression, and therefore when possible write down the name and regard it for a moment, then throw away the memorandum. In this way they are enabled to see the name in their "mind's eye," as well as remembering the sound and other impressions. It is well to get the impressions of as many faculties as possible. Louis Napoleon is said to have acquired his great memory of names by this plan of writing them down. His famous uncle did not need this aid as he always connected the sound of the name with the appearance of the man. The nephew found it impossible to duplicate this and was compelled to resort to the plan above mentioned, and by constant practice he soon acquired the reputation of having inherited his uncle's gift.

Another plan, favored by some, when they happen to forget a name, is to run over the alphabet from A to Z, slowly, in the mind, giving each letter a moment's attention in turn. When L is reached, the missing name "Langtry" will come into the field of consciousness, brought there by the recognition of the initial letter and the association of the balance of the name with that letter. Some vary this plan by writing down the letters in turn until the initial letter is reached and recognized. In this last mentioned variation, the visual memory aids in recalling the name. The same principle operates to notify us of the incorrect spelling of a written word when we have failed to remember the correct spelling by the sense of sound or general memory.

Some have found it helpful in recalling an elusive name if they endeavor to recall the place where they met the owner of the name, the circumstances surrounding the meeting, etc. In other words, they would try to place themselves back just where they were at the time when they met the person, and in this way they often found it easy to recall the name, which apparently came into the field of consciousness along with the mental picture. Others have accomplished the same result by bringing before the mind a picture of any peculiarity in the person's appearance or dress.

Plans of this kind are useful in exceptional cases or in an emergency. But the best plan is to take an interest in names. Study them—analyze them, and you will find that the increased interest will result in clearer impressions and easier recollection.

COMPLETION PRACTICE: THE WAY OF THE DOLMEN ARCH

THE COMPLETION PRACTICES included in previous lesson packets have been intended, among other things, to provide you with appropriate work during the interval between your completion of one grade and your receipt of the lesson packet for the next. This practice occupies a different role, in that there is no further lesson packet in the course—no higher grade in the Dolmen Arch system for you to attain. This by no means suggests that your work with the Dolmen Arch study course and its teachings has come to an end, but rather that your work with them now moves to a different plane or mode. Before you followed the studies that were prescribed to you by the lessons of your grade—now you must prepare to make the studies your own.

In the course of preparing for the grade of Loremaster of the Path, the first grade of the Greater Mysteries in this system, you were encouraged to look back over all the lessons you had received in the grades of the Lesser Mysteries, and relate certain themes covered in the previous grades to one another. Now, as you approach the completion of your training and the beginning of your work as a Free Loremaster, the time has come to review the material you have studied and practices you have done from the beginning of this course until now. In making this review, you should read through all the lesson packets you have received, from the Gradd y Newyddian to the Gradd y Gwyddon Rhydd, and you should also read through your practice journal from the beginning of your Dolmen Arch studies to the present.

This review of all your previous studies in this course has three purposes:

First, if you choose to become a teacher and initiator in the Dolmen Arch tradition, as you will have the right to do upon your completion of the examination for this grade, you will need to have a thorough knowledge and understanding of the work through which you have passed, and through which you will be guiding your own students and initiates. A review of the work is therefore timely, in order to impress on your mind the overall structure of the course and the way that its various elements interact with one another.

Second, it is inevitably the case that a student of this course, or indeed any other, will give more attention to some teachings than to others, and devote more effort to some exercises than to others. In preparing for your own further work in the Dolmen Arch system, it will be well for you to make a list of those teachings and exercises that you do not feel received as much attention and effort in your own training as did others. Once you have prepared this list, it will be of even more value for you to meditate on each item on the list, and seek to determine why it is that each teaching or practice found its way there. There is no need as you do this to justify your decisions at the time, and even less value in blaming yourself for not pursuing this or that part of the studies as intensively as you now think you might have done; the point of the exercise, rather, is to understand what drew you toward some parts of the training and away from others.

Third, as a Free Loremaster you are not only put in charge of the education and initiation of any students you yourself may have—you are also put in charge of your own further education and initiation. This means among other things that it is now your privilege to decide which of the many practices presented to you in this course will be part of your daily and weekly rhythm of Druid practice. All of the exercises that have been included in this course, from the simplest to the most complex and demanding, are capable of far more development than can be attained in the course of three or four months, even of daily work. Which of them you wish to pursue in the days and years to come is entirely open to your choosing.

This, then, is the completion practice for the Grade of the Free Loremaster: to review the lesson packets and your work to date; to list those teachings and practices that received less than your full attention and effort the first time through the course, and meditate on the reasons why each of them falls into this category; and to select those practices that, for the time being, will make up your personal work as you proceed along the path of the Druid mysteries.

Pursue this practice between the time that you request the examination for this grade and the arrival of the response to your examination paper.

About the Author

John Michael Greer *is Grand Archdruid Emeritus of the Ancient Order of Druids in America. He is the author of more than thirty books on a wide range of subjects, including* The Druid Grove Handbook: A Guide to Ritual in the Ancient Order of Druids in America *(Lorain Press, 2011);* The Celtic Golden Dawn: An Original & Complete Curriculum of Druidical Study *(Llewellyn Publications, 2013);* The Gnostic Celtic Church: A Manual and Book of Liturgy *(Lorian Press, 2013);* Paths of Wisdom: Cabala in the Western Tradition *(Llewellyn, 1996);* Inside A Magical Lodge: Group Ritual in the Western Tradition *(Llewellyn, 1998);* The Art And Practice Of Geomancy: Divination, Magic, and Earth Wisdom of the Renaissance *(Weiser, 2009); and* After Progress: Reason and Religion at the End of the Industrial Age *(New Society Publishers, 2015). He is also the translator of Giordano Bruno,* On the Shadows of the Ideas *(Azoth Press, 2017); with Mark Anthony Mikituk of Éliphas Lévi,* The Doctrine and Ritual of High Magic *(TarcherPerigee, 2017); and with Christopher Warnock, of* The Picatrix: The Occult Classic of Astrological Magic *(Adocentyn Press, 2010–11). Additionally, he is the editor of the new edition of Israel Regardie's* The Golden Dawn: The Original Account of the Teachings, Rites, and Ceremonies of the Hermetic Order *(Llewellyn, 2016). He lives in Cumberland, Maryland, an old red brick mill town in the north central Appalachians, with his wife Sara. You may follow his weekly blogging at* Ecosophia: Toward an Ecological Spirituality *(www.ecosophia.net).*

About the Publisher

AZOTH PRESS *is a small independent publishing house which makes its home in the Pacific Northwest. Our purpose is to create extraordinary books by practicing magicians for the practicing magician, with a standard of knowledge influenced by years of dedicated occult study and magical experience. We hope that our books will contribute to the practitioner's evolution and transformation, and also add to the magician's library a collection of unique, hand-made tomes meant to last for generations. Magical books should be Hermetic and talismanic works of art produced by the conjunction of well-written, well-researched, and enlightening content with beautiful design and elegant binding. In line with our goal of creating such magical volumes for practitioners and scholars of the Great Work, all Azoth Press limited-edition books are hand-bound by artisans with decades of experience in the fields of printing and master bookbinding. Each book is manufactured not only to a high æsthetic standard to please the eye and hand, but also to a demanding standard of artisanship and materials, so that each rare volume may be handed down, read, and used in their practice by generations of magicians to come. Please visit our website at* azothpress.com *and follow us on Facebook at* www.facebook.com/AzothPress/.

www.ingramcontent.com/pod-product-compliance
Lightning Source LLC
Chambersburg PA
CBHW042117300426
44117CB00020B/2969